Introduction to Sports Journalism

Matthew H. Zimmerman, PhD
Virginia Tech

Lauren M. Burch, PhD
Loughborough University London

Brian Moritz, PhD
St. Bonaventure University

HUMAN
KINETICS

Library of Congress Cataloging-in-Publication Data

Names: Zimmerman, Matthew (Matthew H.), author. | Burch, Lauren M., author. | Moritz, Brian, author.
Title: Introduction to sports journalism / Matthew H. Zimmerman, Lauren M. Burch, Brian Moritz.
Description: Champaign, IL : Human Kinetics, [2025] | Includes bibliographical references and index.
Identifiers: LCCN 2024013404 (print) | LCCN 2024013405 (ebook) | ISBN 9781492598435 (paperback) | ISBN 9781492598442 (epub) | ISBN 9781492598459 (pdf)
Subjects: LCSH: Sports journalism--Textbooks. | BISAC: SPORTS & RECREATION / Business Aspects | LANGUAGE ARTS & DISCIPLINES / Journalism
Classification: LCC PN4784.S6 Z36 2025 (print) | LCC PN4784.S6 (ebook) | DDC 070.4/46796--dc23/eng/20240618
LC record available at https://lccn.loc.gov/2024013404
LC ebook record available at https://lccn.loc.gov/2024013405

ISBN: 978-1-4925-9843-5 (print)

Copyright © 2025 by Matthew H. Zimmerman, Lauren M. Burch, and Brian Moritz

Human Kinetics supports copyright. Copyright fuels scientific and artistic endeavor, encourages authors to create new works, and promotes free speech. Thank you for buying an authorized edition of this work and for complying with copyright laws by not reproducing, scanning, or distributing any part of it in any form without written permission from the publisher. You are supporting authors and allowing Human Kinetics to continue to publish works that increase the knowledge, enhance the performance, and improve the lives of people all over the world.

To report suspected copyright infringement of content published by Human Kinetics, contact us at **permissions@hkusa.com**. To request permission to legally reuse content published by Human Kinetics, please refer to the information at **https://US.Human Kinetics.com/pages/permissions-translations-faqs**.

The web addresses cited in this text were current as of April 2024, unless otherwise noted.

Senior Acquisitions Editor: Andrew L. Tyler
Developmental and Managing Editor: Amanda S. Ewing
Copyeditor: Kevin Campbell
Proofreader: Deborah A. Ring
Indexer: Nan N. Badgett
Permissions Manager: Laurel Mitchell
Graphic Designer: Dawn Sills
Cover Designer: Keri Evans
Cover Design Specialist: Susan Rothermel Allen
Photograph (cover): Tom Shaw/Getty Images
Photo Asset Manager: Laura Fitch
Photo Production Manager: Jason Allen
Senior Art Manager: Kelly Hendren
Illustrations: © Human Kinetics, unless otherwise noted
Printer: Sheridan Books

Printed in the United States of America   10 9 8 7 6 5 4 3 2 1

The paper in this book is certified under a sustainable forestry program.

Human Kinetics
1607 N. Market Street
Champaign, IL 61820
USA

United States and International
Website: **US.HumanKinetics.com**
Email: info@hkusa.com
Phone: 1-800-747-4457

Canada
Website: **Canada.HumanKinetics.com**
Email: info@hkcanada.com

CONTENTS

Preface vii

CHAPTER 1 Exploring Sports Journalism — 1

The Value of Sports Journalism 1
Content Creators 2
Rise of Social Media 3
Online Media and the Role of Access 4
Female Sports Journalists 6
Social Justice Issues 7
The Power of Sport as a Brand 8
Stories About People 8
What You Can Expect From This Book 8
Summary 10
Discussion Questions 10
Applied Activity 10

CHAPTER 2 The Evolution of Sports Journalism — 11

Development and Expansion of Sport Media 13
Traditional Media's Control of the Narrative 18
Athlete Control of the Narrative 19
Traditional Media Navigate the Challenges 20
The Internet and the Boom of Sports Sites 21
Pivot to Video 23
The Market for Quality Sports Journalism 23
Blurring the Lines Between Journalism and Public Relations 25
Summary 25
Discussion Questions 25
Applied Activity 25

CHAPTER 3 News Gathering and Writing — 27

Sports Writing Basics 27
News Gathering 32
Other Story Forms 40
Media Theory in Sports Journalism 42
Summary 44
Discussion Questions 44
Applied Activity 44

CHAPTER 4 News Gathering in the Digital Age 45
Nonhuman Sources 46
Statistics 48
Analytics 49
Sport-by-Sport Analytics 51
Databases and Other Online Resources 62
Summary 62
Discussion Questions 63
Applied Activity 63

CHAPTER 5 Digital Sports Media 65
Mobile Journalism 66
News Consumers 67
Content Creators 67
Social Media 68
Facebook 71
X (Twitter) 74
Instagram and YouTube 76
Blogs 78
Podcasts 80
Artificial Intelligence 81
Summary 84
Discussion Questions 84
Applied Activity 84

CHAPTER 6 Sports Journalism and Public Relations 85
Public Relations 85
Sport Public Relations 86
Building and Maintaining Relationships With Key Publics 87
Communicating to Key Publics Through News Media 89
Communicating to Key Publics Through Organizational Media 96
Communicating to Key Publics Through Digital and Social Media 97
Crisis Communications 102
Summary 105
Discussion Questions 105
Applied Activity 105

CHAPTER 7 Media Ethics and Law   107

Defining Ethics   108
Ethics, Law, and Writing   110
Managing Bias   114
Social Media and Ethics   118
Sports Gambling and Ethics   119
Workshop Ethical and Legal Dilemmas   120
Summary   121
Discussion Questions   122
Applied Activity   122

CHAPTER 8 Career Paths in Sports Journalism   123

The Traditional Path   124
The Economics of Sports Journalism   126
Online Opportunities   129
Future-Proof Career Advice   133
Summary   134
Discussion Questions   134
Applied Activity   134

CHAPTER 9 The Future of Sports Journalism   135

A Quick Look at the State of the Profession   136
Where Do We Go From Here?   138
Online Media   138
Advancements in Technology and New Competitors   139
Needed Skills   142
Sports Media Startups   143
Women and Minoritized Groups in Sports Journalism   143
Local Engagement   144
Summary   146
Discussion Questions   146
Applied Activity   146

Glossary   147
References   153
Index   169
About the Authors   175

PREFACE

In fall 1993, the lead author of this book sat in a Journalism 1 course, the first course he had taken in college. Through the haze of the 8:00 a.m. starting time, the professor (rest in peace, Professor Combs) said something that resonated well and that continues to make perfect sense. She said that while she knew some students were there as part of the freshman English requirement, a basic journalism course like that one would ideally be part of every college curriculum. Why? "To help people become better consumers of media."

Maybe not every student taking this class and using this text plans to major in sports journalism. Maybe not every student in this class who majors in journalism will end up practicing sports journalism full-time. However, the sports media world exemplifies the major forces at work in the media industry: The rise of corporate-owned media outlets, each with their own business-driven agenda. The intertwining of rights fees and financial interests with various television stations. The observation during a local team broadcast that most teams "also employ the announcers." Local news reporters or bloggers who sometimes write and report as if they're trying to protect their press credentials. The increasing prevalence of sports-related gambling during game broadcasts and in advertising on sports radio shows. Media consumers must be aware of these influences as they develop the ability to discern what is truly reliable in what they are reading, watching, and hearing.

This is not to say that simple consumption and understanding are the major goals of a sports journalism course. The skills learned in a journalism curriculum can be applied in many areas. For example, the effect of public relations, with its similar skill set, on journalism and journalists has been profound (Hutchins & Boyle, 2017). But in an increasingly splintered media landscape, with options for sports coverage occupying many locations on the spectrum in terms of reliability, the wisdom of that professor still rings true.

The authors of this book have each been college professors for more than a decade. They also bring to this textbook professional experience covering everything from high school badminton to mid-major college sports, to international soccer, as well as experience in public relations. Each has changed careers at least once and changed professional jobs multiple times. Based on those experiences, we intend for this textbook to offer students as much information as possible about their potential and myriad options as they go forward in sports journalism.

And with any luck, the principles of news gathering and dissemination will remain relevant even after the tech honchos figure out a way to beam sports directly into consumers' minds.

This book will help prepare the aspiring sports media practitioner for a career in the continually developing world of sports journalism. The field has undergone profound changes just in the last few decades, and this is likely to continue at a rate that will require frequent future revisions in this text. In that way, the business of sports journalism can be seen as a metaphor for sport itself. Sometimes called "the ultimate reality television," sports can be rather predictable at times, but they can also feature many twists and turns and unexpected events in the course of a single contest, and sometimes sports journalists can present narratives that uplift and unite communities (Serazio, 2010). Not every game will be an emotional roller coaster for fans and a constant rewrite for journalists. But the business and practice of sports journalism are now in a constant state of flux, almost like a roller coaster that constantly threatens to disobey the laws of physics.

This textbook is intended to serve as an instruction manual on how to practice multiple aspects of sports journalism. To that end, there are chapters that delve into basic news gathering and reporting, with explanations of the tools needed to start practicing sports journalism. Creating media content in the traditional written and broadcast forms is also covered. Students will also learn about applying journalism skills to digital and online media, as well as the continually evolving world of social media, and about how those platforms can fit into a sports journalist's toolbox.

The effects of the Internet and technological developments are also discussed, and we present the idea that an entire story can be covered just using a smartphone. Not content to adhere to a standard vision of sports journalism, we also describe how a journalist's skills can apply to a public relations career. Beyond the technical aspects of sports journalism work, we also cover equally important aspects such as ethics as they relate to sports journalism, and we present a bit of historical context for how sports journalism has developed over the years. Finally, we offer some thoughts about ongoing and possible future developments, and we ask students to provide their own viewpoints about these topics.

Ultimately, the total package presented in the pages that follow is one we hope is thorough and informative. And also honest. The world of sports journalism continues to evolve, faster than anyone can predict. This includes the people creating this afternoon's newscast, people posting today's instant reactions on social media, those who are planning tomorrow's newspaper, and those who are in the halls of academia with a mandate to try to tell us all what the future may hold. By the end of the lessons and stories contained here, ambitious and thoughtful students should be able to present their own informed viewpoints about the current and future state of sports journalism. And they will also be able to determine what kind of space they might occupy—what kind of contribution they might make to the craft and industry of sports journalism.

Special Features

Several special features are used throughout the text:

- Time-Out sidebars give students the opportunity to think more deeply about a topic.
- Industry Profiles showcase sports journalism practitioners whose career or area of writing illustrates the chapter content.
- Applied Activities allow students to put the concepts learned in the chapters into motion.

Instructor Resources in HK*Propel*

Instructors have access to a full array of ancillary materials within the instructor pack in HK*Propel*:

- **Instructor Guide.** The instructor guide contains a file for each chapter that provides chapter objectives, the Time-Out exercises from the book with suggested responses, the discussion questions from the book with recommended responses, recommendations for how to use the Applied Activities, and additional practical application exercises.
- **Test Package.** The test package includes 180 questions in true-false, multiple-choice, fill-in-the-blank, short-answer, and multiple response formats. These questions are available in multiple formats for a variety of instructor uses and can be used to create tests and quizzes to measure student understanding.

Adopting instructors receive free instructor ancillaries, including an ebook version of the text that allows instructors to add highlights, annotations, and bookmarks. Please contact your sales manager for details about how to access instructor resources in HK*Propel*.

Exploring Sports Journalism

Chapter Objectives

After completing this chapter, you will be able to do the following:

- Determine the relative merits of sports journalism's popular nickname, "the toy department."
- Give a brief overview of some of the technological changes that have affected sports journalism.
- Illustrate the power of sport as a vehicle for storytelling as well as the promotion of ideas.

Sports journalism as a profession has existed for centuries. In the United States, sports journalism grew in popularity largely through coverage of baseball as the sport grew to become "America's pastime" (Anderson, 2001). On September 7, 1979, the Entertainment and Sports Programming Network (ESPN) made its debut, and the birth of ESPN is in many ways the seminal event in the history of what we now understand to be sports journalism. When ESPN creator Bill Rasmussen pitched the idea, the consensus was that no one would watch an all-sports television network. We now know very differently.

In many ways, ESPN pushed—and continues to push—sports journalism forward. As newsrooms in both print and broadcast media have continued to cut budgets for travel, personnel, and equipment, ESPN has pushed the use of new approaches, such as streaming (ESPN+ hits, 2023), and has maintained its reputation for hiring a more diverse workforce than has been typical in sports journalism (Rucker, 2023). ESPN's claim to be "The Worldwide Leader in Sports" has been bolstered and fulfilled by the continued development of technology, bringing the network's multiplatform coverage to audiences all over the globe (MacLean, 2017).

The role of **sports journalism** is to chronicle in real time the events that occur in sport. This goes beyond straightforward game coverage to include personality profiles and analysis. In addition, sports journalists must deal with many forms of criticism both internal and external. Increased competition from online outlets—credentialed and noncredentialed—also presents a challenge for the profession and the craft. Before we get into the meat of this textbook, it is important for aspiring sports journalists to understand some of the issues involved with sports journalism that do not have to do with sport itself.

The Value of Sports Journalism

As a craft and an industry, sports journalism has long been the target of criticisms that tend to diminish its place in the media landscape. Questions have arisen not only about the quality of sports coverage compared to "hard news" coverage but also about the value of sports journalism itself (Weedon et al., 2018). Due to its focus on games and the people who play and plan those games, sports journalism has sometimes been called the "toy department" (Rowe, 2007, p. 385). The **toy department** reputation is largely based on the view that sports journalism's stories fall exclusively in the realm of game previews, game reports, and descriptions of game strategies. Those who regard sports journalism as the toy department contend that it omits coverage of off-field news about social issues and other topics more challenging than diagramming a Cover-2 or a Box-and-1 (Rowe, 2007).

Sports journalists also have had a reputation for being supporters of home teams, athletes, and leagues (Anderson, 2001) and therefore being reluctant to cover stories that might jeopardize their relationships with sources (Rowe, 2017). But the need to maintain cordial and even (at times) friendly relationships with sources is part of all journalism, and especially part of sports beat reporting (Anderson, 2001).

Ultimately, as this book will make clear, the notion that sports journalism is somehow less than the news or features department is very short-sighted and fails to take into account all of the varied forms of sports journalism and the opportunities they present.

Sports journalists face more serious issues than just being called "the toy department." Concerns about the effects of media ownership cross over from the front page into the sports pages (Weedon et al., 2018). As of 2024, ESPN is owned by ABC, for instance. And The Walt Disney Company owns ABC. Does that affect coverage? For a decade, Disney owned Anaheim, California's two professional sports teams, the Anaheim Angels and the Mighty Ducks of Anaheim (now, respectively, the Los Angeles Angels of Anaheim and the Anaheim Ducks). Did this ownership have an effect on ESPN's coverage? Does working for Fox Sports represent an association with the rest of the Fox media world?

For a sports reporter, issues can arise off the field, ice, or court that involve legal analysis, criminal activity, scholastic malfeasance, economics, and societal situations. For example, the continued discussions about name image and likeness (NIL) compensation for high school and college athletes, fake classes taken by students in major Power 5 athletic departments, athletes making political statements, and labor issues between athletes or arena workers and franchise owners are all sports journalism stories. They are the types of stories that can come up in the course of reporting on sports.

It is true that what is often lost in the training and practice of sports journalism—and journalism itself—is the need for critical thinking and investigation (Rowe, 2017). The toy department criticism manifests when sports journalists are perceived as taking the side of sport's power brokers (Anderson, 2001).

A sports reporter must be versatile and adaptable to any situation. One of the authors of this book covered two high school sporting events four years apart that both ended in gun violence off the field. How do you pivot from watching high school soccer or football to seeking information on a drive-by shooting? What kind of a change in mindset and approach must be taken in such situations, however unlikely they might be? Sports features events that are very public and that draw large crowds. A good sports reporter is ready to cover the star player's issues with grades just as quickly as diagramming the movement in a 3-4-3 formation.

Taking the temperature down a bit, it must also be noted that a good sports journalist is ready to tell personal stories about individuals and their triumphs. About people who often achieve things that make them seem larger than life. A good sports journalist, in other words, can do it all and is comfortable telling any kind of story, and telling it well, in words, visuals, graphics, or a combination of these.

Time-Out

As you begin your journey into the world of sports journalism, take a moment to think about your dream job.

1. List your top five desired careers in sports journalism.
2. Next, list your top five desired locations to practice sports journalism. These can be cities, states, or countries.
3. Compare the two lists to determine your top three job and destination combinations. What kinds of opportunities exist in the locations you chose? Were they what you expected? Explain your answer.

Content Creators

The expansion of media outlets and opportunities has offered a chance for fans to become more involved with sport than ever before (Oates, 2016). With video games, radio shows, podcasts, and television shows dedicated to analysis, and an increase in general interest and technology to provide a place to discuss those interests, fan examinations of sport have proliferated like never before. As sports on television became more popular, a more dispassionate mode of analysis started to develop and became favored in national broadcasts (Oates, 2016).

As technology evolves in a way that adds options for traditional media outlets' coverage, sports journalism faces competition not only from the official sites, but also from fan sites. Independent bloggers can present their viewpoints without worrying about whether they will lose access to coaches and athletes (McCarthy, 2013). As other sources of media proliferated, so did opinion-driven content. With this type of writing becoming the dominant

Among the opportunities for students in sports journalism is social media coordinator for official team feeds.
Michael Gonzales/NBAE via Getty Images

form online, news organizations' guidelines for their journalists' social media use included warnings against even retweeting, in order to avoid any appearance of expressing a personal viewpoint (Orellana-Rodriguez & Keane, 2018). As blogs gained some popularity, these nontraditional media earned the reputation for basing their viewpoints on the reportage from trained and paid reporters (McCarthy, 2013). Sports blog *Deadspin*'s debut in 2006, with the motto "Sports News Without Access, Favor or Discretion," indicated that the sports journalism business no longer belonged to traditional journalists. And yet, perhaps in a nod to the aspects of print journalism that worked well, blog posts are created with headlines and images meant to draw readers (McCarthy, 2013).

Rise of Social Media

The use of X (formerly known as Twitter), Facebook, Instagram, YouTube, and other social media platforms to create and share sport-related content is not unique to newsrooms (English, 2016). This means that sports journalists face competition from many sectors, including from the average fan, to create stories, break news, and share content. Thus, sports journalists must know how to effectively use social media in order to compete.

Social media's role in traditional sports journalism is not only to promote stories, but also to interact with readers. As social media became more popular with users, the use of X to promote traditional media coverage was thought to have the potential to increase newspaper and online readership (English, 2016).

However, journalists must be careful with their use of social media. Orellana-Rodriguez and Keane (2018) noted that the Associated Press, Reuters, and Agence-France Presse all enacted guidelines for journalists' use of social media. These are the world's three largest news organizations, and each has a large sports section. Journalists' use of social media can invite such a level of scrutiny that who the journalists follow or unfollow can create speculation. Reuters notes in its rules for journalists on social media that a simple follow can potentially reveal an anonymous source (Orellana-Rodriguez & Keane, 2018). This makes sense in a media world where star athletes or celebrities following or unfollowing each other can be perceived by observers as indicating potential free-agent destinations or marital issues. For instance, when Kobe Bryant unfollowed Dwight Howard after their single tumultuous season together with the Los Angeles Lakers, every NBA fan knew because it was reported widely on social media.

For decades, journalists have often resisted newer forms of media, but as traditional outlets began to embrace technology, this action paid some dividends. Research has indicated that using social media to promote traditional media content can have a positive effect on readership (Hong, 2012). While bloggers were at first (perhaps mistakenly) dismissed as unworthy and not at all engaged in true competition with traditional media, social media platforms presented both a challenge and an opportunity for traditional media outlets (Boyle, 2013, p. 96).

Jobs in Sports Journalism

The list of potential jobs in sports journalism has expanded greatly since the early 2000s, largely due to the use of Web 2.0 technologies in journalism. Just since 2010, jobs have emerged with media organizations and sport organizations in which trained students can use the skills taught and discussed in this textbook.

A quick note: When possible, you should not work for free. Your work is valuable. However, some internships remain unpaid, and each person must decide whether the opportunity fits with their career goals and their ability to pay rent.

- *Print journalist.* This can include working for newspapers or magazines, but the role has now expanded to include any kind of writing for an outlet. This includes blogs, online outlets, and the more traditional outlets.
- *Television journalist.* Work for television and cable stations as a writer, videographer, or reporter. Trained and experienced students can also create video content for websites and can produce and edit media content.
- *Radio journalist.* Work for radio stations as a writer, on-air host, or producer. In addition, similar roles are available working for podcasts, a market that has shown no signs of slowing its ongoing boom.
- *Public relations practitioner.* Those who have been trained in sports media skills (e.g., writing, reporting, video, audio, editing) can apply those same skills to working in public relations. These roles can be found with sport organizations as well as media organizations and with advertisers that work with teams and leagues.
- *Social media practitioner.* More and more, sport organizations as well as media organizations have concluded that social media is an excellent way to reach their target publics. Those who have become proficient in the use of social media (e.g., Facebook, Twitter/X, Instagram, TikTok, YouTube) can find roles producing media content for these platforms. In the recent past, many PR professionals were asked to simply add "social media practitioner" to their list of other job duties, but there are now specialized positions devoted to creating social media for organizations.

Online Media and the Role of Access

As previously mentioned, journalists and journalism outlets can use social media to promote content and potentially increase the number of eyes and the level of attention on that content. However, the rise of social media platforms has also made it difficult for consumers to discern what is the straight news and what is opinion, speculation, or simply untrue. This makes it especially important that traditionally trained journalists contribute reliable information. Many readers do not distinguish between traditional media outlets, which must follow news coverage norms, and individuals who simply have an Internet connection and a screen name (Boyle, 2013).

Because online media did not initially have the same level of respectability, and the sheer cachet, that legacy media outlets did, online entities were at first barred from the sports media club, which included access to events and personnel (Suggs, 2016). That access improved as teams began to credential prominent bloggers and fan sites. In addition, teams began to increase sports coverage on their official sites. After decades of dominance, traditional media now face competition from online media that may have a similar level of access, and from official team sites that never have to worry about their credentials being pulled for a negative story (Suggs, 2016).

The idea of access means something different for every type of media outlet. Even sports reporters at major outlets are not always guaranteed access to the athletes' sanctum sanctorum, the locker room or clubhouse (Suggs, 2016). For *Deadspin*'s first decade-plus, the lack of access was a badge to wear proudly, as if to proclaim that their viewpoints were not influenced by the need to maintain good relationships or to enter locker rooms and clubhouses. Sports information directors often grant access more readily to a national outlet than to a local one (Suggs, 2016) because ESPN swooping in to cover a story means much more potential publicity for their programs.

Industry Profile

Tricia Whitaker

As the sideline reporter for the Tampa Bay Rays, Tricia Whitaker fulfills a different kind of media role than those addressed through traditional sports journalism education. But while part of her job is, as she notes, "to tell the truth, tell the game story, but always with a twist of optimism" about what occurs with the team, the core tenets of sports journalism training and experience still apply.

"You could work for a team, or you can work for a local station; you still need to ask good questions," Whitaker said (personal correspondence, February 2021). "It doesn't matter who you work for. You still have to know how to phrase those questions, you have to know how to frame a story. And the basic skills of journalism are so important."

Majoring in communication and culture as an undergraduate, Whitaker worked for student-run outlets as a reporter and interned with the Indiana Pacers while in school. Working for the team's official media, she had the opportunity to cover the team when the Pacers were jockeying with LeBron James' Miami Heat for Eastern Conference supremacy. That experience helped lead to Whitaker's first professional job, working in Green Bay, Wisconsin. Her first assignment, fresh out of college, was to cover a Packers road playoff game in San Francisco.

"I was terrified; I've never been so nervous in my life to be on TV," Whitaker said. "I was so scared, because I'd never done anything like that before. But I did it. I was thrown into the fire, and it was the best thing that ever happened to me."

After two years in Green Bay, Whitaker returned home to her native Indiana to work for an Indianapolis TV station for four years. Since January 2019, she has been the Rays' in-house reporter. Being embedded with the Rays each season, traveling on the team plane and staying in the same hotel, has helped crystallize Whitaker's personal storytelling brand.

"I realized—I like the Xs and Os of the game, don't get me wrong—but I really enjoy telling stories, deeper than game stories," Whitaker said. "I really enjoy getting to know the player, I really enjoy getting to know the coach, I really enjoy getting to know their families. Because I am the bridge from the fan to the team. When you get to know who they are, in my opinion it makes watching them on the field in their game so much more interesting and valuable, and I can connect to it more."

During her first season with the team, the Rays qualified for the 2019 postseason and started a trend. They qualified for the postseason in each of Whitaker's first five seasons with the team, including advancing to the World Series in 2020. Along with all the team's wins, Whitaker's social media posts featured images of her narrowly avoiding postgame Gatorade showers intended for clutch players, as well as Whitaker being doused with beer while conducting clubhouse interviews after the team clinched a playoff berth. And as she notes, that's part of the game.

"Women have worked for decades to be accepted in the clubhouse," Whitaker said. "We finally are, and somebody wants to be like, 'They're being so mean to her!' No! They're treating me like I'm a part of the team. This is what women have worked for—before I even came along—for decades. Don't ruin it. It was awesome."

With experience working both in traditional media and relatively newer in-house roles with professional teams, Whitaker noted that standard sports journalism approaches translate directly to each type of job. In the MLB off-season, she returns home to teach a sports broadcasting course in The Media School at her alma mater, Indiana University. So, what advice does Tricia Whitaker have for aspiring sports journalists?

"Be willing to get out of your comfort zone, and don't say no to opportunities," Whitaker said. "Learn everything. Learn how to shoot, learn how to edit, learn how to produce, learn how to do social media, learn how to host, learn how to report, learn how to do packages, learn how to do podcasts, host radio shows, because nowadays, you can't do just one thing. You have to do everything."

And perhaps just as importantly, "Be a good person, because at the end of your career, you'll want to look back and remember the relationships you formed, and people will remember you for how you made them feel," Whitaker said. "And if you made them feel insignificant because you thought you were better than them, or if you made them feel like they didn't deserve your time of day, they're going to remember that. And you don't want to be remembered for that."

In an examination of the coverage of scandals that beset the international soccer governing body FIFA, Rowe (2017) noted that sports journalists tended to avoid such challenging topics. The ability to not only analyze strategies and roster moves but also to engage in deeper dives into the "why" of sport itself is integral to sports journalism training and education. Too often, sports journalists tend to become part of the fabric of what they cover. Journalists might share a social media post about how proud they are to have covered a team, or how much they've enjoyed seeing someone grow as a person and as an athlete. But as Rowe (2017, p. 528) points out, it is better for sports journalists to remain "inquiring and skeptical" in their work.

Female Sports Journalists

Another aspect of sports journalism that cannot be ignored is the demographics of the industry. Research from the early 2000s indicated that female sports journalists faced extra challenges compared to their male counterparts (Hardin & Shain, 2005). The industry has tended to be populated mostly by males at all levels, from editors to bosses to reporters (Rowe, 2017).

Representation in newsrooms has been an ongoing issue in terms of newsroom demographics' effects on coverage and on readership and viewership. But opening the newsroom to a more diverse set of voices occurs at a glacial pace. In a survey of women who worked in sports media, Hardin and Shain (2005) found that some female sports journalists had become more accepting of the idea that changing coverage norms was difficult and perhaps impossible.

While more than half of the respondents in Hardin and Shain's (2005) survey indicated that they were satisfied with their professional positions, female sports journalists also reported instances of workplace sexual discrimination. Respondents also asserted that it was more difficult for female sports journalists to do their jobs than for males, although opportunities for women were considered to be more plentiful than ever. Female sports journalists also indicated that women's sports do not receive the level or the type of coverage they merit—they often mentioned the need to pointedly inform their colleagues about the importance of covering women's sports and events (Hardin & Shain, 2005).

Female sports journalists who have left or considered leaving the industry indicated that lack of advancement opportunities and the overall effect on their nonwork life were key factors (Hardin & Shain, 2005). As Hardin and Shain (2005) pointed out, the lack of female leadership in newsrooms can serve as a deterrent to encouraging young women to pursue and stick with a career in sports journalism.

Using Film to Learn About Sports Media

In a case of crossover between media, film can be an effective way to learn about sports media history and practices. Brugar (2016) examined ESPN's ongoing *30 For 30* documentary series, noting the effectiveness of using such films in the classroom. The entries' narrative filmmaking covers international as well as institutional topics, with opportunities for student learning arising from the diverse set of on- and off-field issues featured in the films. ESPN had previously positioned itself as an arbiter and disseminator of sports history with its SportsCentury specials, which appeared in the late 1990s—a decade before the *30 For 30* series—to commemorate the network's 20-year anniversary (MacLean, 2017). While unlike, for instance, the *New York Times'* *1619 Project*, ESPN's *30 for 30* releases do not officially include materials intended to be used in the classroom; the material can supplement what an instructor is trying to impart to students.

The widely praised documentary *Pony Excess*, which examined the effect of the NCAA's so-called death penalty on Southern Methodist University football, can be used in contexts such as sports history for coverage of current NCAA enforcement, as well as sports journalism coverage of sports law issues. Other films are windows into past behaviors of sports media, such as *The Marinovich Project* or *Fab Five*. Also valuable for a sports journalism context are the *30 For 30* shorts included in the series. *Judging Jewell* depicts the media frenzy around Richard Jewell, a security guard falsely accused of planting a bomb at the 1996 Atlanta Summer Olympics.

Social media give sports journalists an opportunity for a more public face or "brand," but they also come with potential and profound negatives (DiCaro, 2021). Social media platforms enable people to send direct and harassing messages to anyone who is registered on these platforms, including athletes and reporters (Feringa, 2024). Major issues include inconsistent workplace policies for the use of social media by news and media organizations, and individual companies' inability to protect their workers from harassment, which can include threats of violence (DiCaro, 2021).

With some media consumers who are determined to judge female pundits more harshly, any minor or major misstep can become a larger story. And as in any profession, female sports journalists can be very protective of the integrity of their work. In fall 2023, longtime TV sports broadcaster Charissa Thompson said on the *Pardon My Take* podcast that in her days as a sideline reporter, she would "make up the report" when a coach hadn't been available at halftime or a similar situation (Reedy, 2023). Backlash was swift, with many female sideline reporters expressing disappointment at the remarks (Lenthang, 2023). Considering the fact that female sports journalists have had to deal with a harsher level of scrutiny, Thompson's statement was a major breach of public trust and an embarrassment that her peers could not ignore. However, in an example of the speed with which society tends to move on to the next story, the controversy somehow passed quickly. In what may be an example of the positive use of social media to attempt to defuse a controversy involving a female sports journalist, Thompson posted an apology on her Instagram feed (Lenthang, 2023; Reedy, 2023), and she continued in her roles with Fox Sports and Amazon Prime Video.

Social Justice Issues

Over the years, sport has been portrayed and accepted as a venue in which race does not matter, as long as a person can play the game. After Jackie Robinson broke baseball's color barrier in 1947, sports media and sport power brokers presented the false idea that athletics were free of racial strife and in fact presented opportunities for equality (Smith, 2006). However, often strict rules are enacted in professional leagues dominated by African American athletes, such as drug-testing requirements and restrictions on the ability to celebrate during a game (Oates, 2016).

In previous cases, such as when members of the St. Louis Rams football team took the field in 2014 making the "Hands up, don't shoot" gesture, coaches and team executives proclaimed that sport was separate from politics (Oates, 2016). However, more recent protests during the national anthem and displaying of the American flag have proven to be more difficult to avoid for people in sports, from athletes to coaches to owners. The increasing prominence of sport as a venue for protest and social activism has led to a reexamination by media members as well. Sports media members who previously might have kept their viewpoints to themselves now use social media to express their political opinions.

Sports media have proven to be a potent force in bringing social issues to the forefront. In summer 1968, during the heart of the American civil rights movement, *Sports Illustrated* published a series called "The Black Athlete: A Shameful Story." By connecting social activism and the fight for civil rights with sport and the athletes who were speaking out on social issues, the magazine affected fans' perceptions of the importance of these issues (Smith, 2006). On a side note, *Sports Illustrated* would later draw criticism for asking in 1997, "Whatever happened to the white athlete?" (Oates, 2016).

Two decades after Jackie Robinson won the Rookie of the Year award as a Brooklyn Dodger, African American athletes were urged to boycott the 1968 Mexico City Olympics. While the boycott itself did not occur, American track and field athletes Tommie Smith and John Carlos held up their fists in a Black Power salute on the medal stand. The *Sports Illustrated* series, which had been in motion for a couple of years, had validation (Smith, 2006).

Time-Out

In what ways can fictional portrayals affect perceptions of real-life professions like sports journalism?

1. Name five depictions of sports journalists in fiction, in any medium (e.g., books, movies, television).
2. What were some characteristics they shared? What made each portrayal unique?
3. Were the portrayals positive, negative, or mixed?

The Power of Sport as a Brand

In an examination of beer and liquor advertising in two Super Bowls as well as in two *Sports Illustrated Swimsuit Issues* from the early 2000s, Messner and Montez de Oca (2005) noted that in addition to eliciting a purchase intention, the advertisements for these products also helped create a form of masculine identity connected with the purchase and consumption of alcohol. In addition, alcohol advertising during sporting events or in connection with sports media can tend to perpetuate a viewpoint that sport is at its purest when males are watching in a group (Messner & Montez de Oca, 2005).

Messner et al. (2000) wrote of what they identified as the "Televised Sports Manhood Formula." This included 10 categories pertaining to "gender, race, aggression, violence, and consumerism" (p. 380), which were interpreted to influence young males' perception of sports.

As writing and presentation styles in sports journalism have evolved, one aspect that has remained is the use of metaphors commonly used to describe military combat (Jenkins, 2013). Perhaps, then, it was no surprise when in 2009, the U.S. Department of Defense paid millions of dollars to partner with the NFL in honoring military personnel (Berr, 2018). In the following years, the U.S. military would also partner with other professional leagues in cross-promotions for which the Department of Defense paid millions of dollars. And it wasn't just partnerships with the NFL, which in television viewership, attendance, and revenue is the recognized 800-pound juggernaut of U.S.-based sports. The deals included an event with Major League Soccer's Los Angeles Galaxy, which was enjoying a wave of popularity in David Beckham's final season (Hogg, 2015).

The sporting world itself uses these metaphors as well, with talk about battles and going to war with opponents, and teams such as MLB's San Diego Padres wearing alternate uniforms meant to evoke military images and support (Jenkins, 2013). The use of patriotic imagery in sport, including playing the U.S. national anthem prior to games, has led to criticism of athletes who did not participate in the anthem's traditions (Jenkins, 2013). True, there is a bit of distance between sports journalism's use of military metaphors and actual promotional partnerships with military entities. However, the use of a sporting event or athletic team to help promote products and ideas can be seen in every single sports broadcast, every publication, every notation that a product is "the official airline/soft drink/hamburger/beer/etc." of a certain sporting franchise or league. While U.S. Department of Defense partnerships with the NFL ended in 2015 (Gregory, 2020), this symbiotic cross-promotional relationship between sporting entities and advertisers is a core aspect of sports media.

Stories About People

Sports journalists have the opportunity to write what some journalists call "the first draft of history." Even in recent times, sports journalism has proven effective in creating hero and villain narratives, designed to uplift and unite communities (Serazio, 2010). This is no surprise because sport is seen as an opportunity for people to engage in self-actualization through the use of skills both physical and mental (Beck & Bosshart, 2003). Especially in broadcast media reporting, narratives often feature athletes fighting through injuries or physically dominating opponents (Messner et al., 2000).

What You Can Expect From This Book

The steady decades of radio, TV, and print media providing sports coverage have given way to a new and often fluctuating paradigm. As sports journalism continues to move forward in an uncertain media world, unexpected changes can occur that have far-reaching implications. In July 2023, the *New York Times* announced it was closing its sports section. Having acquired sports website The Athletic the previous year for $550 million (Chapman, 2023), the *Times* would now rely on that site's national and international coverage for its sports material, with the *Times*' sports journalists reassigned to other sections (Reilly, 2023).

In early 2024, an even larger stalwart of sports journalism announced mass layoffs. After going from a weekly publication to becoming a seasonal one, *Sports Illustrated* magazine's decline reached its ultimate nadir. *SI* owner Authentic Brands Group revoked *SI* publisher The Arena Group's license after the latter missed a licensing payment (Wile, 2024). In the wake of this event, the SI Union told Front Office Sports that Arena Group had informed them that there would be mass layoffs, possibly affecting the entire staff (Perez, 2024). Authentic Brands also told the media that it intended to keep the *Sports Illustrated* brand alive (Reedy & Bauder,

2024), but the future of the magazine and the content on the official website remained uncertain.

The loss of two former sports media juggernauts may not resonate for today's students as much as it does for previous generations. If current sports journalism students have seldom picked up a newspaper, it is fair to ask how often they read *Sports Illustrated*. Print media do not have the same cachet as in past years, and this textbook will reflect that. The following chapters feature a mix of information about the history of sports journalism (e.g., why things are the way they are) as well as a heavy amount of content pertaining to the practice of sports journalism.

Chapter 2 provides an overview of important historical events in the development of sports journalism. As stories about sports are often not about chronological events, but rather events and decisions building upon one another to create the who, what, when, where, and why, this chapter builds the case for why things are the way they are and where they might go in the future.

Chapter 3 is an overview of written journalism, with details about not only the craft of a story, but also the news gathering process itself. Emphasis is placed on source cultivation as well as on how the classic written form of newspaper journalism has transitioned into the modern era. In addition, the chapter covers the determination of what makes a good story idea. An important skill for any journalist is the ability to discern what is news, and what might be interesting for readers to know. This chapter includes the seven news values as well. It also includes notes on the classic inverted pyramid story structure and the lead—that is, how the story can grab readers quickly and arouse their interest in reading the rest of the story. Then the nut graph, to explain why we are here. This chapter also discusses two media-related theories, agenda setting and framing.

Chapter 4 discusses news gathering. The discussion of news gathering in the digital age goes beyond creating content for online and into the importance of analytics, statistics, and how the digital world has expanded our knowledge about what is possible in sports media. Nonhuman sources are also discussed. Sometimes the best source is not a person; people may have experience and knowledge but also personal biases. And human sources are no longer so readily available, both due to ongoing changes in the relationships between sport entities and media and due to changes resulting from the COVID-19 pandemic. Gone are the days when a reporter could show up to practice and speak with anyone as they came off the field, court, or ice. With access more heavily constrained, chapter 4 explains the importance of nonhuman sources and the need for modern sports journalists to learn about what WAR and VORP mean.

Chapter 5 discusses new and emerging tools of sports media. Not just hardware like smartphones and digital recorders, but also online platforms such as blogs, Facebook, X (Twitter), Instagram, and YouTube. The chapter discusses the arcane term *backpack journalist* from a time before technology surpassed journalists' ambitions. The chapter also looks at the role of artificial intelligence and its role is sports journalism.

Chapter 6 is about how sports journalism skills translate easily to public relations. In the past, there was a stigma in which traditional journalists identified PR people (hopefully in a humorous manner) as "sellouts." Our chapter explains the fact that PR now uses not only the skills but many of the principles of journalism.

Chapter 7 asks the questions, What is good? What is ethical? Does athletes' status as public figures affect the ability of journalists to tell their stories? And should it? These ethical questions are discussed in a chapter that brings value not in providing indisputable and concrete answers, but in starting the discussion. Legal issues related to sports media are discussed as well.

Chapter 8 features perhaps the most important information in the major: potential jobs in sports journalism. These potential roles have expanded greatly in just the last decade or two. MLB teams didn't all have an in-house sideline reporter at the turn of the century, for instance. And by the time this textbook is in its second edition, the potential roles will have expanded again, in ways few will be able to predict. But this chapter describes what we know now, with the ongoing march of technology. It also includes an in-depth discussion of the task ahead for any aspiring sports journalist: Work harder than you think you need to. Then increase that personal work ethic. Learn, write, shoot, edit, become better than you think you can be. And even then, corporate ownership might make career decisions for you. It is vitally important that each sports journalist understand that they must create value with their work, and that this value should therefore be honored whenever possible. Put another way, don't work for free! . . . if you can help it.

Chapter 9 is a discussion of the main issues facing sports journalism in the modern age and what may be the biggest challenges going forward. The democratization of sports media means that there will continue to be an increase not only in competition, but also in the amount of deliberately created misinformation. Sports journalists' role in being reliable chroniclers of sport is covered, as is the need to counter misinformation.

Summary

There are many aspects to the world we call sports journalism. For the individual sports journalist, the ability to adapt not only to situations and different conversations is very important, but also the ability to adapt to new ways to tell stories. It's important to cultivate and maintain human relationships, but also keep a good relationship with the tools of the trade. Among sports journalism's challenges are adapting not only to the expansion of a journalist's personal brand and voice, but also to the new exposure to fans who have views ranging from the very positive to the very negative. This overview is an entry into the world of sports journalism as a major and as a profession.

Discussion Questions

1. What drew you to this major or this class? Why is sports journalism something that interests you as a potential career?
2. What do you hope to learn in this course about sports journalism?

Applied Activity

Choose three pieces of sports journalism that you have consumed (i.e., read or watched or listened to) in the past week. What made these the topics or media you chose? Have you decided to focus on producing content in a specific medium? Why or why not? Share your answers in a class discussion.

(Media start with being able to express viewpoints in front of others. Any shyness about sharing your opinions and viewpoints should be addressed now.)

The Evolution of Sports Journalism

Chapter Objectives

After completing this chapter, you will be able to do the following:

- Illustrate key moments and events in the development of sports journalism.
- Understand the evolution of sports journalism from print to streaming.
- Discuss sports journalism from the viewpoint of practitioners.

National Basketball Association (NBA) superstar LeBron James sat in a room full of youngsters, with a Boys & Girls Clubs banner prominent in the background. It was July 2010, and host Jim Gray asked James, a free agent at the time, what his next NBA destination would be. After a dramatic pause, the answer arrived. To an ESPN audience of millions, James announced that after seven seasons with his hometown Cleveland Cavaliers, he was going to "take [his] talents to South Beach" and leave for the Miami Heat. While a thousand memes and jokes were soon launched based on his unusual choice of words, James' "Decision" also very publicly signaled a massive change in the very nature of sports media. ESPN's broadcast of **"The Decision"** was not made with the input of the news department, the intent being to shield the news department from any scrutiny. However, the event used the main ESPN station with the program presented as a breaking news story both live and in later reports (Banagan, 2011).

In the face of decades of sports media hegemony held by sports journalists themselves, James' "Decision" was seismic. It was done completely through the filters of James' free-agency choice, a massive media event controlled mostly by James' own camp, and a monumental moment for the history of sports media. It signaled a change from the long-accepted roles of traditional media and the subjects they cover. That change has been gradual, but it is also inexorable. While ESPN's involvement in "The Decision" caused critics both from within and without to ask questions about the network's pursuit of traditional journalism on a consistent basis, it also showed that ESPN was very aware of how athletes would like to be covered going forward. It was a seminal moment in sports journalism, as athletes began to exert more control not only over their own careers, but also over their media coverage (Banagan, 2011).

After "The Decision," decades of understanding that media members would provide the filters and the viewpoints through which sport would be perceived by readers, listeners, and viewers were at an end. The traditional media suddenly were put on notice that the old cliché about the need for adaptability finally applied. No, the old methods didn't come to an immediate end on that July night. And as of this writing, traditional media still have a role to play in the coverage of sport in the United States and around the world. However, from the moment LeBron James broke his own story on his own terms, the sports media world would include athletes creating their own media, telling their own stories.

"Changes." "Innovations." "Metamorphosis." "Challenges."

Any discussion of sports journalism since the turn of the 21st century has been likely to include at least one of these terms. Whether one was a veteran columnist, a young television reporter, a media mogul, or someone seeking to make a name by promoting their blog or YouTube channel on social media, the buzz around sports journalism

LeBron James and "The Decision."
Larry Busacca/Getty Images for Estabrook Group

has long been that "challenges" are being met by "innovations" that are bringing "changes" as sports journalism experiences an ongoing "metamorphosis." Gone are decades of only being able to listen to a game on the radio, watch highlights on the 11:00 p.m. news, and read all about it in the following morning's newspaper. The traditional media hegemony was not quite being completely replaced, but it was undeniably—to the consternation and protests of traditional media practitioners and power brokers—morphing into something else, something different and not necessarily respectful of the old school. The new media were not wholly new in content, though the types of voices that have become popular would probably make 1940s sports writing pioneer W.C. Heinz and his contemporaries blush. Rather, sports journalism has completely changed in terms of access, for readers and practitioners alike.

As technology changed how sports journalism was practiced and delivered, industry leaders sought new ways of telling stories. The opportunities presented by the Internet led to the most profound leaps forward for sports journalism since NBC broadcast a college baseball game between the Princeton Tigers and Columbia Lions in 1939 (Columbia University Athletics, 2009). No bears were part of that day's proceedings, other than the emergence of television as a viable vehicle for sports news and live games. Once that first national broadcast occurred, sports on TV soon joined radio as a preferred method of enjoying live events from a distance.

Sport is an opportunity for people to engage in self-actualization through the use of skills both physical and mental (Beck & Bosshart, 2003). As part of that, fans engage in their own self-actualization, whether through group identification or through a connection with the athletes' athletic achievements. These achievements can include overcoming major challenges. Like print journalism, broadcast sport often features narratives about athletes fighting through injuries or physically dominating opponents (Messner et al., 2000), narratives that an audience wishes to relate to. And these stories have been told in an ever-expanding variety of ways.

For decades, innovations occurred not by creating new modes of content delivery, but within the existing media.

- New camera angles were created.
- Sideline reporters emerged as a standard part of a broadcast.
- Battery-operated transistor radios became popular.
- Typewriters were replaced with computers.
- The triad of print, radio, and television dominated the sports media landscape.

That dominance by the media was concurrent with a dominance of sports discussion and thought by the decision-makers at the various traditional media outlets. Reporters, editors, publishers, producers, and owners all had a hand in shaping daily and ongoing sports journalism coverage, their influence permeating much of what would be known as the first draft of sports history. Even when traditional media began to (grudgingly) make room for the various forms of online media presentation offered by the Internet, traditional media power brokers—and other practitioners operating under a traditional media paradigm—still retained most control over which stories would be told. But changes not only in the ways in which messages have been transmitted, but also in the messages and nature of sports media itself, have also taken hold in more recent years. The effect of public relations, with its similar required skill set, on journalism and journalists has been profound in terms of journalists wondering about their own place in the media landscape (Hutchins & Boyle, 2017).

The current media landscape, with what is known as "traditional media" being joined—and in some cases, overwhelmed—by consumer choices, was predicted by some experts and observers. In 2004, researchers who identified their work as being from the "Museum of Media History" created *EPIC 2014*, a short Flash video depicting a vision of future of media usage. Some of their predictions involved social media pioneer sites that soon faded (Friendster, we hardly knew you), and conglomerate mergers that did not come to pass such as Googlezon, a merger of Google and Amazon. But the video perceptively predicted a world in which user choices would dominate the media landscape, with individual news curated according to each person's desires (Farivar, 2014).

Development and Expansion of Sport Media

Sport is representative of a community's ideals and culture (Beck & Bosshart, 2003). While nowadays people have a great deal of control over the media content they consume, sports occupy a larger place in the zeitgeist both domestically and internationally (Billings & Hundley, 2010). As sport has developed over time, the ability to communicate the norms, rules, and expectations has been paramount in that development (Beck & Bosshart, 2003). Therefore, sports media have developed along with sport itself as an ongoing point of interest worldwide.

Time-Out

What are the five most important sports news events and stories of your lifetime? Of the last five years?

1. List those events. Number them in order of importance, according to your recollections.
2. What was the primary medium on which each event was covered?
3. How do you think each would have been covered in the decades before online media?

Printed Sports Media

The first sports-centric publications were magazines in England, including *Racing Calendar* (1751), *Sporting Magazine* (1792), and *Sporting Life* (1821) (Beck & Bosshart, 2003). The first recorded instance of a sports story appearing in a newspaper occurred in 1733 with a report of a local boxing match in the *Boston Gazette* (Blackistone, 2012; Slater & Zimmerman, 2021). In 1817, England's *Morning Herald* became the first newspaper to feature a sports-specific section.

Organized sport began to proliferate in the latter half of the 19th century. By 1870, the telegraph allowed print publications to report sports news from other locations besides local events. By the start of the 20th century, national sporting publications had come to France (*L'Equipe*) and Italy (*La Gazzetta dello Sport*, *Corriere dello Sport*), with Spain's *Marca* following later. The United States' premier sports-related magazine, *Sports Illustrated*, joined the group in 1954 (Beck & Bosshart, 2003). In the decades to come, these general magazines would also be joined by multiple publications, many of which thrived as vehicles for deeper, more analytical coverage as opposed to day-to-day game reports.

Newspapers

Newspapers have historically been the dominant medium for sports journalism. By the end of the 19th century, newspapers would become the primary medium covering sport in America (McChesney, 1989). McChesney (1989) wrote that this is when sports journalism emerged as a distinct genre of journalism and became an "indispensable section of the daily newspaper" (p. 55). It was also the time when many sports journalism practices emerged—including the game story, a play-by-play recap of a game.

Throughout the 20th century, sports continued to be heavily mediated. Most people who follow games and matches are not there in person but are either watching them on TV or listening to them on the radio. Each technological change forced newspaper sports journalists to change their work routines. One of the most obvious changes to the way sports journalists did their jobs came with the growth of game broadcasts—first on radio, then on television. Game broadcasts forced newspaper journalists to change their focus. "Sports writing has become an adjunct to television, its primary role now to find the story behind the story" (Oriard, 1998). Instead of writing game stories that relied almost solely on play-by-play descriptions, sports journalists began using their stories for more analysis and more detail, and they also began interviewing players and coaches to get their views on the game. This began in the 1920s and 1930s as a response to radio broadcasts (Bryant & Holt, 2006) and continued with the growth of television coverage in the 1950s and 1960s (McChesney, 1989). The quote became a critical part of sports journalists' work, a way to differentiate themselves from other media (Vecsey, 1989), and like other journalists, reporters were judged on the quality of their sources (Boyle, 2006).

McChesney (1989) wrote that TV coverage changed some of the ways in which newspaper sports journalists did their jobs. Stories became less likely to be recaps of the game and more reliant upon statistics, analysis, and background. By the mid-1980s, ESPN had become popular as a cable channel dedicated to 24-hour sports coverage, and in *USA Today*, the one true national print newspaper, sports received 25 percent of the available space every day, compared with 12 to 20 percent in most local newspapers (McChesney, 1989).

Despite the growth of broadcast media and their widespread influence over sports and sports media, newspapers remained the dominant medium for sports journalism. "Newspapers also have the chance to take you into the locker rooms, into interview areas and places quick radio/TV sound bites do not," said Bryce Miller when he was the sports editor for the *Des Moines Register* (Gisondi, 2011).

In the digital age, written sports journalism remains popular. From corporate giants like ESPN and Yahoo! to former blogs turned digital news sites like Bleacher Report and The Ringer, to the growth of individual blogs, message boards, recruiting sites, and local digital news outlets over the past two decades, sports media and digital media have been a perfect match.

Radio

Radio provided the opportunity for sports reporting and consumption to occur in real time. The first sports radio broadcast was of a boxing event in 1921 (Beck & Bosshart, 2003). By the mid-1920s, there were five stations in the United States in the then-new medium of radio when Harold Arlin of Pittsburgh voiced the first live sports play-by-play broadcast, a professional baseball game between the Pittsburgh Pirates and Philadelphia Phillies (Sheridan, 2023). In 1927, millions of Americans listened live to a Jack Dempsey fight.

The new medium for enjoying sport was not without its contemporary critics, however. In an early example of sports power brokers wondering whether new media could take away from their bottom line, there was concern even in the 1930s that with radio as an option, fans would stay home instead of filling venues (Beck & Bosshart, 2003).

Television

Today's students are used to having many opportunities to watch sports on television, with broadcasts from all over the world occurring on ESPN, Fox Sports, Bally Sports' various regional networks, other regional networks, Sky Sports, NBC Sports, BBC Sports, and CBS Sports, to name a few. It wasn't that long ago, though, that televised sports were limited to ABC, NBC, CBS, and Fox.

The first sporting event to air on television was a college football game in 1939 featuring Columbia University and Princeton (Columbia University Athletics, 2009). However, the first notable expansion of sports broadcasts on television occurred in

1961 with the birth of ABC's *Wide World of Sports* (Finn, 2021). While college football and professional baseball had become mainstays on U.S. television, *Wide World of Sports* promised in its opening narration that it was "spanning the globe to bring you the constant variety of sport." This meant American audiences were exposed to everything from the exploits of legendary daredevil Evel Knievel, to the Tour de France, to cliff divers in Acapulco, to golf's British Open. In addition, *Wide World of Sports* was the first broadcast home for events that now receive national broadcasts, including the Indianapolis 500 and the Little League World Series. The show also innovated with players wearing mics during games, slow motion, and split-screen broadcasts (Finn, 2021), elements that remain a large part of any sports broadcast today.

The next big moment for sport and television was the launch of ESPN in 1979. In its early days, ESPN broadcast slow-pitch softball tournaments along with college football games, seeking an audience and enough content to please that audience for a new 24-hours-a-day, seven-days-a-week sports television station. (See the sidebar for more information on ESPN.)

As sport became more popular in the latter part of the 20th century, the need for more sports coverage emerged. Newspapers hired more staff, professional leagues found their games being in demand for television network airing, and the emergence of cable television in the early 1980s meant that a lot more sports would become available to view. While ESPN's initial search for investors faced the challenge of convincing anyone that an all-day sports

ESPN: The (Self-Proclaimed) Worldwide Leader in Sport

Calling itself the Entertainment and Sports Programming Network proved to be prescient—and very wise—for ESPN. While ESPN has at times been criticized for falling short of traditional journalistic principles in its dealings with individual athletes, teams, and broadcast partners, that E at the start of the network's acronym has allowed it over the years to become, with no apologies, a one-stop location for people who want to experience everything from basketball to the annual Fourth of July hot dog–eating contest.

ESPN also pioneered new revenue streams in pay television, asking cable companies for an extra fee just to carry ESPN and later, its sister stations ESPN 2, ESPNews, and ESPN U. One major factor in ESPN's early and meteoric growth was a move that seems simple and obvious in the 2020s, but which 40-plus years earlier was brand new and decidedly outside the previously established norms of sports broadcasting. After the 1979 NCAA Men's Basketball Tournament final between Larry Bird's Indiana State Sycamores and Magic Johnson's Michigan State Spartans drew massive ratings, it seemed possible that there was more of an audience to tap for what would later become March Madness. At that time, only the Final Four national semifinals and the final were broadcast.

Sensing an opening, ESPN purchased the rights to the earlier rounds of the tournament, anticipating that fans of schools that might not reach the Final Four would still enjoy seeing their teams compete. This proved to be correct, as the popularity of the tournament continued to grow and ESPN reaped the benefits. As cable television slowly found its way into American households, hotels took advantage of the situation. Just as today hotels might offer potential patrons free Wi-Fi or HBO, in the early 1980s they would advertise the fact that their rooms had ESPN available so that groups could rent rooms and gather to watch their alma mater compete in the NCAA tournament.

As ESPN grew, broadcasts brought the international yacht race the America's Cup into homes, with live broadcasts of Australian Rules Football on ESPN 2 helping 1990s insomniacs get their sports fix. ESPN's claim to be "The Worldwide Leader in Sports" has been bolstered and fulfilled by the continued development of technology, bringing the network's multiplatform coverage to audiences all over the globe (MacLean, 2017). The development of ESPN Radio and ESPN.com further added to ESPN's reach, as now ESPN content could be consumed in the car or on the computer.

network would find an audience (Shales & Miller, 2011), soon cable outlets like the Golf Channel and the Speed Channel were serving enthusiasts for the links and the track, respectively.

The NBA's rise illustrates how quickly broadcasting and sports changed. In 1980, the deciding game of the NBA finals, a Los Angeles Lakers victory over the Philadelphia 76ers, was shown on the West Coast on tape delay (Krawczynski, 2017). Within a decade, NBA broadcasts had become ratings winners on NBC (Curtis, 2018). As of this writing, the NBA's television contract with ESPN and TNT pays the league approximately $2.6 billion per year to broadcast the regular season and playoffs. The next contract is expected to include lucrative streaming rights in addition to broadcast rights (Adgate, 2023). In 2024, the NBA was also expected to gain a new windfall with negotiations for a new rights deal expected to yield multiple broadcast partners (Friend, 2024). The NBA was expected by observers to attain a new deal potentially worth between $60 billion and $72 billion in its 2024 negotiations, up from the previous $24 billion deal signed in 2014 (Friend, 2024).

The NBA is not alone in having lucrative broadcast contracts.

- The National Football League's (NFL's) various partners include ABC, NBC, CBS, Fox, and Amazon Prime, with YouTube carrying NFL Sunday Ticket. These various deals are slated to net the league more than $125 billion before 2033 (Ozanian, 2023).
- Major League Baseball (MLB) features its own proprietary streaming opportunity, for which fans can pay a fee ($129 in 2024) to watch every game for their favorite team, other than locally blacked-out games. In addition, MLB is partnered with Fox ($729 million per year), ESPN ($560 million), and Warner Bros. Discovery ($535 million), as well as Apple ($85 million), which shows Friday evening games (Fisher, 2023).
- National Hockey League (NHL): Not every professional sports league has seen its broadcast rights skyrocket in value. NHL commissioner Gary Bettman had hoped for a deal worth $750 million a season and had to "settle" for multiple partners paying more than $600 million total, including ESPN getting back into NHL broadcasting after a lengthy absence with a $400 million per year package (Schram, 2021). The NHL also has a Canadian broadcast deal worth $4.2 billion (U.S. dollars) over 12 years (Schram, 2021).
- Women's National Basketball Association (WNBA) commissioner Cathy Englebert said in an appearance on CNBC following the 2024 NCAA Women's Basketball Tournament Final Four that she was optimistic about the league's next TV contract. The 2024 Women's Final Four had earned record TV ratings; Englebert said that the women's sports had been undervalued, and the WNBA hoped to double its rights fees in potential deals with multiple broadcast partners (Squawk Box, 2024).

Table 2.1 shows current broadcast partners for various leagues.

TABLE 2.1 Broadcast Partners for Selected Sport Entities in the United States

League	National broadcast partner	Local/regional broadcast partner
National Football League	Fox, CBS, NBC, ESPN, Prime Video, NFL Network	N/A
Major League Baseball	Fox, ESPN, Turner, Peacock, YouTube, Apple TV+, MLB Network	Negotiated by teams
National Basketball Association	ESPN, Turner	Negotiated by teams
National Hockey League	ESPN, Turner, Hulu	Negotiated by teams
NCAA (Men's Basketball Tournament)	CBS	N/A
Big Ten Conference	Fox, NBC, CBS, Big Ten Network	N/A
English Premier League (United States contract)	NBC, Peacock, USA	N/A

Reprinted by permission from G.E. Clavio and M.H. Zimmerman, "Governance and the Sport Media Industry," in *Governance in Sport: Analysis and Application*, edited by B. Tiell and K. Cebula (Champaign, IL: Human Kinetics, 2020).

Industry Profile

A.J. Perez

A.J. Perez knows that the best way to get noticed as a sports journalist is by being a diligent, motivated, and observant reporter. As part of an NJ.com team of reporters covering Super Bowl XLVIII in February 2014, Perez was in the room when a man took the mic during game MVP Malcolm Smith's postgame press conference and asserted conspiracy theories about the 9/11 terrorist attacks in New York and Washington, D.C. Perez was immediately on the case.

"I was like, 'This is a story,'" said Perez, who had covered local police in his early career (personal correspondence, February 2021). "Having a background in open records, I can find almost anybody's phone number."

Perez's story explaining how the microphone grabber snuck into one of the most secure sporting events was cited by multiple outlets. It wasn't the first time Perez was in the right place at the right time to cover a story and recognized it as such. As an auto racing reporter for the Long Beach *Press-Telegram* in 2005, Perez covered a confrontation between then-IndyCar rookie Danica Patrick and Jaques Lazier. That story getting picked up led to an opportunity at *USA Today*.

"I was not a NASCAR writer when I went to *USA Today*—I had covered two NASCAR races," Perez said. "If you're a reporter, and you know what you're doing, you can fit into any job. Just be versatile."

After three years at *USA Today*, Perez worked for Fox Sports, CBS Sports, FanHouse, and NJ.com, largely covering hockey, a sport for which he had a strong affinity. That came in handy when he returned to *USA Today* and his editor pitched Perez a story about what it would be like for a rec league goalie to take shots from Washington Capitals superstar Alex Ovechkin.

The hook? Perez was that rec league goalie. So, just after he competed in a Tough Mudder event, Perez—who also had become a personal trainer by this time—returned to the D.C. area and suited up.

"Then I flew back from Vegas, and I took shots off Ovechkin," Perez said. "I was fortunate because we didn't have a shooter. Our producer was tossing the pucks to Ovechkin for the one-timers, so I had the advantage there. He was a little off his game because of that."

Perez's toughness against one of the great goal scorers in hockey history has crossed into his career as well. Circumstances have meant that even experienced, knowledgeable reporters can find themselves between jobs, and Perez is no exception. But Perez notes that being able to sift through records and documents is something that should still bring great value, even as sports journalism continues to adjust to changing times.

"I would like to think that people who go through court records, who go through police records, who know who to call . . . we saw it with Tiger," Perez said, referring to reportage surrounding Tiger Woods' 2021 automobile accident. "There's fewer people doing that kind of thing, so when something like that happens there's not the reporters there who have the knowledge to do it."

Perez also noted that he had honed over the years a writing and reporting style that was largely presented as quicker hits, reporting that cuts through the noise and goes straight to the most important aspects. A modern style that can adapt to a world where many people now consume news on smartphones.

"Now we have a notice that tells us how long a story will take to read," Perez said. "You're almost incentivized to keep it shorter and more concise."

Perez's adaptability helped lead him in late 2020 to Front Office Sports, where he is a senior reporter whose byline can be found on stories ranging from the activities of sports media corporations, to the Coyotes moving from Arizona to Utah, to a court case involving Brett Favre.

"I always call it quick enterprise," Perez said. "That's what I specialize in; I don't like doing stories that take forever to write and they're 4,000 words. I like doing stuff that's digestible. It's exclusive, but it's not something that's gonna take me two or three weeks or a month, two months, to do."

Perez also offered a few thoughts for students and reporters who are just starting out.

"It's being there, being recognizable, don't be late. That kind of thing," Perez said. "Don't try to hit a home run your first week on the job. Just grow into it, and don't stress over getting beat the first couple months on a beat. You're going to get the same sources as everybody else eventually. So as long as you're cordial and accurate in your reporting, that's what they care about most."

In light of the demonstrated appetite for sports programming and the passion of local fan bases, regional networks and TV deals for professional sports began to spring up in the late 1980s. Teams in larger markets have been able to reap the benefits, such as MLB's Los Angeles Dodgers' 25-year TV deal for $8.35 billion (Crupi, 2023). However, teams outside the largest markets have not had an easy time finding lucrative TV deals. In early 2023, Bally Sports, which carried local TV rights for a total of 37 franchises in MLB, the NBA, and the NHL, declared bankruptcy (Clemens, 2023). The loss of the television revenue stream was expected to be devastating to the financial prospects of those teams, in addition to the ability of fans to see games. Part of the fallout included losing the rights to two MLB teams, with others possible as the company failed to pay its bills. In January 2024, Bally Sports owner Diamond Sports Group announced a deal that would bring Amazon Prime in as a part owner and broadcast partner, offering a chance for Bally Sports to survive and retain broadcast rights to its various remaining teams (Folk, 2024).

Similarly massive amounts of money for broadcast rights are also flowing into college athletics. Each conference can negotiate its own media rights deals, thanks to a 1984 U.S. Supreme Court ruling. The NCAA had controlled television rights and determined which matchups appeared on national television until the University of Oklahoma and the University of Georgia led a lawsuit and won (Mawson & Bowler, 1989).

Even in the wake of the COVID-19 pandemic, college sports brands remained valuable to potential partners. In 2020, ESPN and the Southeastern Conference (SEC) agreed to a deal that would pay $300 million per season, an increase from the previous $55 million per year in the conference's CBS deal (Caron & Crupi, 2020). The two entities also partner in the SEC Network. Not to be outdone, the Big Ten made agreements with three broadcast networks. The conference's deal with Fox, CBS, and NBC began in 2023 and is worth billions (Reedy, 2023).

The gap between the Big Ten and SEC and the expansion of other "Power" conferences is already more than tens of millions per school per year and is expected to widen (Holton, 2023). These post-expansion windfalls for the SEC and Big Ten caused schools in the remaining Power Four conferences to take notice. In 2023, *Sports Illustrated* reported that a group of schools in the Atlantic Coast Conference (ACC) had discussed exploring an attempt to withdraw from the conference's Grant of Rights television agreement, which does not expire until 2036 (Steinberg, 2023). A top-earning school in the ACC, for instance, received approximately $40 million in 2022, while in 2024 it was estimated that schools in the Big Ten and SEC might receive $75 million, with that figure expected to escalate in the coming years (Holton, 2023).

Clemson sued the ACC in a South Carolina court, joining Florida State in challenging the league's right to charge schools hundreds of millions of dollars to leave the conference. The league's exit fee was said to be in excess of $140 million (Russo, 2024).

The market has the potential to become unsettled in other ways as well. The increased payouts to collegiate athletic conferences also occur in the wake of ongoing legal battles over college athletes' rights and increasing opportunities for financial compensation (Baker & Brison, 2015).

Streaming

As noted in the discussion of various broadcast partners, streaming continues to gain popularity. However, the cable-based television deals are still important. Apple's deal with Major League Soccer, for instance, gives the U.S.-based soccer league a streaming home, but the league also has a deal with Fox to broadcast games from 2023 to 2026, including playoff matches (Quillen, 2022). Further, as the major U.S. professional sports leagues all have opportunities for fans to purchase streaming for their favorite teams or for entire leagues, the most lucrative deals continue to be from traditional broadcasting. Many sports consumers might watch games on ESPN Plus, but their subscription fees still go to the main entity of ESPN. Also, as consumers confronted the need to pay for multiple streaming services just to watch their favorite shows, ESPN, Fox, and Warner Bros. Discovery announced that in fall 2024 they planned to launch a merged streaming service (Associated Press, 2024). So while streaming is important technology, and the future of broadcasting will feature more and more streaming services, the most lucrative deals for sport remain anchored—if not always featured—on more traditional services.

Traditional Media's Control of the Narrative

For decades, the sports media's relationship with athletes and organizations consisted of sports reporters covering events and producing feature stories on those athletes and organizations. As the

All the Stats That Fit in a Box: Henry Chadwick's Seminal Contribution

New York–area sports journalist Henry Chadwick, a cricket fan originally from England, had an idea. The year was 1859, and Chadwick decided to create a way to present all of the statistics from a baseball game in one tidy package. Inventing the term *strikeout* along the way, Chadwick created the first baseball box score (Pesca, 2009).

The game was so long ago that Brooklyn had two teams, the Stars and the Excelsiors. They provided the material for Chadwick's first venture into an aspect of the game that would endure long after Brooklyn ended up with no Major League Baseball teams. The box score eventually became important for rotisserie participants, reporters looking to include statistics in their stories, and everyone from casual to hardcore fans.

Within each box, a story is told. How many batters did each pitcher face? Who was the most important hitter? Did fielding miscue play a part in the game result? It was all there in the newspaper, and now online.

The box score was invented largely as a way to show readers the game in a time before sports photography. Even as more ways to report the game have come along, the box score remains integral, as those seeking information, and perhaps nostalgia, rely on the details it contains (Kurkjian, 2010).

---

years passed, that coverage would become more investigative and would also expand to include a focus on news that had nothing to do with statistics and great—or not so great—plays, spotlighting off-field (as well as off-ice and off-court) issues as they occurred. All of what occurred on the field, ice, or court—and the stated viewpoints of the people involved with those events—was filtered for public consumption through people with training or experience in the practice of sports journalism who were tasked with observing people and events, then describing and interpreting what had occurred.

When newspapers were the dominant medium, reporters relayed their own recollections and viewpoints of the games and the people who played them, with those people's voices also included . . . at the discretion of the writer. The choices of which voices and events to include, and how they were included, belonged to the writers and their editors.

As technology and sports media evolved to include the broadcast medium, radio presented an opportunity for sports enthusiasts to hear events relayed in real time. While pre- and postgame interviews were largely unfiltered conversations, the events themselves were still described through the eyes, experiences, and knowledge of the broadcaster, or more simply, through the broadcaster's judgment. Many of these broadcasters carried their own biases into the booth and provided not just information, but also an affinity for those who wanted to listen to someone who would root, root, root for the home team. Broadcast sport often features narratives of athletes fighting through injuries or physically dominating opponents (Messner et al., 2000). In that context, a broadcaster's ability to lend drama and gravitas to the storytelling through familiarity with teams and athletes can be vital to connecting the audience to an athlete's struggles.

By the mid-20th century, televised sports enabled viewers to witness events live and make their own judgments about what happened. That is, provided the proper camera angles were available. The ability to see a game's minute details on television has improved exponentially, with multiple replays of every moment showing people at home whether the officials got the call right, whether that was a catch, a successful tag, a double fault, or a goal that should have been determined to be offside. Still, even as technology has evolved, the choice of which games are available for viewing and which camera to switch to at a given moment is still made by a producer.

Athlete Control of the Narrative

Four years after "The Decision," New York Yankees legend Derek Jeter spearheaded his first post-retirement gig. Partnering with other professional athletes, Jeter started *The Players' Tribune*, an online outlet featuring first-person accounts written—sometimes with the assistance of professional journalists—by athletes themselves. *The Players' Tribune* isn't necessarily intended as a rebuke of media coverage, or a commentary on traditional media. Rather, its stories are written as if traditional media do not exist, with original and often notably personal descriptions of the lifestyles and life experiences of athletes. There are stories of draft preparation, injury rehabilitation, inspiration from family and mentors, the glow of a championship, and the frustration of a loss in a big game or match. *The Players' Tribune* has given many athletes the chance to tell their own stories, in their own words, without a traditional media filter. As with social media (chapter 5), the message is taken straight to the readers.

The Players' Tribune's mission also spotlights athletes who write about the issues that affect them and are important to them individually, including discussions of race, gender, and levels of compensation. For example, in the midst of a years-long legal battle between U.S. Soccer and the U.S. women's national team over financial compensation, WNBA and U.S. Olympic basketball legend Sue Bird weighed in with a column that not only discussed the soccer situation (with a nod to her significant other, U.S. soccer stalwart Megan Rapinoe) but also addressed the ongoing collective bargaining discussions in the WNBA (Bird, 2019). As discussions of the issue of systemic racism in the United States dominated conversation in July 2020, retired and former Pro Bowl Cleveland Browns offensive lineman Joe Thomas penned a column titled "Just Being 'Not Racist' Isn't Good Enough" (Thomas, 2020). That same month, European soccer stars addressed incidences of racial injustice through a video titled "Not Born Racist."

Months before the launch of *The Players' Tribune*, the traditional media still played a role in partnering with athletes for major announcements. It was not necessarily a last gasp, but perhaps "The Decision" will be remembered as the last time an athlete didn't use a proprietary outlet or their own social media account. While James' exclusive ESPN broadcast perhaps paved the way for more athletes to try to control their own narratives, James himself went back to a somewhat old-fashioned method. The same blurred lines would soon appear again as James' 2014 return to Cleveland was announced exclusively in an article in *Sports Illustrated* by writer Lee Jenkins (James & Jenkins, 2014).

Traditional Media Navigate the Challenges

Years before athletes began to establish their own vehicles for messaging, traditional journalism practitioners also tried to create their own versions of sports media utopia. America Online's (AOL's) FanHouse recruited writers and editors from newspapers and magazines in building an outlet that featured recognizable talent, including columnists such as Kevin Blackistone and Lisa Olson. FanHouse had begun in 2006 as a less mainstream sports blog site, and it started its campaign to hire more reporters and columnists away from traditional outlets in January 2009. The online edifice would not last, as a sale to legacy media outlet *The Sporting News* in January 2011 precipitated mass layoffs and the end of AOL FanHouse, as it had become known (Sandomir, 2011). Many of the alums scattered throughout sports media, sharing their tales and descriptions of a place many felt might have been the greatest place they had ever worked.

While it did not last long, FanHouse's demise shared some noteworthy characteristics with a more legendary (that is, at least among old sports journalists), and even more short-lived, attempt at sports media utopia. In January 1990, *The National Sports Daily* had debuted, flush with cash and with plans to spend it. Intent on dominating the sports media landscape, *The National* (as it was quickly known) used the financial might of founder Emilio Azcarraga Milmo to build a staff of known quality sports journalists, led by editor in chief and longtime *Sports Illustrated* writing legend Frank Deford.

Ever since the early 1990s, when sports journalists of a certain age and era talk about the most desirable traits of a sports media outlet both as a place to work and as a source readers appreciated, *The National* is often mentioned as the ultimate example. Over the years, certain print sports sections have gained acclaim among sports journalists. The 1970s and 1980s *Boston Globe* of Bob Ryan, Dan Shaughnessy, and Will McDonough. *Sports Illustrated*'s old stable that featured Deford, Jim Murray, Roy Blount Jr., and Dan Jenkins, with later writers such as Rick Telander, Gary Smith, and Jackie MacMullan taking up the mantle as *SI* built and maintained its legend over a period of decades.

The National had Deford, famous for being a longtime voice in sports journalism who could claim friendships with people such as Boston Celtics and NBA great Bill Russell. It had well-known columnists in Dave Kindred and Charles Pierce. It had a humorist—then just finding his voice and niche—in Norman Chad. It had strong and dependable beat writers in Chris Mortensen, Ed Hinton, and Johnette Howard. It had a veritable boatload of money that management, the major beat writers and columnists, and the rank-and-file were eager and able to spend. *The National* immediately declared its intention to cover the major American sports better than anyone, starting with editions in the United States' three largest cities featuring the local NBA star on the cover in each one: Chicago (Michael Jordan), Los Angeles (Magic Johnson), and New York (Patrick Ewing).

They produced a daily sports-only newspaper that emulated popular and similar publications from overseas such as Italy's *La Gazzetta dello Sport*. They left no reporting stone unturned, famously paying to send a writer to Cameroon to report a story on local reaction to the Indomitable Lions' unexpected run to the 1990 FIFA World Cup Quarterfinals. They expanded circulation and local coverage to cities beyond those first three, looking to spike circulation numbers in the face of a reluctant advertising market. The budget and the mandate to cover everything to the best of their ability, the encouragement to write lengthier pieces, plus the massive travel budget, were a sports journalist's dream. The daily—and quite thick in terms of page count—paper dedicated to sports only, including the box score of every game played the day before in the United States at press time, was a sports enthusiast's dream. A half decade before the Internet started becoming part of everyday life, *The National* stood tall and without true competition in the American written and print sports journalism market.

And by this moment, just about every student reading this early chapter of a book on sports journalism is probably wondering, "Why in the world haven't I heard of *The National Sports Daily*?"

Ultimately, *The National* fell victim to a major reason why it is often difficult for great business ideas to last. After the initial burst of excitement and spending money as if the spigot would never turn off, and perhaps partially due to ownership realizing how long it would take for the publication to turn a profit, it simply ran out of money (French & Kahn, 2011). A year after its first publication, *The National*'s budget was cut by millions of dollars, and within months the paper was completely finished. Just 18 months after starting, *The National*'s final issue intoned, "We Had a Ball: The Fat Lady Sings Our Song." In a cruel irony, the fate of *The National* was that of most upstart sports leagues throughout the years: They made a splash and, as a result, ran through their financial capital quickly in an unsuccessful attempt to maintain that early status as the Hot New Thing. In a further twist, the financial extravagances practiced by *The National* would be mirrored a decade later when the dot-com boom became a bust.

The Internet and the Boom of Sports Sites

Students reading this book for their classes understand that the Internet has not been around forever. But those same readers also have never known a world without the "information superhighway." Ads started to show up on afternoon television in the early to mid-1990s for providers like Prodigy and AOL, the latter with its well-known bootup sound of electronics struggling, then quieting to "Welcome!" users to the World Wide Web. By the end of the 20th century, faster connection speeds expanded the possibilities for sites, with a higher number of visual elements for site visitors to enjoy.

The Internet provides a platform for broadcasts of and information about sporting events (Beck & Bosshart, 2003), but more notably in these times, it also provides an opportunity for fan commentary in real time. Today, sites such as ESPN, CBS Sports, *Sports Illustrated*, and MLB.com all provide statistics, video, information, stories, and podcasts for visitors on the various types of hardware on which the Internet is viewed. However, the path to get to the comparative efficiency of today's Internet was not an easy one, and the various sites are still constantly trying to find the best ways to present sports news and information, with as few autoplay ads as possible.

To understand how communication moved from traditional media (e.g., newspapers, television, and radio) to include digital outlets such as web pages and later social media platforms such as Facebook and X (formerly known as Twitter), it is helpful to outline the evolution of online communication. Digital media provide access to information on a next-to-immediate basis, and this immediacy brings advantages in increased reach and readership, taking communication from a local or state level to national and often international. The technology that enabled this shift to online communication had humble beginnings.

The concept of online networking was based on a global set of interconnected computers from which anyone could quickly and easily access data. This concept, while revolutionary, was missing one key component—how to make computers talk to each other to share small packets of information, known as **packet switching**. To test the feasibility of packet switching, an experiment was designed in which two computers were connected to each other, one in Massachusetts and the other in California, through a low-speed dial-up telephone line. The computers were able to run programs and retrieve data, leading to a network called ARPANET.

To accommodate mass consumer use, high-speed networks were developed and connected in a shared infrastructure, creating the information superhighway, which we now know as the Internet. By the mid-1990s, affordable personal computers and access to the Internet enabled online communication, a crucial element of digital media. Early forms of online communication, known as Web 1.0, provided a way for users to connect with each other around shared interests. Web 2.0 enabled content creation (Cormode & Krishnamurthy, 2008).

Web 1.0

One of the earliest forms of **Web 1.0** that facilitated online content consumption was traditional websites. Websites also offered individuals the ability to simultaneously consume content and exchange information with others through comment areas placed at the end of a web page. This effectively made websites both a mass medium and a form of interpersonal communication (Eighmey & McCord, 1998).

With increased website presence, digital journalism gained prominence, largely influenced by the availability of Internet service providers such as AOL and web browsers such as Internet Explorer. By 1996, most major news outlets had a digital version of their product. Text and photos from print versions were posted online, with the occasional addition of video.

Although the content remained similar, the differences in content consumption were significant. Traditional print media contain topical sections and are bound by space limitations. Digital versions of the same publications included sections, but they also featured searchable toolbars, grouped content, and linked content within text. Thus, anyone could create a unique way to consume news and information.

The addition of news aggregators attached to service providers such as AOL and Yahoo! only increased the availability of sports content and the ways in which people could consume that content. AOL or Yahoo! news aggregators could now pull stories from multiple outlets and arrange them by topic. Readers no longer needed to visit multiple publications for their sports news, and by 2008, the Pew Research Center (Pew Research, 2023) reported that more Americans were getting their news from the Internet than from printed newspapers.

Web 2.0

Interactive features that allowed users to create content led to the rise of **Web 2.0** at the turn of the century. Message boards grew in popularity and led to the proliferation of sites meant for specific audiences (e.g., Friendster, Classmates, Rivals, MySpace) to connect them with others who had similar interests (Cormode & Krishnamurthy, 2008; Wolcott, 2008). Rivals.com was a hub for individualized sites that hosted coverage and message boards for collegiate athletic programs. Fans could pay a monthly fee for access to premium articles on recruiting and premium access to the message board on which to discuss those recruits. Other similar sites sprang up, and soon they began to hire former sports journalists to replace coverage previously provided by fans with a passion but with neither training nor experience in writing about sports.

The interactive features of Web 2.0 allowed for the emergence of content creators and mobile journalism, especially through social media and outlets such as blogs and podcasts. Facebook, X, Instagram, and YouTube are the Big Four social media platforms. There are other platforms that have proven popular, but these four have endured over a period of years and present the widest set of options in terms of how sports media practitioners might apply sports journalism principles to their work. The Big Four have proven to be effective platforms for both media organizations and sport organizations to communicate information quickly and efficiently to their target publics and other interested consumers. While other social media platforms, such as Snapchat and TikTok, have gained a noteworthy following, the staying power and user-friendliness of the four in question dictate that they will be the main focus of sports journalism education for the modern era.

Online video was highly desired from the start, and users sat through grainy and slow-loading videos for years before finding their oasis. YouTube was created in 2005, and so quickly did it become well-known as an efficient way to stream video that when *Time* magazine named its 2006 Person of the Year as "You," the representation of the computer video screen on the *Time* cover was identical to YouTube's interface (Zimmerman et al., 2011). Instagram was created in 2010 as a photo-sharing platform (Blystone, 2020), and it was acquired by Facebook only two years later for $1 billion. As an indicator of the various platforms' machinations and utilization independent of each other, the acquisition was said to be spurred by Facebook's wariness of X's growth (Rodriguez, 2019).

As social media have become more ubiquitous, journalists at traditional outlets have used social media technologies to connect with fans and sometimes to engage in **crowdsourcing**—that is, seeking information via social media posts soliciting such information. While journalists have often resisted newer forms of media over the years, once traditional outlets started to embrace technology, it began to pay some dividends. Past research has indicated that using social media to promote traditional media content can have a positive effect on readership (Hong, 2012).

Pivot to Video

The fading of the initial dot-com boom in the early 2000s forced legacy media sports websites to make some personnel changes due to financial difficulties. Fox Sports was the hardest hit, with layoffs occurring shortly after a hiring binge in the early 2000s. More recently, Fox Sports was an example of the difficulty of managing content across platforms. In June 2017, Fox Sports' online platform announced that there would be a "pivot to video," resulting in 20 writers and editors (the entire writing staff) being fired from the website (Marchand, 2020). Fox Sports' "pivot" was part of a wave of similar moves. MTV laid off writers it had hired to create long-form articles. *Sports Illustrated* laid off multiple writers amid a push for more video. Online media companies including Vocativ, Mic, and Vice also sought to replace writers with videographers (Curtis, 2017; Kelleher, 2017).

The "pivot to video" made sense on some levels. Online video had gained in popularity as the ability to stream (e.g., bandwidth, faster Internet connections) improved (Kelleher, 2017), with a chance to use the medium for advertising that could be placed where a news consumer could not simply click away (Curtis, 2017). In addition, the newspaper industry's earlier failure to recognize the online trend had media companies worried (Kelleher, 2017). The advertising implications of this pivot were clear. Users could click away from pop-up advertising, but they would have to watch an ad placed in front of a video before they could watch the video (Curtis, 2017).

As noted in popular blog site The Ringer, the pivot to video was the latest in a history of attempts by media companies to gain and regain readership and viewership by announcing a change in approach (Curtis, 2017): newspapers announcing they would publish fewer long-form stories in a pivot to more of a *USA Today* style. News aggregation. More analysis. Podcasts. Anything to entice an audience that may in the end be impossible—or at least, massively difficult—to attract anyway. While media companies have tended to allow media outlets driven by new technology to gain a foothold and sometimes overtake the old—or, as they might prefer, "existing"—technology and media outlets, they did not give up without trying to look like they were keeping up with the media zeitgeist.

Now the phrase "pivot to video" represents not a renewed focus on a viable and important medium, but rather a sign of upper management lacking a clear plan for the future. But how did it turn out for the sports site that started the trend? By fall 2020, Fox Sports was reversing the decision, asserting a new need for people who could create original content for the site, including writing and podcasting in addition to video (Marchand, 2020).

The Market for Quality Sports Journalism

Despite some past failures, new high-quality sports media ventures are not necessarily financial losers. Quite the contrary. Sports coverage often is a revenue driver for a media outlet. But as outlets such as FanHouse and *The Players' Tribune* have led to further endeavors in the quest for sports media perfection, slower and steadier growth has become the better management approach.

The emergence of ***The Athletic*** resulted from such an approach. The sports media site started modestly with reporters in Chicago first and later Toronto before expanding to cover most of the United States and selected markets in Canada. Like its online predecessors, *The Athletic*'s hiring practices consist largely of poaching writers and editors from existing legacy media outlets. Notably, the ownership of *The Athletic* drew pointed criticism for stating that their goal was to "pillage" newspapers (Draper, 2017). In addition, *The Athletic*'s promotional model seemed to rely heavily on having every new reporter promote their own hiring on social media. Whether they were covering the Los Angeles Dodgers or the Buffalo Sabres, American college football or England's Premier League, each new reporter wrote a "Why I'm Joining *The Athletic*" piece detailing their career, their new role with *The Athletic*, and their belief in the site's business model and goals (Clavio & Moritz, 2021). Links to these were then tweeted by the new writer, often with a mention of *The Athletic* offering a discount for new subscriptions. For instance, in fall 2020, the site featured an offer for a subscription to *The Athletic* for the cost of a single dollar per month. There are regular discounts for new subscribers and college students as well.

The Athletic's stability soon begat aggressive expansion. As *The Athletic* grew in popularity, the site hired writers and podcasters to cover most stateside markets. Fans could name just about any city, team, or league, and it probably had at least one beat writer *The Athletic* had hired away from whatever their previous gig happened to be. Writers from newspapers and magazines, writers from websites, independent bloggers—many found a home at *The Athletic*. In 2018, *The Athletic* announced new coverage of soccer, including the U.S.-based Major League Soccer and the National Women's Soccer League as well as England's Premier League.

However, like most companies and media outlets, *The Athletic* was not immune to market forces. Layoffs began in June 2020, with the media company losing 46 people, or 8 percent of its staffing (Draper, 2020). As with Fox Sports' layoffs two decades earlier, this may have been a symptom of overexpansion because the job losses included beat reporters for teams in all four of the major sports, college beat writers, a person who analyzed film of Los Angeles Lakers games, a podcast producer, and a pair of boxing writers. *The Athletic* also announced a 10 percent pay cut for all employees, while executives noted that it had raised $50 million in venture capital earlier in the year, enabling it to keep the cuts to a lower level (Draper, 2020).

The Athletic's experience indicates that there remains a market for quality sports journalism. Subscriber rates were high—though spiked by frequent discounts—and more than $140 million in venture capital had been raised between 2016 and 2020. There's really no way to describe layoffs in a positive manner, but the company had only been around for four years, and 46 employees made up only 8 percent of the workforce, indicating a huge and rapid expansion. And as occurred after *The National*'s demise three decades before, most of the reporters who lost their positions with *The Athletic* landed well with other sports media outlets. However, the end of *The Athletic*'s rapid rise should tell media moguls and journalists to always be prepared

The Year Sports Stopped

When the deadly COVID-19 pandemic occurred in 2020, sports joined society itself in coming to a complete halt. And while people were soon able to shop for essentials, sports stopped in March 2020 and didn't return until months later. MLB, the NHL, and the NBA eventually decided their championships in abbreviated seasons played in nearly fan-free bubbles while the world waited for scientists to develop a vaccine.

During the height of the pandemic, sports journalists saw their usual schedules thrown into not only disarray, but nonexistence (Velloso, 2022). One of the most out-front reactions was radio hosts finding another way to fill the air. Some went with broadcasts analyzing historical events in sports, for instance. Locker room access was lost (Curtis, 2020a, 2020b), which was sensible considering the situation. However, that access did not return as society returned to normal, though some journalists noted that access had already been lessening prior to the pandemic (Velloso, 2022).

It must also be noted that, as The Ringer editor Bryan Curtis wrote while making clear that locker room access was a privilege, "Of all journalist whining, sports writer whining is the least sympathetic" (Curtis, 2020a).

Velloso (2022) interviewed a dozen sports journalists about their experiences during the COVID-19 pandemic. The group consisted of newspaper reporters, digital outlet reporters, and reporters for official team media. The subjects noted that without games to write about, they instead engaged in more feature stories and analysis.

Related to the loss of locker room access, teams' and leagues' move to video press conferences meant more limitations on who the sports journalists had a chance to speak with. In a postgame or post-training locker room, a reporter can approach any available player; this proved to be a profound change in terms of how it affected coverage.

Ultimately, a "return to normal" for sports has led to the continuation of lucrative broadcast deals, with fans able to watch sport on more platforms than ever before. For sports journalists, however, their previous version of normalcy has been slower to appear.

for the many twists and turns of the industry. And there are still hundreds of employees at *The Athletic*, working from north to south and sea to shining sea, including many who would say that it might be the best job they've ever had.

Blurring the Lines Between Journalism and Public Relations

Sports journalism is part of the creation of collective memory, which includes mythmaking around events (Serazio, 2010). Message creation in public relations involves many of the same skills as news reporting, and many former journalists find themselves working in roles that pertain more to positive message creation than to unbiased coverage. It is important to consider each outlet and the focus of its coverage, as sports media shape history and perceptions of identity (Billings & Hundley, 2010). Ultimately, sports journalism narratives can affect public perceptions, for better or for worse (Serazio, 2010). The impact of sport goes beyond local communities, with implications for national pride as well (Beck & Bosshart, 2003).

The distinction between sports journalism and public relations becomes less clear when journalistic outlets are used in partnership with athletes' or organizations' public relations goals, as when ESPN aired live exclusive coverage of NBA superstar LeBron James' famous "Decision" (Banagan, 2011). Nothing is certain about the future of sports journalism as a field of practice or study. After all, ESPN was expected to fail when it debuted in September 1979 (Banagan, 2011). But events and trends indicate that as traditional outlets lose prestige and personnel, and outlets that focus on controlled messaging become more prominent, it will become more common to use sports journalism skills to produce content that years ago might have been considered public relations. The difference between traditional journalism and public relations leads us to constantly examine how to train aspiring sports media practitioners for these seemingly divergent roles (Hutchins & Boyle, 2017).

Summary

Sports journalism's genesis occurred in 1733 with a newspaper story on a local boxing match. Since then, developments in technology as well as public interest have led sports coverage to evolve far beyond—and perhaps, without—newspaper, radio, and television. Now games can be viewed on streaming services on a supercomputer that fits in your pocket. And when the games are done, there is no shortage of places to go—on that same smartphone—for information about what you just saw, and what might be next. Throughout the history of sports media, outlets in print, broadcast, and online have reacted to and searched for the next big sporting event, and how best to deliver its information to an eager fan base. The training students will receive from this textbook can be applied across multiple platforms while each person strives to keep up with ongoing changes in industry trends.

Discussion Questions

1. As more broadcast options continue to emerge, what is the place for the written word in sports journalism?
2. What do you think is the next great development in sports journalism technology? Can new sports still find a niche among sports enthusiasts?

Applied Activity

Choose a national sports website (e.g., The Ringer, *The Athletic*, ESPN.com, CBSSports.com). Analyze its latest 25 pieces of content and answer the following questions:

1. What is the most commonly occurring type of content? Written, audio, video?
2. What topics are covered most often? Game analysis? Issues away from games?
3. Which sports receive the most coverage? Why do you think that is?
4. What are the benefits and shortcomings of the site, in terms of accessibility and usability?
5. Which kinds of content will make you return to the site? Why? What would keep you from coming back? Why?

News Gathering and Writing

Chapter Objectives

After completing this chapter, you will be able to do the following:

- Identify and define the different types of stories that sports journalists routinely write, and illustrate how they are an integral part of sports journalism.
- Demonstrate the basics of writing sports journalism, including story ideation, story structure, and news value, and provide advice for clear, concise writing.
- Describe the best practices for interviewing athletes and coaches, from selecting sources to interview to conducting the actual interview.
- Emphasize the value of engaging in research before doing interviews, and provide advice on how to conduct that research.

Late in a game, whether in a stadium or an arena, there are few better places to be than in a press box. As the minutes tick off the clock, and the deadline creeps closer and closer, there is an energy in the press box or along press row. Reporters who had spent the game talking, chatting, and joking gradually go silent with focus and concentration. Their laptops clatter as everyone types with purpose. When the game is over and the first deadlines arrive, reporters send their first stories back to their offices. The game has ended, but the true work has only begun.

"The press box is beginning to vibrate, with hundreds of writers filing on deadline, the adrenaline kicking in, all the talent and the skills and the experience being called into play" is how retired *New York Times* sports columnist George Vecsey described the scene among reporters at Super Bowl XX (Vecsey, 1989, p. 64).

That's the ultimate purpose of sports journalism—to provide readers with an accurate and honest reflection of what happened in a game, and what is happening with a team.

The purpose of this chapter is to introduce the basics of news gathering and writing in the context of sports journalism. First, the chapter details how print media—both newspapers and their digital media counterparts and successors—have been the dominant platforms for sports media coverage. It will then describe the basics of writing and news gathering techniques for sports journalism, with an emphasis on game coverage.

Sports Writing Basics

This section covers the fundamentals of sports journalism. You'll learn the basic structure for sports stories and the basic news values that guide journalists in general and sports journalists in particular. You'll begin to learn what to write about and how to write.

Story Structure

The cornerstone of sports journalism is the game story.

> "Game coverage is central to sports journalism. A reporter's work schedule, story selection, and sourcing decisions are almost always centered around the games of the team(s) he or she covers. An editor's planning of his or her section—both in print and online—almost universally centers around game coverage. Sports themselves revolve around games—from the NFL to high school football—so it's natural that sports journalism has its roots in games. In fact, it can be argued that no area of journalism is so intrinsically tied to a part of their coverage as sports journalism is to games." (Moritz, 2014, p. 97)

Types of Sports Journalists

Before we dive into the basics of sports writing, it's important to understand the differences between the types of sports journalists.

- **Beat writers** provide the day-to-day coverage of a team, conference, or league. They traditionally cover all of a team's games, home and away (although the economic challenges to the industry that are described in later chapters are changing this), and they cover all news that happens in and around teams. Larger beats at larger outlets sometimes have multiple journalists assigned to a single beat.
- **Feature writers** focus their work on longer-form pieces. These can be profiles (stories about people), stories about trends and issues, or other pieces that don't necessarily fall into the day-to-day grind of a beat.
- **Columnists** are the opinion writers of the sports pages. They write regularly, though not every day, and tend to focus on personality-driven pieces.

One of the most important aspects of writing any piece of journalism is the story's structure. The most basic sports game story structure is the **inverted pyramid**, which is a format that prioritizes information in a news story according to importance (figure 3.1). The first paragraph—the lead—contains the most salient, newsworthy, and important information. You don't want to "bury the lead," or have the most important information too low in the story, where the reader may miss it. Each paragraph that follows includes slightly less newsworthy information; these paragraphs provide supporting information that details the issue or event through quotes, background information, and statistics, studies, and reports.

The inverted pyramid story structure comes from the Associated Press. The idea behind it is that a newspaper could take a story to fill a hole on a page and cut from the bottom of the story to make it fit. Ideally, the story can be cut at any place from the bottom up and still make sense to the reader.

The Lead

In an inverted pyramid story, the **lead** (sometimes spelled *lede*) is the most important part. It contains the most important information. It is the first part of the story the reader will see (after the headline and byline), and it is the only part of the story that is virtually guaranteed not to be cut. If we're being honest in a largely social media–driven media world, there's a good chance it will be the only part of the story an audience member actually reads.

The lead has to do a lot of work. It has to convey a lot of information in a short amount of space. Ideally, the lead to an inverted pyramid story should be about 35 to 40 words. In that space, it should address the classic journalism questions—who, what, when, where, why, and how—or at least as many as possible that pertain to the story.

If the basic unit of sports journalism is the game story, then an inverted pyramid game story would focus on the most newsworthy aspects of that game. The most basic story structure emphasizes the team that wins the game and the final score:

East High School defeated Brightman Tech, 34-7, in a non-league football game on Friday night at East High.

Fine. But kind of boring, right? So let's add a top individual performance.

Rob Butler rushed for 189 yards and three touchdowns to lead East High School to a 34-7 North Division home victory against Brightman Tech on Friday night.

Look at all the work that lead does. It answers the basic questions:

- Who: East High School and Brightman Tech
- What: East High beat Brightman in football, 34-7
- When: Friday night
- Where: At East High
- How: Rob Butler's 189 yards and three touchdowns

In writing a game story, it's crucial to identify the central point of the story. What is the most newsworthy element of the game? Who played the best game? What was the biggest play? The lead should focus on the most clear and compelling way to start your story.

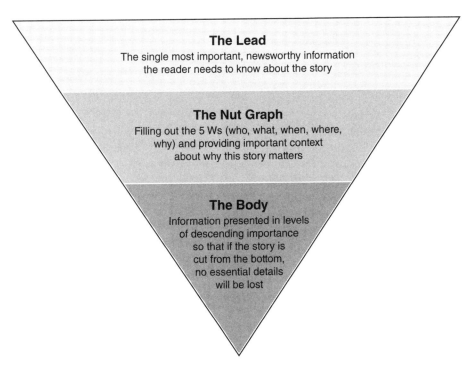

FIGURE 3.1 Inverted pyramid of story structure.

Nut Graph

After the lead, it is important to provide readers with context. They know the basic information about the game. **So what?** That's the question the writer needs to answer in what is called the "nut graph." The **nut graph** provides readers with the valuable context of the information that was in the lead. If the lead does the work of answering the six core questions, the nut graph builds on that information and answers "so what?"

In our East High versus Brightman example, a nut graph may look something like this:

> The victory keeps East High in first place in the North Division with just two weeks left in the regular season.

Or

> The victory snapped East High's four game losing streak, while Brightman Tech fell into a tie for second place with the loss.

Notice what an inverted pyramid game story is not. It is not in chronological order. It's incredibly rare for a game story to be written chronologically. This is one important way that newspaper writing is different from broadcast writing. In writing for radio, TV, or online video highlight packages, the game is often presented chronologically. All the major plays in the game are presented in the order in which they happened. A basketball highlight package would never begin with a buzzer-beating three-pointer. But the lead of a game story absolutely would feature that buzzer-beater. Think of the inverted pyramid as a summary of the most important parts of the game rather than a chronological retelling of the entire game.

A good newspaper-style sports story is concise and focused. It includes all of the essential information but no extraneous details. To keep your story concise and focused, use only the background information readers need in order to understand that day's story. Don't include play-by-play from parts of the game that had no impact on the final score. Don't feel obligated to quote everyone that you interview. Use only the best quotes to enhance the story. (We have more to say on quotes in the interview section of this chapter.)

Alternative Leads

The basic inverted pyramid story is the kind you will often see in stories written by the Associated Press. In a lot of ways, it is the building block of all journalism and game coverage. For students and young reporters, learning it is akin to a young musician learning scales—it's the format upon which all other stories are based. It can also be very effective for high school sports roundups or stories, where the audience of people who already know the outcome or who were at the game is smaller. There's nothing wrong with using the basic inverted pyramid structure. If a writer is ever in doubt about what to do, they can do worse than to start there.

But what if we want to do more with a game story?

What if, instead of just recapping the game, we want to tell a deeper story? What if we are writing about a game that many in our audience have already seen, about which they already know the details? In the age of digital and social media, when highlights are available in real time and on various platforms, is a recap the best way to write a game story?

Let's take Super Bowl LI as an example. A basic inverted pyramid lead could look something like this:

> Tom Brady threw for 466 yards and two touchdowns to lead the New England Patriots to a 34-28 come-from-behind overtime victory over the Atlanta Falcons in Super Bowl LI on Sunday.

That is certainly correct. But does it come close to really capturing the story of that game, in which the Patriots rallied from a 28-3 deficit to force the first overtime Super Bowl? Not at all. To do so, we can look at **alternative leads**. These are ways to structure and start stories that move beyond the basic who-what-when-where-why-how structure of the inverted pyramid. They expand our storytelling options, allowing writers to capture the meaning or the spirit of the game in a way that is better suited to our digital world. These leads can also be a little bit longer since they are doing more than conveying the basic information of an inverted-pyramid lead. If the basic lead is 35 to 40 words, an alternative lead can run a little longer—50 to 75 words.

> "The purpose of a game story used to be very simple—to tell people what happened in the game, because games weren't on TV a lot and if you weren't there, you didn't know what happened. In the era of TV being everywhere and every game being televised and the Internet giving you instant information, the game story is much more about a trend, or a subplot within the game." (Mike Harrington, *Buffalo News* columnist, personal interview, Jan. 7, 2020)

Let's look at some potential alternative lead styles. The taxonomy of these leads comes from Lloyd and Guzzo (2008).

Anecdotal Leads

In an **anecdotal lead**, the story begins with an anecdote (hence the clever name of this style). The writer leads with a scene that captures the essence of the game, the people involved, the impact. Essentially, this is a little scene or a story within the larger context of the game itself. An example of this comes from Dan Wolken of *USA Today*, who wrote about Serena Williams' loss to Naomi Osaka in the semifinals of the 2021 Australian Open.

> "As she left the court after a comprehensive semifinal loss to Naomi Osaka, Serena Williams twirled around, took a long look at Rod Laver Arena and put her hand to her heart. It was the kind of slow, heartfelt goodbye that naturally leads to some questions when a tennis player is 39 years old and sees their rivals getting younger, faster, fitter and more confident.
>
> After yet another loss late in a Grand Slam to a young superstar, each one a bit less competitive than the last, Williams is running out of options and running out of time to sneak in one more major title.
>
> And she knows it." (Wolken, 2021)

Serena Williams leaving Rod Laver Arena.
Matt King/Getty Images

Situational Leads

A **situational lead** is one in which the story begins with a description of the unique circumstances of

Writing Quick Hits

- The final score is always winning score–losing score (with golf scores being the notable exception), even if you are writing it from the perspective of the losing team.
- The teams' records can go in parentheses next to their names at some point in the story. Don't feel the need to include a separate sentence with their records. That's an inefficient use of space and words.
- Write relatively short paragraphs. Between one and three sentences is best for print or digital media. Paragraphs that are much longer become big blocks of text on the page, are not pleasing to look at, and create friction for the reader. Also, it can be useful to vary the paragraph length as a storytelling technique. A series of short paragraphs can propel a reader through parts of a story more quickly, while longer paragraphs slow the reader down.
- When you are punctuating quotes, it's best practice to start the paragraph with the quote itself, rather than identifying the speaker first. Instead of

   Serena Williams said, "It felt good to be back out there. I feel like I'm playing better than I have in a long time.

   Write

   "It felt good to be back out there," Serena Williams said. "I feel like I'm playing better than I have in a long time.

- When you quote a source, the best practice in terms of using names is as follows:
    - If it is the first reference to an individual in a story, you would use "said FULL NAME." "It felt good to be back out there," said Serena Williams.
    - On second and subsequent references within a story, you would use "last name SAID." "It felt good to be back out there," Williams said.
- Don't feel the need to set up quotes too much. This is another way newspaper writing differs from TV highlight writing. You don't need to introduce quotes too much, and it's important not to repeat information leading up to the quoted material.

   Serena Williams said she felt good to be back on the court after a long layoff. "It felt good to be back out there," Williams said.

- Punctuation always goes inside quote marks.

the game or the performance. It sets the scene of the story. In essence, it's the writer thinking, "OK, here's the situation..." and the lead is what comes next. An example of this comes from Chuck Culpepper, writing about the Villanova–North Carolina NCAA men's basketball championship game in 2016:

> As a roaring basketball game in a roaring football stadium distilled to one final, soaring shot making its descent, 74,340 seemed almost to hush. The hush would not last. Kris Jenkins's cocksure three-pointer from the right of the top of the key swished down through the net and into deathless fame, and all manner of noise broke out and threatened to stream through the years.
>
> Villanova's players surged into a pile. Villanova's coaches hugged and hopped. Jaws dropped. Fans boomed. Streamers fell. North Carolina's players walked off toward hard comprehension. The scoreboard suddenly read 77-74, and Villanova, a sturdy men's basketball program with an eternal Monday night glittering from its distant past, had found another Monday night all witnesses will find impossible to forget. (Culpepper, 2016)

The Intriguing Statement

An **intriguing statement** is a coy, interesting, ironic sentence that begins the story. The point of this lead is to intrigue the readers, to make them say, "Huh ... well, I've got to see what happens next." The most famous example of this occurred during the 1956 World Series after Don Larsen's perfect game for the New York Yankees. With the help of legendary columnist Dick Young, *Daily News* beat writer Joe Trimble wrote the following lead:

> **Time-Out**
>
> Let's practice writing a game story. To do this, find a college basketball game (either men's or women's) from a smaller school (low-level Division I or Division II, III or NAIA). Any sport would do for this exercise, but the statistics and information available after a basketball game (box score and play-by-play) make it easier to write a story without having seen the game. Picking a smaller school that you are not previously familiar with will help you focus on the mechanics of writing a game story without leaning on your prior knowledge or opinions about a team, player, or game.
>
> Download copies of the game's official box score and official play-by-play.
>
> 1. Write a 250-word inverted pyramid game story based solely on the box score.
> 2. Using both the box score and the play-by-play, write a 500-word inverted pyramid game story.
> 3. Rewrite your LEAD only, using one of the alternative lead styles discussed in this chapter. The lead should be no more than 50 to 75 words.
>
> By the end of this assignment, you will have written three different items: a 250-word inverted pyramid game story, a 500-word inverted pyramid game story, and a 50- to 75-word alternative lead.

An imperfect man pitched the perfect game yesterday. (Eskenaz, 2016)

A more contemporary example comes from the South Bend (Ind.) *Tribune*, with this lead from Anthony Anderson from a Notre Dame–Tennessee women's basketball game:

Somehow, some seemingly inconceivable way, the greatest successful comeback in Notre Dame women's basketball history didn't even include what would seem an automatic accompaniment—a fantastic finish. (Anderson, 2018)

The Change in Direction

A **change in direction** is an abrupt shift in the story. You start out leading the reader to the right and then cut back to the left. This can be handy in comeback games, like the aforementioned Super Bowl LI. Here's an example of what that might have looked like:

Matt Ryan and the Atlanta Falcons were cruising, up 25 points in the third quarter and seemingly en route to their first Super Bowl championship. Tom Brady and the New England Patriots erased those dreams in a comeback for the ages.

Humor

A humorous lead is self-explanatory. It is a funny statement or observation or moment from a game or match that stands out to the reporter. A word of caution: Humor is very, very difficult to do well. What a reporter finds funny or amusing may fall flat to readers—or worse, be offensive. One example of humor as a lead comes from one of this book's coauthors:

Since Sunday was Dr. Seuss Day at NYSEG Stadium, the children's author may have described the game like this:

The Baysox of Bowie remained very hot

While the Binghamton Mets were most certainly not. (Moritz, 2007)

News Gathering

So far, we've talked about *how* to write a story for the sports section. But all of the mechanics, all of the technical knowledge about structure and leads and nut graphs are only half of the story of sports writing. It's important to know *how* to write a story. But it is equally important to know *what* to write about. This section of the chapter will be dedicated to that "what?" question. It will examine news gathering in the context of sports journalism. It will begin with a discussion of news values, followed by research strategies and interview techniques.

Sports News Values

Mike Abdo, who served as the sports editor for *The Times Herald* in Olean, New York, had a philosophy about what went on his sports pages. "News," Abdo would frequently say, "is what people are talking about."

In a way, this is a simplistic way of looking at news judgment. After all, an important part of all journalism is to shine a light on what the public doesn't know yet, to introduce things into the public agenda. Giving people what they are already talking about feels like the shortcut to clickbait, infotainment, and a watered-down sports section.

But on a day-to-day, story-to-story basis, there are worse guidelines to follow. If you cover a game where a basketball player hits 12 three-pointers, your game story probably shouldn't focus on her team's interior defense.

This idea—what are people talking about—gets at the heart of the question of news values.

We've established that when you are writing a basic news story, you lead with the most important information. Cool. How do you do that?

One of the most important yet often underappreciated skills for a sports journalist—any journalist in fact—is **story ideation**. Simply put, it's knowing what can be categorized as "news."

All news—be it politics, crime, or sports—is a social construct. This simply means that news doesn't exist naturally in the world. It's defined by journalists, through shared values and work routines passed down through years of on-the-job training (sociologists call this process isomorphism). This is where the idea of news values comes in.

News values are the measures by which journalists evaluate events and decide how newsworthy those events are. It's important to note that news values are qualitative measures; there's no numerical scale, no points, no ranking system that a reporter can use to determine what to lead with or what's the most newsworthy element of a game, practice, or event. Reporters often talk about news value as almost a sixth sense—when they see it they know it. After a while, it becomes an instinct.

Every journalism textbook describes news values in a different way:

- Filak (2019) uses the acronym "FOCII" (p. 13): fame, oddity, conflict, immediacy, impact.
- Lloyd and Guzzo (2008) list six traditional news values: personality, impact, timeliness, proximity, quantity, and human interest.
- Dating back nearly a generation, Fedler (1993) calls timeliness, importance, prominence, proximity, and oddities the "characteristics of news" (p. 116).

You can see the similarities running through the different authors and through time.

For our purposes, a useful distillation of news values comes from the University of North Carolina at Pembroke (UNCP, n.d.):

- Impact
- Timeliness
- Prominence
- Proximity
- Conflict
- Currency
- Bizarreness

These are not listed in any kind of rank order. Remember—news judgment is a qualitative exercise, not a quantitative one. First, let's define these terms:

- **Impact:** Who does this story affect? How many people does it affect? What is the effect it has on these people?
- **Timeliness:** When did something happen? News is what's new, so the more recently something happened, the more newsworthy it is. A scoop is when news is reported before it happens.
- **Prominence:** News is about people, and the more famous or important society deems people, the more newsworthy stories about them are. A man having lunch at a Park Avenue restaurant in Rochester, New York, is not newsworthy—except when it was then-President Barack Obama.
- **Proximity:** How geographically close to your readers does the event happen? The closer it happens, the more newsworthy it tends to be.
- **Conflict:** The core of almost all storytelling is conflict (Shoemaker & Reese, 2013). If there's a disagreement between people or groups, that makes for news.
- **Currency:** If a subject, topic, or person is being discussed and is culturally relevant, this is an example of currency. Topics like this are just generally alive in the culture—there aren't necessarily daily events about them, but they permeate the culture. Examples include the AIDS crisis in the 1980s and the climate crisis in the 2000s.
- **Bizarreness:** This is what journalism scholars Shoemaker and Reese (2013) have called

deviance. Anything that's weird, wacky, or way out of the ordinary would be an example of bizarreness. A plane landing safely shortly after takeoff isn't bizarre—unless it lands in the Hudson River and everyone survives.

Now let's take each one from a sports perspective.

- *Impact:* What does this particular game mean in the big picture of a team's season? Is it the playoffs? Is a playoff berth on the line? With a game, how much does a play or a player affect the outcome? A missed field goal in the first quarter is likely to be far less newsworthy than a missed field goal as time expires.
- *Timeliness:* Remember, news is new. In sports journalism, this is built into our coverage because so much of what we do is event-driven. Yesterday's or tomorrow's game will be more newsworthy than a game that happened earlier in the season. Today's free-agent signing is more newsworthy than last month's signing. (As we'll see in subsequent chapters, this news value has become even more heightened in the digital media world.)
- *Prominence:* Star players, star coaches, and star franchises tend to be seen as more newsworthy. What LeBron James or Megan Rapinoe do on and off the court and field is more newsworthy than similar actions by their reserve guard or defender teammates. News involving the New York Yankees or the University of Connecticut women's basketball team gets better coverage than something that occurs with the San Diego Padres or the Niagara University women's team. Because of her prominence, how Naomi Osaka does in a tennis tournament can be seen as more newsworthy than the tournament's final outcome. (Side note: If this sounds like a bit of a self-fulfilling prophecy, where stars get more coverage because they already get coverage, well, you're not wrong.)
- *Proximity:* In terms of geography, teams that play close to the media outlet are more newsworthy. The *Indianapolis Star* is not going to be running a lot of stories about the Miami Marlins. However, in sports terms, proximity also applies to leagues, conferences, and divisions. Boston and Toronto are 550 miles apart, but each city's newspapers will run stories about the other city's baseball and basketball teams because they're all in the same divisions.
- *Conflict:* In a way, all sports are conflict (games, matches, etc.). But beyond that, conflict exists when there is a contract dispute between a player and a team, a controversy between a team and a league or between a city and an owner, or a feud between two or more people. Allegations of cheating (think Deflategate), recruiting violations, and legal issues involving athletes and team officials are also examples.
- *Currency:* Like in news, in sports there are issues that transcend the day-to-day coverage and are a part of the culture. Examples in the late 2010s and early 2020s include concussions and player safety in football (and other sports) and the controversy about the economics of college sports and the potential of paying college athletes.
- *Bizarreness:* Weird, unexpected things happen in sports. Sometimes, they're so weird and unexpected they become stories of their own. A quarterback fumbling during a football game is hardly news in and of itself. A quarterback fumbling after running into his offensive lineman's backside—Mark Sanchez's infamous "butt fumble"—is newsworthy.

Let's break this down even further, taking it out of the realm of the journalism textbook and into the world of sports. Some news values to ponder as you cover games include the following:

- *The result:* Who won, who lost, the final score. Blindingly obvious, yes, but who beat whom by how much is the atomic element of sports journalism.
- *The key players:* Who was the winning pitcher, the key hitter, the high scorer? Who had the best game, either quantitatively, qualitatively, or both?
- *The key plays:* Obviously, if there is a game-winning shot, a walk-off hit, a buzzer-beater, that's newsworthy. But other important plays—especially ones late in the game—deserve mention in your story.
- *The context:* What does that final score mean in the big picture of the team's season? Is a winning streak extended or a losing streak snapped? Was a playoff berth clinched? A championship berth earned?

Time-Out

Look at the following list of headlines from ESPN.com (Taken Jan. 3, 2024):

Panthers' Tepper fined $300K for drink toss at fans
NFL reminds players to 'clearly' report as eligible
Iowa's Clark beats buzzer, MSU with 3 from logo
Jets cut RB Cook to allow him to join contender
Grambling women post record 141-point victory
Djokovic loss in United Cup ends Australia streak
'Talented' Thunder stay hot, top NBA-best Celtics
Osaka ousted early in return to tennis by Pliskova

Take each headline one at a time.

1. Determine what news value (or values) each one demonstrates or relies on.
2. List, in order of importance, the news value (or values) the story demonstrates and how it does so.

There's no right answer; your interpretation may vary from those of your classmates.

Research and Reporting

Knowing how to apply news values to your team or game comes from the reporting and research you do before arriving at the field or gym. Knowing who the star players are, who is on a hot streak, and what the game means to both teams comes from the reporting you do before the game. This background work is vital to sports journalists. You cannot write a good story without putting in the reporting work.

That reporting starts with reading and research. For professional and most college teams, game notes are prepared by the team's public relations staff or the school's sports information department. These notes contain statistics, facts, and figures about each team. It's important to read through these before the game for both teams involved so that you know what is going on with each team. In addition, read up on both teams before the game. Use the Internet and social media to find stories from earlier games. The more reading you do, the better informed you will be. That will help you understand what you see during the game, and it will help you to tell your readers what happened, why it happened, and why it matters. (You'll learn more about these sources of information in chapter 4.)

During the game, make sure you actually watch the action. That may sound like the most obvious advice in this book. But with the constant siren call of digital and social media looming in the background on our phones and laptops, it's worth a reminder. Keep running notes throughout the game, either on paper or in a computer file. If you're covering softball or baseball, keep score. If you're covering football or basketball or volleyball, keep a running play-by-play record. This keeps your head in the game and makes writing the story afterward easier.

Interviews

One of the things that makes journalism stand out from other forms of writing is reporting, and the most visible and important aspect of reporting is interviewing sources. For print media, interviews for game stories virtually all happen after a game.

Access to sources varies from sport to sport, level to level, and it can depend on the organization or organizations involved.

- For Major League Baseball, the clubhouse is open for two and a half hours before the game, until an hour before first pitch.
- In pro hockey, teams often have a morning skate the day of the game, and media have access to players and coaches after that.
- In pro football and pro basketball, there is generally little pregame access. Interviews for game stories happen immediately after the game.
- Coaches generally hold a formal press conference after each game. Sometimes, star players also come to a press conference.

Industry Profile

Mike Harrington (The Buffalo News)

Mike Harrington

Mike Harrington is there. Every day.

After more than 30 years as a sports journalist in Buffalo, New York, Mike Harrington's secret is simple.

He is there. Every day.

Whether it is with the Buffalo Sabres as a hybrid hockey beat writer and columnist, or covering the Buffalo Bisons and the Cleveland Guardians' organization, he's always at the park or the arena.

"I want the players and coaches to think of me as part of the furniture," Harrington said in a personal interview. "That I'm always there. I just think they feel like 'we're here every day, how are you gonna really tell the story properly if you're not?' It matters that people think that sources need to think that you understand what's going on, that you're connected, and that you understand what they're dealing with. And I think I don't care if they like me at all, but they need to respect the fact that I'm there all the time and I know what's going on."

Harrington has been a full-time sports reporter for the *Buffalo News* since 1987, covering everything from high school sports to college basketball to pro baseball and hockey. He estimates that he's written between 250 and 300 stories each year—around 9,000 to 10,000 for his career.

Harrington has covered professional baseball in Buffalo since 1993 and is a member of the Buffalo Baseball Hall of Fame. In 2007, after more than a decade covering college basketball, he moved on to the hockey beat.

"I knew everyone in basketball," he said. "I knew conference commissioners. I had Final Four referees coming up to the press table to say hi to me before games. Now I'm throwing all those sources away. And I have nobody. I know nobody in hockey at all, and I'm 42 years old."

So how did Harrington build sources on a new beat in the middle of his career?

"You gotta be there every day," he said. "You just gotta be there and they have to see you every day. When I started on the Sabres, I would get to practice like 20-25 minutes early and I would always be in the seats as they came on the ice. Well (a colleague) told me that (then-Sabres coach Lindy) Ruff noticed and commented that I was there every day early. So, you kind of develop trust that way a little bit. They see you a lot, you develop trust and people talk. Your name gets spread around a bit. You never stop building those relationships."

That every-day access leads to some interesting stories and exchanges, none more memorable for Harrington than one that happened in 2012. After a Sabres loss in Chicago, Harrington had a pointed exchange with Ruff, the longtime Buffalo coach. As Ruff walked away from the small postgame scrum, he turned to Harrington and yelled, "Hey Mike! YOU coach the team!"

The next night, the team was in Winnipeg for their next game. After the morning skate, Ruff met with reporters, including Harrington. Ruff looked at Harrington and said, "Are we still friends?"

"We're always friends," Harrington said to Ruff. "Sometimes, we just disagree."

"My biggest regret, always," Harrington remembered years later, "was I should have gone to a sporting goods store in Winnipeg and shown up the next day with a goddamn whistle!"

- At the pro level, locker rooms are open by league rules after each game, and interviews are conducted in front of a player's locker. Access tends to be a little more restricted at the college level, and each team has different rules about whether or not locker rooms are open.

- For high school sports, access tends to be much more informal. Interviews tend to be done on the field immediately after the game.

Non–game day access varies between sports and levels. Some sports, like the NFL and college football, tend to be highly regimented in their schedules and in the opportunities they give media to speak

Sources Are People

One point to remember: Our sources are people.

It can be easy to think of the people we write about as characters in a story. We view the details of their lives as fodder for our stories, dramatic hooks that make for interesting reading. We talk about them as if they were chess pieces for us to move around. We discuss their performance as if they were nothing more than numbers on a spreadsheet, nothing more than statistics and a salary.

But they are actual people with actual human emotions.

The difficult childhood or traumatic injury or devastating loss that makes us want to write about them is actual trauma they have to live with. It doesn't mean we can't or shouldn't write about them. It does mean that we, as sports journalists, should approach our subjects—especially profile subjects—with a high degree of empathy.

with players. If media want to speak with a player or coach for a longer story or outside of regular availability, interviews can be scheduled either through the PR or sports information departments or through a player's agent.

Conducting an Interview

The first step to a successful interview is understanding what kind of story you are looking to write and what you need from the interview. The type of story you are writing will influence what kind of interview you conduct. This is an obvious but often overlooked aspect of interview advice. Different stories require different interviews. For a long-form feature profile on an athlete, you will want to have an interview that is as much a conversation with the subject as it is a formal question-and-answer session. That requires different preparation and a different mindset than an interview for a game story being written on a tight deadline. In the latter situation, a reporter simply doesn't have time for a leisurely conversation with a manager or a player. It's quick questions, quick answers, and back to the computer.

The mechanics of the interview are pretty straightforward. A reporter should always record an interview, either with a smartphone app or with a digital recorder. It's useful to take notes while recording. This way you are covered in case of a technological meltdown.

It can be helpful to prepare a list of topics you want to address with your source. Beginning reporters often feel a need to list the questions they plan to ask, but you should avoid this temptation. A list of questions can become a de facto script you may feel compelled to stick to. It may discourage you from asking follow-up questions, which can yield the best information. Allow the interview to go to a place you didn't expect—some of the best information can come from those detours. Your list of topics will enable you to get back on track easily.

This is where reporting becomes a circular, iterative process. The preparation you have done—your own reading that morning, your study of the game notes—works to inform the interview. The more research and reporting you have done beforehand, the more informed and well-rounded your questions will be, the better your interview will be, and the better your story will be. "Preparation is as important as execution," is how two-time Pulitzer Prize–winning journalist Eric Nalder puts it. Nalder suggests never doing an interview without doing previous research. Even as little as five minutes of reading will improve your interview (Nalder, 2010).

When you are interviewing, short questions are often the best; ask "Why?" "Why's that?" "What's that?" and "What do you mean by that?" We've all seen interviewers ask long-winded questions that are as much about them showing off their knowledge as they are about getting information to inform their readers. John Sawatsky, a noted interview coach who has worked extensively with ESPN, said that the perfect question should be like a clean window:

"A clean window gives a perfect view. When we ask a question, we want to get a window into the source. When you put values in your questions, it's like putting dirt on the window. It obscures the view of the lake beyond. People shouldn't notice the question in an interview, just like they shouldn't notice the window. They should be looking at the lake.... Stained-glass windows are beautiful to look at, but it's all about the window, not about the view." (Paterno, 2002)

Sawatsky advocates journalists ask questions that are lean, open, and neutral:

- **Lean questions** are short in length and conceptually simple (Gay, 2012).
- An **open question** is one that allows for a yes–no answer but forces the subject to answer in a way that is expansive.
- A **neutral question** does not have any editorializing or loaded words.

Here's an example. Instead of asking, "LeBron, how frustrated are you right now with what's happening?" try "LeBron, how are you feeling about what's happening right now?"

By introducing the word *frustrated* in the first question, the interviewer inadvertently limits the topic. The respondent can focus the answer on that word—for example, "I'm not frustrated"—and move on. The question becomes not about what's happening around the Lakers but about that word *frustrated*. The second question—without the limiting word—is much more open-ended. It gives the player the opportunity to talk more expansively. Rather than injecting a word (or in this case, a feeling) on your own, you give your subjects a chance to talk themselves.

Who to Quote

In conducting interviews after a game or match, it is important to interview the key stakeholders. The coaches of both teams will be interviewed, as will the key players in the game. The player who scored

Dumbest Guy in the Room

Throughout his career as an award-winning columnist and a best-selling author, Joe Posnanski has had a secret to his reporting.

He embraces the idea that he is the dumbest person in the room.

"I didn't hide from that," Posnanski said on an episode of *The Other 51* podcast (Moritz, 2019a). "If you put it that way and you're that disarming and you're that honest, not everybody's going to be with you, but most people will—especially when you make it clear you're not there for any threatening reasons at all. You're there because you want to learn."

It can be tempting for inexperienced reporters to try to look good in front of the people they are interviewing. The interview setup can be intimidating, and it's natural to want to look good in front of your sources and, in some cases, reporting peers.

But for Posnanski, the worst thing a reporter can do in an interview is fake it.

"What they really don't like is you pretending that you know as much as they do," Posnanski said. "I think that's really offensive to people."

One of the secrets to dealing with this is to lean into your lack of knowledge. There's no shame in being the dumbest person in the room. Be open about it and embrace it, with humor and humility. "This may be the dumbest question you get today, but . . ." That can instantly disarm your subject and turn an adversarial relationship into a mutually beneficial one.

It was a lesson Posnanski learned early in his career as a sports journalist. While covering a minor league baseball game as a 21-year-old, he found himself sitting in the press box next to Baseball Hall of Famer Billy Williams, who was then a roving hitting instructor for the Chicago Cubs.

"Mr. Williams, I have a question for you, and I know it's really, really stupid, and I apologize," Posnanski said to Williams. "I'm just wondering if you could explain the difference between a curveball and a slider."

Posnanski said you could hear the other people in the press box groan at such a basic question. But Williams didn't.

"He spent the next 20 minutes—it was like getting a TED Talk on pitching," Posnanski said. "He spent the next 20 giving me a master class on the difference between a curveball and a slider, and how different sliders work—this is how (Bob) Gibson's slider went; this is how (Steve) Carlton's slider went—and I use that information to this day. This is 30 years ago, and I use that information to this day.

"And he said at the end—I will always remember this—he said, 'Don't let 'em laugh, don't worry if they laugh at you, don't worry about it, because they don't know.' And I think that's right. Nobody in that press box and very very few people in the world know the difference between a curveball and a slider the way Billy Williams does. So, that was a real eye opener for me."

the most goals, the winning pitcher, the skier who won the race, the golfer who won the tournament. In some individual sports, there are incremental leaders who should be interviewed—in tennis, this may be the highest-seeded player to play that day, or the winner of any kind of featured match on the main court. In golf, it would be whoever is leading after each of a tournament's four rounds. If there is a game-winning shot or score, the players involved in that play will absolutely be interviewed.

In addition, team leaders are important to interview and quote. This can be a star player, a veteran who's been on the team for years, or the team captain. Even if this player did not play a significant role in this game, they can often provide important context about the game and what it means to the team. Also, there are players and coaches who sports journalists will describe as "a good quote." All this means is that they are people who say interesting things in interesting ways. Even if they don't play a role in a game, their quotes can be entertaining, informative, and surprising. They are the people whose quotes breathe life into stories.

Integrating Quotes Into Stories

Quotes should never exist in a story just to exist. Quotes should never simply take up space. Quotes should be clear and should propel the reader through the story. "A good quote … must advance the story" (Gisondi, 2011, p. 11). Quotes should

- be authoritative,
- showcase the personality of the players and coaches, or
- surprise the reader in some way.

Quotes allow journalists to offer different voices in their stories, to get inside the heads of the participants in a game to show what it was really like. Quotes should illuminate the story, not confuse the reader. At their best, quotes breathe life into stories.

Elements of Good Quotes

- Provide clarity and avoid confusion
- Avoid clichés
- Show authority
- Show character
- Convey emotion
- Highlight a variety of voices
- Provide diverse points of view

So what makes a good quote?

First and foremost, a quote should be clear. It should not confuse the reader or leave readers wondering what the person meant. It should not be filled with too much technical jargon that ordinary fans aren't familiar with. It should fit the context and the structure of the story. It shouldn't feel out of place. What the person is saying should be easy to understand.

Let's talk about clichés. There are clichés in every aspect of life and in every form of journalism. But they feel more prevalent and prominent in sports writing. Whether it's a coach saying, "We just didn't execute our game plan," a player saying, "We played hard and just wanted it more," or a player in training camp saying they are in the "best shape of their life," athletes and coaches will often speak in vague clichés. Avoid clichés whenever possible. Reporters can use the interview techniques described later in this chapter to move their interviews beyond clichés and into more meaningful quotes.

Quotes that don't employ clichés are authoritative. In the 2019 season, after a loss to the Carolina Panthers, then-Houston Texans quarterback Deshaun Watson was asked about a long pass he missed on. Video of his response went viral on social media:

"Do you know what coverage they were playing? I'm just asking. It's Cover 4, so what the safeties are doing, they're playing deep, and they're guarding No. 2. The corners sink, and they trap [No.] 2. So what they're doing is keeping everything in front, the linebackers are playing anything that crosses.

"[Luke] Kuechly is playing the middle. He stops everything that crosses the middle. He jumps everything that—and the safety is charging No. 2. So if the safeties are playing low, then we can't take that. We have to hit double moves. We did the post, because [Eric] Reid stepped up on 2, with the out [route], over the top, I didn't hit that. Same thing with [DeAndre] Hop[kins] in route—safety jumped up, he went vertical, I didn't hit it. That was the only two. After that, they played back, Cover 2, 6, bust, which is safety Reid comes in between Kuechly, the outside linebacker plays deep, I gotta get rid of the ball." (Ruiz, 2019)

Truth be told, there's probably a touch too much technical, inside football jargon in that quote (see our above rule on clarity), but it is the definition of an authoritative quote.

> ## Time-Out
>
> Let's put some of these reporting lessons into practice by creating the foundation for a news story.
>
> 1. Select a story or an issue that is in the news. Pick something that is being widely covered in sports media and that fits the news values discussed in this chapter.
> 2. Do background research by reading at least three news stories on the issue.
> 3. Find three sources to interview for this story. Make sure they are people who are knowledgeable on this issue, whether they are stakeholders involved in the story or fans who are connected to it. Conduct a 5- to 10-minute interview with each source.
> 4. Write one paragraph of background information on the issue, and select the best quote from each of your three interviews.

An authoritative quote says something in the words of the stakeholders better than the journalists can. If you as a reporter can say it better than the quote, don't use the quote. Paraphrase it while still attributing it to the person. Instead of "'This is our third win in a row,' said coach Tara Smith," you can write "Tara Smith said that this was the team's third victory in a row."

Good quotes also show character. Again, they are interesting things said by interesting people in interesting ways. They also convey emotion. The exuberance of a team winning a championship. The devastation of a team that lost in overtime. The anger of a player who thinks a referee missed a key call. The awe at a star's play. Great quotes don't describe what happened, they describe what it felt like.

In addition, good quotes contain a variety of voices. They should not all express the same feelings or say the same thing. Diversity of point of view is critical. Don't just quote the winning team. Don't always just quote the quarterback or the starting pitcher. The more different voices a story has, the more complete the story will be, and the more the reader will learn and understand.

Using Your Senses As a Reporter

One final note for reporting (for now, at least): Reporting is so much more than interviewing sources and quoting what they say. Using your senses enriches your reporting and makes your stories deeper and more interesting.

- Sight: What was the person wearing? How did they appear? Describe what you observe a source doing as well as what they say.
- Hearing: What sound did the crowd make? Does an interview subject's tone of voice change when you ask a specific question?
- Smell: What do you smell? Is it the sweet scent of champagne in the locker room as a team celebrates a championship? The sweat of the player immediately after the game?
- Touch: Was it especially hot or cold in the arena? How does the sand feel under our feet at a beach volleyball tournament? When you shake a player's hand, how does her hand feel?

Don't limit what you write to simply what your sources say.

Other Story Forms

Of course, sports journalists do more than cover games and write news stories about player moves and coaching decisions. They write feature stories that tell interesting stories about athletes, and they write columns expressing their opinions. These are the stories that give sports journalism life and that connect readers to their favorite teams and athletes.

Profiles

We've spent most of this chapter talking about writing game stories (and, by default, sports news stories). While they serve as the backbone of sports journalism, they are far from the only stories sports reporters do.

One of the most common types of nongame story done by sports journalists is the profile. A **profile** is a feature story that is about a person—in our context, usually a player or a coach. Profiles can vary in length. Magazine profiles can run several thousand words, and the very best of these stand as some of the finest long-form writing anywhere. A newspaper profile may run as short as 500 to 600 words.

The key to a good profile story comes before you've typed a single letter, interviewed a single source, or done one bit of research. The key is picking an interesting subject. Prominent athletes are easy profile subjects, but they are not the only people worth writing about. Some of the best profiles, big and small, are about athletes who aren't stars. What makes a good profile subject?

- *Conflict:* The cliché version of this (which you're going to avoid, obviously) is "overcoming adversity." It seems like every athlete has a story—real or imagined—of adversity they had to overcome. But conflict in an athlete's life makes for an interesting story. If the subject had to overcome a difficulty or a setback—be it a troubled childhood, injuries, illness, the loss of a scholarship—this can make for a good story hook.
- *Moments:* Does the subject have a special time that defines their life or profession? Did they win a big game, hit a big shot, score a memorable goal, or have a memorable season? That moment can serve as an anecdote to help tell the subject's story.
- *History:* What is the player's life story? How did they get to the point where a reporter is interviewing them for a story about their life? Does the subject's past explain why they act as they do today?
- *Relevance:* Do the subjects' situations or actions provoke interest from people who have little in common with each other? In other words, is this person someone whose story we'd care about?

In all profiles, it is helpful to have a news peg. The **news peg** is what connects the subject to the reader. It's the answer to the question, "Why are you writing about this person today?" It could be that a new coach has been hired, or that a player moves into the starting lineup for the first time or is having the best stretch of play of their career. It could also be an anniversary of an event or game that leads to writing about one of the participants.

A key element of good sports journalism, especially in feature stories, is the principle of "show, don't tell." This means writing in an active voice and using the details you find in your reporting to paint a picture of the story for the reader. Don't write that a player is the hardest worker on the team. Write that they are in the gym an hour before practice, shooting free throws alone. Don't write that a player is close to her parents. Write that immediately after every game, she texts her dad. The details will come from your reporting. The more you do, and the more senses you use in your reporting, the richer your story will be.

Zig When Others Zag

One of the best pieces of reporting advice comes from Steve Buttry, a longtime reporter and editor turned digital journalism coach:

> "When you find yourself running with the pack, take a moment to consider what the pack might be missing. If everyone is looking to the right, look to the left, at least briefly. You can usually catch up with the pack pretty quickly if you don't find an exclusive. The pack isn't hard to find. But you won't find the exclusive without leaving the pack. Sometimes the pack is really on the big story. But if you always follow the pack, all you will have is the same story as everyone else." (Buttry, 2009)

We've all seen the pictures of interview scrums where a player or a coach is surrounded by dozens of reporters, cameras and microphones all getting the same quotes and comments. A way to stand out can be to find a player who's not being interviewed by as many reporters. If there is a story angle that interests you that is a bit off the beaten path, pursue it. If it interests you, there's a really good chance it will interest readers.

Steve Politi, a Newark *Star-Ledger* columnist known for his quirky columns on the Masters golf tournament—like where the champions' green jackets are dry cleaned, and how Arnold Palmer (the golfer) ordered an Arnold Palmer (the drink), said on *The Other 51* podcast,

> "In the industry, there is a reluctance to sometimes break out of that box. You get in a groove where you're at the Super Bowl and they give you the availability schedule and you know who you're gonna talk to on a certain day, you know what the big topics are, it's hard to say 'Wait a minute, why am I going to write the 47th best Tom Brady column this week?'" (Moritz, 2019b)

Column Writing

Columnists are the rock stars of the sports pages. Instead of a simple byline, they get their picture in the paper next to their work. Instead of having their work simply driven by the news of the day or the result of a game, they get to pick and choose what they write about. Instead of being objective and neutral in their perspective, they get to express their opinions. They get side gigs as radio and TV hosts.

If beat writers are the foundation of the sports section, then columnists are the decorative flourishes. "They are writers who found their voice and developed perspective, and they try to bring passion and energy to their work every day" (Wilstein, 2002, p. 70).

Generally, we think of columns as works of opinion. But they are more than just that. Yes, columnists often write that a coach should be fired, a player should be traded, or a team choked in a big game. But there's more to column writing than spouting opinions. Columnists come in all kinds—from bold and brash to thoughtful and poetic to brazenly funny.

> "Columns come in a variety of sizes ... and flavors: analytical, angry, breezy, comical, controversial, descriptive, evocative ... on through the alphabet ... indignant, ironic, irrelevant, mournful, newsy, philosophical, poignant, scornful, and more, down to zingy." (Wilstein, 2002, p. 70)

The best columns are rooted in the same journalism and reporting practices that fuel the best beat writing. Columnists should attend the games they write about in person, interview the people they are writing about, and be accountable to the people they write about. The same news judgment, eye for detail, and interviewing acumen that fuel good feature writing fuel the best columns. More than any other genre of sports writing, a columnist's job is to capture the spirit of the thing.

An example of this comes from the legendary Red Smith, the great columnist for the *New York Herald Tribune* from the 1940s through the 1960s. Smith's column from the 1951 National League playoffs—in which the New York Giants beat the Brooklyn Dodgers on Bobby Thomson's famous walk-off home run—stands as an all-time classic. Here is Smith's lead from that game's column:

> Now it is done. Now the story ends. And there is no way to tell it. The art of fiction is dead. Reality has strangled invention. Only the utterly impossible, the inexpressibly fantastic, can ever be plausible again. (Smith, n.d.)

And the final paragraph, which shows Smith's remarkable eye for detail:

> Ralph Branca turned and started for the clubhouse. The number on his uniform looked huge. Thirteen. (Smith, n.d.)

Media Theory in Sports Journalism

While this book's intended focus is on more practical applications in sports journalism, the *why* of certain types of coverage and actions pertaining to them must also be addressed. The two main media-related academic theories discussed here are agenda-setting and framing.

Agenda-Setting

A theoretical approach that resulted from an examination of political news coverage in North Carolina in the early 1970s, **agenda-setting** exemplifies the power of media to steer discussion and attention toward certain topics (McCombs & Shaw, 1972). To be clear, agenda-setting is not about telling readers—or, more appropriately for today, "news consumers"—what to think. Rather, it addresses the fact that media coverage can tell readers and viewers and listeners what to think *about*.

Decision-makers at media outlets decide on the topics for discussion—that is, the issues and events that will receive news coverage. The media landscape has changed greatly from the days when it consisted mainly of newspapers and magazines, television, and radio; now it features those outlets plus more individualized production of blogs, podcasts, and YouTube channels. But in all of these channels, there are still people deciding what kind of information agenda to set. Someone chooses each day what we hear about, no matter if we watch Kellerman versus Stephen A. in the morning, or a panel of Blackistone, Cronin, Isola, and Gutierrez in the late afternoon.

Organizations and teams hire people with sports journalism backgrounds to work on their web offerings, including the official sites and the teams' social media. This offers interested fans a chance to see another perspective, straight from the team's interests. And in protecting those interests, much of what a team posts will have a positive viewpoint on the happenings surrounding that franchise. This was not a new idea; sports information directors know very well how to finesse a 47-32 basketball loss into trumpeting the fact that a "record low number of points allowed defensively" is the main takeaway. By marrying sports journalism presentation norms with organizational goals and values, the official site thus practices agenda-setting as if it were a traditional media outlet (Zimmerman et al., 2011) with the core aim of telling readers and viewers, "Please talk about this topic, and while you're at it, go ahead and ignore the other one(s)."

Agenda-setting's applications occur elsewhere. Journalism practitioners seldom discuss—or likely, even think of—applying media theory to affect their news reporting approaches, but the process of story choice and story presentation often illustrate agenda-setting decisions.

Framing

Framing theory was first put forth by Goffman in 1974. While agenda-setting is a manipulation of topics without expressing a viewpoint or opinion, **framing** seeks to present readers and viewers with a clear and stated point of view about a topic. Framing can portray a topic or event as being important as part of a larger whole. Scholars note that media framing usually can be categorized as either episodic or thematic. **Episodic framing** is coverage that treats each occurrence of an incident as independent of others. **Thematic framing** presents an ongoing issue, with each event being part of that issue (Gross, 2008).

A good example of the two types of framing involved the coverage of concussion-related issues in professional football and hockey in the United States. NHL star Sidney Crosby of the Pittsburgh Penguins had his early career derailed by a series of head injuries. These were typically covered as separate incidents until the conversation around the long-term effects of repeated head injuries, such as chronic traumatic encephalopathy (CTE), became too big to ignore. Similar issues occurred with coverage of the National Football League. Head injuries were often dismissed as "getting your bell rung"—separate incidents—until the connection of cumulative head injuries to the deaths of several retired football players raised an issue that the league and the media had to begin to address in a more honest manner.

Media Theory in Action

On May 2, 2012, the sports world lost one of the greatest defensive players in NFL history. Hall of Fame San Diego Chargers linebacker Junior Seau took his own life by gunshot in his Oceanside, California, home (Merrill, 2012). A postmortem examination revealed that Seau suffered from chronic traumatic encephalopathy. He became the latest deceased former NFL player to be diagnosed with the brain condition that had football observers worried about the future of the sport (Fainaru-Wada & Fainaru, 2013). Seau was also the third former NFL defensive player to commit suicide while suffering the effects of CTE. The others had been two safeties with a reputation for vicious tackling, Andre Waters and Dave Duerson.

The effects of CTE had become a prominently discussed issue in NFL circles, and the loss of Seau prompted an immediate discussion of whether he also suffered from CTE, which in the case of athletes has been shown to result when a person suffers repeated blows to the head (Mayo Clinic Staff, 2021). This is an example of media outlets covering an issue in a thematic manner. When the issue of concussions in sport first began to attract attention in media coverage in the early 2000s, each incident was treated as an individual case, not indicative of a larger trend. Episodic framing was the norm. However, when the findings on CTE began to attract attention, sports media decision-makers determined that concussions in sport merited more thematic coverage.

Within hours of Seau's passing, outlets from *Sports Illustrated* to the San Diego *Union-Tribune* featured the news in their online sports sections, many including speculation about the possibility that Seau had CTE. The media response was appropriate. One of the game's greatest defensive players had taken his own life at age 43 while possibly suffering the aftereffects of brain trauma. The event sent shock waves through the league that would eventually lead to rule changes at all levels of football. NFL broadcast partner ESPN eliminated a regular segment that highlighted big hits during games. "Jacked Up!" had featured a montage of such plays, with the ESPN studio crew gleefully yelling the phrase at the appropriate times (Gordon, 2013).

This brings us to ESPN's initial coverage of Junior Seau's tragic suicide. While other outlets had the news of Seau's passing prominently displayed, ESPN moved slowly. Earlier that day, NFL commissioner Roger Goodell had enacted suspensions for four players involved in Bountygate, a scheme by the New Orleans Saints' defensive coordinator to offer cash prizes for extra-hard hits, some of which resulted in injury (Fleming, 2012). And for most of the day, the ESPN.com front page reflected what was being discussed on the network's morning shows, its afternoon shows, and at the top of *SportsCenter*. Despite the tragic passing of an NFL great, ESPN stayed with the story it had planned on covering. The network soon got to the Seau news; it's just that when all the other online sports front pages featured Seau, Bountygate was the topic on ESPN (ESPN News Services, 2012).

Bountygate had been the topic on ESPN for a few days as the story developed and new details were revealed. *First Take* talked about it, and the midday shows talked about it. The afternoon shows talked about it, Kornheiser and Wilbon included it on *Pardon the Interruption*, and the panelists on *Around the Horn* talked about it before it led *SportsCenter*. Bountygate was ESPN's story, and they were bound to stick with it as long as possible even in the face of news that shattered the sports world.

ESPN's daily activities fit into agenda-setting.

Summary

The basics of sports writing are the same as the basics of news writing. The basic story structure, the reporting techniques, the judgments and decisions reporters make when covering sport are fundamentally the same as those made by reporters covering politics. Good, sound journalism is good, sound journalism, regardless of whether it is sports or news.

This chapter has outlined the basics of news gathering and writing in the context of sports journalism. It detailed the basic structure used in covering games and writing news stories, showed how the basic story format can be expanded on, introduced the news values used in sports journalism, gave basic news gathering and interview advice, and described different types of sports journalism.

The core values of sports writing and reporting are simple—accurately reflect what happened in a game and what is happening with a team.

Discussion Questions

1. Much of this chapter focused on the writing of game stories. Why is that? Why are game stories so fundamental to sports journalism? In the digital age, do you believe this is still the case? Why or why not?
2. Why are reporting, interviewing, and research so important to sports journalism? How are columns and features improved by reporting?

Applied Activity

You've practiced writing. You've practiced reporting. To combine the news writing and reporting skills that you have learned in this chapter, you will cover a sporting event in person. Pick an event either at your school or at a nearby college or high school—these events are often easier to get access to than a professional game—and write a 650-word game story for immediate publication.

You are responsible for all aspects of game coverage:

- Requesting media credentials from the appropriate office. You can do this by finding the media relations or athletic communications office on a team or school's athletic website and contacting the staff. Often, there will be a link or form to fill out to request credentials. For high school games, you can contact the host school's athletic director. There is no fee for media credentials.
- Conducting all necessary pregame research, including reading any game notes provided by both teams (at the college and pro level) and looking up previous stories to know the context of the game.
- Attending the game in person.
- Acting as a professional reporter.
- Attending any postgame press conference, selecting players and coaches to interview, and asking them questions.
- Writing a well-structured, complete, well-written, and well-reported game story that clearly identifies and describes the most newsworthy aspects of the game.
- Completing the story within 24 hours of the game's start.

News Gathering in the Digital Age

Chapter Objectives

After completing this chapter, you will be able to do the following:

- Identify reputable nonhuman sources of information and know how to use them in your reporting.
- Define many of the major analytics used in American professional and college sports.
- Understand how to turn statistics—both basic and more advanced—into compelling sports stories.

In 2012, the Detroit Tigers' Miguel Cabrera narrowly won the American League (AL) Most Valuable Player (MVP) award over Mike Trout of the Los Angeles Angels of Anaheim. Cabrera led the league in batting average, home runs, and runs batted in (RBIs), becoming the first AL player to win the Triple Crown in 45 years. Trout had better numbers in many of the advanced metrics that have risen to prominence throughout the 2000s. In the *Detroit Free Press*, columnist Mitch Albom (2012) gloated not for his hometown player but for the traditional approach to sports.

> In a battle of computer analysis versus people who still watch baseball as, you know, a sport …
>
> And this WAR statistic—which measures the number of wins a player gives his team versus a replacement player of minor league/bench talent (honestly, who comes up with this stuff?)—is another way of declaring, "Nerds win!"
>
> We need to slow down the shoveling of raw data into the "what can we come up with next?" machine. It is actually creating a divide between those who like to watch the game of baseball and those who want to reduce it to binary code. (paras. 26-27)

Michael Wilbon of ESPN (and a longtime *Washington Post* columnist) has been a loud and persistent anti-analytics voice for years. Writing for *The Undefeated* (2016), he wrote the following:

> The greater the dependence on the numbers, the more challenged people are to tell (or understand) the narrative without them. Makes you wonder how people ever enjoyed or understood the dominance of baseball king Babe Ruth or boxing champ Joe Louis or Masters Tournament co-founder Bobby Jones. (para. 12)

Jason Whitlock, then of Fox Sports, went one step further in 2011, saying that "stat geeks are ruining sports" (Lucia, 2012, para. 1).

It's become a common point for sports columnists of a certain generation and disposition to use their space to rail against the growing analytics movement. As the modern cliché says, don't be that guy. This chapter teaches you how not to be that person.

This chapter provides instruction on the use of nonhuman sources in sports journalism. This includes the basics of finding information on official sites (e.g., used for rosters, schedules, statistics) and also the use of databases and analytics in sport analysis. With new ways to talk about sports (e.g., Corsi in the National Hockey League, WAR in Major League Baseball, SP+ in college football), sports journalists must have a working knowledge of these elements, which have grown and continue to grow in popularity among fans, team front offices, players, coaches, and other writers.

To quote Shea Serrano in his book *Basketball (and Other Things)*,

> "One of two things just happened in that stats section above. Either you started reading it and were like, 'Wow, this is interesting.' Or you started reading it and were like, 'Nah, (forget) this,' and then skipped it. If you're in that second group, all you need to know is that whenever a stat gets mentioned somewhere, high numbers are good and low numbers are bad." (Serrano, 2017, p. 5)

Nonhuman Sources

In the previous chapter, you learned about how to find human sources for your stories. Which players and coaches to interview, how to ask the best questions and get the best answers, why it's important to cultivate sources and develop relationships with the people on your beat, and so on. All of that remains the core of sports journalism. So why are we dedicating an entire chapter in a book about sports journalism to how to use analytics and other nonhuman sources?

For one thing, the "holy war" that *Moneyball* author Michael Lewis described between traditional scouts and users of advanced analytics (Law, 2017) is over, and the analytics users have won. Just about every team in major sports around the world has some kind of analytics department. Almost every decision a team makes in terms of roster construction—who to draft, who to sign, who to trade and for what—is informed at least partially by analytics. How a team plays on the field—when a baseball team shifts its defense, what kinds of shots a basketball team looks for—is informed at least partially by analytics. Given this fact, it's important that sports journalists have at least a basic working knowledge of the statistics and analysis used by teams.

From a more pragmatic and practical standpoint, being able to use analytics and other nonhuman sources in your sports reporting is a crucial skill to have. Starting in the 2010s and now going forward, teams have started locking down the access that journalists have to players and coaches. The access to sources we described in chapter 3 is changing; teams and leagues are starting to restrict which players are available to the media for interviews. Assistant coaches are not allowed to talk to reporters anymore. More and more interviews happen in a formal press-conference setting. Reporters cannot count on being able to interview all the human sources they are used to, which means you must be adaptable and find new sources of information.

This is even more true in the aftermath of the COVID-19 pandemic. During the pandemic, sports leagues and college conferences strictly limited reporters' access to players and coaches due to social-distancing guidelines. Reporters who were used to traveling to away games and diligently working the locker room found themselves covering games from their couches and conducting group interviews with players via Zoom (Kane et al., 2020). Even reporters inside a league's official bubble couldn't rely on getting in-person interviews (Moritz, 2020). There is no guarantee that access for sports reporters will ever again approach the levels that were considered normal and expected before the pandemic. Given these restrictions, the ability to write and report using nonhuman sources and analytics becomes even more valuable.

So, when this happens, what do you do? How do you do your job well? How do you cover your beat and keep your readers informed about their favorite teams or athletes when you don't have human sources? After all, there is always a story due by deadline.

Journalism is more than just interviewing human sources. Websites, media guides, and databases provide a treasure trove of information for sports

Michael Lewis, the author of *Moneyball*.
Steve Jennings/WireImage

journalists. They are places to find story ideas, to do reporting, and to find statistics and data to analyze.

Lastly, there's no such thing as too much knowledge. Simply put, nothing bad can come from knowing about these statistics and analyses. Anything that makes your stories more informed and more well-rounded will help give your readers a better understanding of their favorite teams.

Let's start with the basics.

Media Guides

Before the digital age, a sports team's **media guide** was its equivalent of a Bible. Printed at the beginning of every season and distributed to every media member, the guide contained every bit of information a reporter might need about a team. It contained the opening-day roster, with bios and statistics for every player—ranging from multiple-page entries for star players to short paragraphs for the last players off the bench—coach, and front-office executive. There were detailed team statistics from the previous season and from the team's entire history. Want to know the Buffalo Sabres' all-time record in games played in Vancouver? (It's 20-32-12.) (Buffalo Sabres won-loss records, n.d.). How about the 14th-highest-scoring game by a Philadelphia 76er? (Wilt Chamberlain, 53 points on Jan. 25, 1966, versus Los Angeles.) (1920_mediaguide_v3.pdf, n.d.) The media guide held all the answers.

In the digital age, that information has, of course, moved online. English Premier League club Ipswich Town F.C. was the first sports team with a website, going online in 1990 (Who was the first football club to have an official website?, 2016).

Major League Baseball teams still have printed media guides, at least for the big-league clubs. Minor league clubs have phased out printed guides. Some NFL and NBA and WNBA teams still print media guides, but teams in those leagues are moving more and more to online-only guides. The NHL has moved its media guides completely online, as have many college sports programs. Interestingly, every team still produces the classic media guide. It's just that instead of going through the time and expense of printing them out, they are published online as PDFs.

Team Websites

In contrast to the media guides, team and league websites are not written with the media as a primary audience. Rather, the public, the various teams' fans, are the primary audience. The website is a way for teams to sell tickets, promote upcoming events, and link to a sport organization's official store. Since the mid-2000s, teams have also had "official reporters" who act as quasi-journalists covering the teams (Ioakimidis, 2010). But a team's website is still a wonderful place for a reporter to start.

Access the Indiana Fever's website, and let's look at it as a reporter would (Official Indiana Fever website, n.d.). As you can see, there is an overload of information available—podcasts, social media links, news stories, and videos. Fans can buy tickets and merchandise, request a donation for a charity fundraiser, and sign up to take part in an in-game time-out activity. There's even a link to GIFs for social media users.

For our purposes as sports journalists, there are several places to look for information and story ideas.

- On the Team drop-down menu, there is the official roster (with links to each player's bio) and information on the entire coaching staff and front office.
- The Schedule tab has, of course, the team's schedule and results.
- The News tab is useful for the News Releases link, which contains all the press releases put out by the media relations team.

It's important to spend time getting familiar with the official website of any team you cover. They are invaluable resources for finding story ideas, doing research, and preparing you for an interview with a player or a coach.

Time-Out

1. Go to your college's athletics website. Using only the official website, generate a list of 10 potential story ideas from the information you find there. They can be specific (about a player or a team) or general, but the goal is to generate a list of stories you could pitch to an editor.

2. Think of your favorite current athlete, college or pro. If you don't have a favorite athlete, pick one at random. Find their current official bio on their team's web page. Using only this information, create a **listicle** of "10 things you never knew about (Insert Athlete's Name here)." Include a combination of statistical and anecdotal information.

Statistics are an important part of a sport journalist's arsenal of information.
Steph Chambers/Getty Images

Databases

In addition to team websites and media guides, there are a number of statistical databases that are available to sports journalists. These databases are collections of statistics for both active and historical athletes in most major sports. We will go into more detail about these sources later in this chapter, after detailing the types of statistics and analytics available to sports journalists.

Statistics

Statistics have been an important part of sports and sports journalism since the beginning of both. Sports journalism and baseball have been intrinsically intertwined since the sport's beginnings in New York City in the 1850s and 1860s. Henry Chadwick, a newspaper reporter who was covering cricket when he first discovered baseball, is widely credited with inventing many of the statistics still used in baseball, including batting average, the concept of earned and unearned runs, and recording strikeouts with the letter K. Chadwick's most famous work was creating the box score, a statistical summary of each day's game. That fact is immortalized on Chadwick's plaque in the Baseball Hall of Fame (BBHOF, n.d.).

Statistics served a vital purpose in those early days of sports journalism. As Chadwick's biographer Andrew Schiff wrote, "The box score was the only way of showing the game, there really was no photography. So the writer really was the person at the center between the fans and the player at the game" (BBHOF, n.d.).

A central element of every newspaper sports page for generations has been the agate page. This page contains the standings, scores, schedules, box scores, and other statistical information. Through the years, even as sports journalism has evolved, statistics have remained at the heart of what sports journalists do.

As technology and access to information improved, so did the availability and the analysis of statistics. In 1971, the Society for American Baseball Research (SABR) was formed. Inspired by that organization's name, Bill James began writing about baseball from a more statistical point of view, calling his approach **sabermetrics**. It was the birth of the analytics movement in sports.

Analytics

Analytics is the use of advanced statistics to evaluate teams and players. They have become incredibly important to front offices because they are used primarily in roster construction. The use of analytics has trickled down to sports journalism too.

Analytics have been controversial in sports and sports journalism in the early 2000s. But they aren't going anywhere, so as an aspiring sports journalist, you should get to know what they mean and how to use them.

Some of the critiques and criticisms of the analytics movement have emanated from members of the mainstream sports media. These are not critiques of the statistics in terms of how they are used and how they are developed—for example, the fact that OPS+ is a mathematically dubious stat because the denominators used are different (Jaffe, 2017; Law, 2017). Instead, these are offhand remarks from sports journalists who mock and degrade the analytics movement:

"I was told there would be no math."

"They're too complicated."

"They tell us what we already know."

"They take the fun out of sports."

Let's take these complaints one by one and address them.

I Was Told There Would Be No Math

Journalists are famously allergic to math. We're word people whose favorite subjects in school were English, history, creative writing—anything but math. It's important to remember that in analytics, we don't do the math. The math is done for us. What we're doing is analyzing the information and contextualizing it for our readers.

Also, sports journalists trade in numbers and statistics from the day we watch our first game. The most math-hating sports reporter can multiply by seven (thanks to football) or figure out a batting average based on available hit and at-bat information.

They're Too Complicated

Counting stats like wins, home runs, and touchdowns is easy to figure out and understand. WAR, PER, and the newer range of statistics feel more complicated. But are they really?

Let's take batting average as an example. Off the top of your head, what does batting average measure? There's a good chance that "how often a baseball player gets a hit," or some variation of that, was your answer. After all, the old chestnut holds that the best baseball players fail seven of 10 times, right?

But as you may also know, batting average does not measure how often a player gets a hit. It measures how many hits a player gets per at-bat. An at-bat does not refer to every time a player comes up to hit. That's a plate appearance. If a player draws a walk, is hit by a pitch, hits a sacrifice fly or a sacrifice bunt, or reaches base because of the catcher's interference, it does not count as an at-bat. Why not? Because the rules say so.

Considered at some distance, batting average is not a simple stat but instead a pretty complicated one that measures how often a player gets a hit, but only when that player doesn't do one of these four things that are incredibly common and often quite useful. In fact, in three of them (walk, hit by pitch, catcher's interference), the batter gets on base but doesn't get credit in this stat.

Or look at wins for a pitcher. What could be more basic and straightforward than a pitcher win? One team wins, and that team's pitcher gets credit for it. Of course, that's not true. The MLB rulebook defines a winning pitcher as follows:

> The Official Scorer shall credit as the winning pitcher that pitcher whose team assumes a lead while such pitcher is in the game, or during the inning on offense in which such pitcher is removed from the game, and does not relinquish such lead … if the pitcher whose team assumes a lead while such pitcher is in the game, or during the inning on offense in which such pitcher is removed from the game, and does not relinquish such lead, is a starting pitcher who has not completed (1) five innings of a game that lasts six or more

innings on defense, or (2) four innings of a game that lasts five innings on defense, then the Official Scorer shall credit as the winning pitcher the relief pitcher, if there is only one relief pitcher, or the relief pitcher who, in the Official Scorer's judgment was the most effective, if there is more than one relief pitcher. (What is a win (W)?, n.d.)

So what feels like a straightforward stat is actually pretty complicated—and explained in a notably lengthy run-on sentence—and oftentimes is decided not by the play on the field, but by an observer watching the game from the press box.

(There are all manner of issues with using pitcher wins as a statistic, which we'll address later in the chapter.)

The point is that while new statistics may feel mathematically complicated (and often are), the traditional baseball card stats we've used for generations are complicated as well. They're just accepted because they've been around for a long time and we happen to be familiar with them.

The point of sports journalism is not to avoid what's complicated or unfamiliar, but to explain these concepts to our readers.

They Tell Us What We Already Know

Do we really need to evaluate a player's efficiency rating to know that Diana Taurasi is one of the greatest players in basketball history? Or that Tom Brady has the single-best QBR of all-time?

The fact is that most advanced statistics do reinforce what the traditional stats tell us. Advanced stats are simply ways to better contextualize what we watch on the field and what we read in the box score, or ways to give us a more well-rounded, nuanced understanding of sports. So yes, when you look up the top-five players ranked in John Hollinger's NBA and WNBA PER rankings (explained later in this chapter), there will not be any surprises. They'll almost always be the superstars whom you expect to be among the best players in the league.

Stats are also value neutral. They're not positive or negative. And no single analytic is perfect. Some might tell more information about a player than others, but there's no such thing as a perfect statistic. Stats are simply numbers that are a direct result of what a player does in the games.

Analytics have always been a part of sports. They've become more advanced as the technology that tracks and measures the games has gotten more fine-tuned, but the use of stats is nothing new. In his book on statistical forecasting, Nate Silver (2012) quotes an anecdote told to him by a longtime baseball scout:

> "Well, let's face it guys, what's the first thing we do when we go to the ballpark? We go to the press room, we get the stats. We get the stats! What's wrong with that? That's what you do." (p. 95)

They Take the Fun Out of Sports

At the core, this is the heart of many of the traditional sports arguments against analytics. The columns by the Whitlocks and Alboms and Wilbons and Plaschkes of the world are all, in a lot of ways, rooted in this idea that analytics take the fun out of sports. Sports is supposed to be fun, a break from the world, and then these nerds with their spreadsheets come in talking about their equations and not watching sport the *right way*.

There's so much wrong with this line of reasoning. First of all, it perpetuates a dangerous form of toxic masculinity, where intelligence is mocked and put down needlessly and foolishly. It's incredibly uncreative and outdated (because all smart people must be nerds, and all nerds must love spreadsheets, right?). It also suggests that there is a right and proper way to be a sports fan, and that can't involve math. But plenty of kids grow up loving math *and* sports. Front offices all over professional sports are now populated with such people. There's no proper way to be a fan or an observer of sports.

What analytics provide us in sports journalism is another tool. Another club in our bag, to use a golf metaphor.

A common way this can be useful is when you are doing a profile on a player and your interviews from his teammates and coaches yield quotes like, "He's just a winner, man. He does the things that don't show up in the box score. He's got a lot of confidence, and he lifts us up." Fine quotes, but a little vague. They don't really tell you or your readers anything useful or interesting about your story's subject. But using advanced analytics to go beyond the typical box score stats may help you paint a more well-rounded picture.

At a time in our industry when access to players and coaches is decreasing, due both to increased control by teams and to restrictions put in place due to the COVID-19 pandemic, the ability to understand advanced analytics, use them in your stories, and make them understandable to your readers is an invaluable one.

Industry Profile

Ben Lindbergh

Ben Lindbergh

For someone who writes about baseball from an advanced analytics point of view, Ben Lindbergh has what might be a surprising background. Lindbergh, the former editor of Baseball Prospectus and current senior editor at The Ringer, was an English major in college.

"During and after college, I did internships for baseball teams, but I missed producing work for public consumption and I learned that my statistical chops couldn't compare to those of the math and computer science experts who were working as team analysts," Lindbergh said in an email interview. "Writing and editing (and later, podcasting) was better suited to my skills and more in line with my passions and lifestyle."

Lindbergh, the coauthor of two books that look at baseball from an analytics perspective (*The MVP Machine* with Travis Sawchik, *The Only Rule Is It Has to Work* with Sam Miller), was introduced to the sabermetrics movement through the writing of Rob Neyer at ESPN and through reading Baseball Prospectus and the website Fire Joe Morgan.

"I found it intriguing that there were hidden layers to a long-established sport, and that some of the common beliefs about baseball might be misleading," he said. "I wanted to know what I was missing. But I probably wouldn't have been hooked if not for the great writing of the sources I cited above. The language and arguments grabbed me more so than the stats."

Lindbergh said he views statistics as tools he uses in his reporting—the same as archival research in traditional reporting.

"If I think analytics and statistics can shed some light on a certain subject, I'm happy to flick that switch," he said. "But it's vital to frame the inquiry correctly and to be aware of what the stats are (and aren't) saying and whether there are any limitations to the data or confounding factors that could be steering you wrong."

Lindbergh's career in sports writing has been guided by asking interesting questions and seeking analytical answers to them. In *The Only Rule Is It Has to Work*, he and Miller take jobs as general managers of an independent baseball team in California and are given complete freedom to build the team around analytics-based strategies. In *The MVP Machine,* he and Sawchik report on how baseball teams are using analytics to better develop prospects and players.

"Most of my articles start with a question—something I'm wondering and want to try to explain to satisfy my own curiosity," Lindbergh said. "If *I'm* not curious, why should I expect the reader to be? Then I try to figure out what work on the question has already been done, who or what might be able to help me get closer to an answer, and how to get access to the info I need. Sometimes the stats supply the 'what' but not the 'how' or the 'why,' in which case the stats are just the starting point, a springboard to the next step. It's also important to keep in mind that not every question calls for a statistically-derived answer."

At the end of the day, it comes down to the story he is telling. The use of analytics and advanced statistics is not an end in and of itself but is a way to tell a story that resonates with readers.

"If I do that job well," Lindbergh said, "reading the results won't feel like doing math homework."

Sport-by-Sport Analytics

Now that we've sold you on why you should use analytics, it's time to start understanding them a little better. For each of the major sports (basketball, baseball, American football, soccer, and hockey), we break down the most basic statistics you probably already know. These are the traditional stats. Jaffe (2017) and Law (2017) call these baseball card stats, but these apply to all sports, not just baseball. We call these *card stats*. We also provide context and tell you why these stats are at worst flawed, at best incomplete. Then we define some of the more popular advanced analytics (what we call *advanced stats*) for each sport and tell you what they measure, where you can find them, and how you can use them as a reporter.

A bit of explanation before we get going:

- This is by no means an exhaustive list of advanced analytics. It's not even the be-all and end-all of beginners' lists. This is meant as a starter kit, so to speak, to help you (and by extension your readers) use and understand some of the advanced stats that are being used in sports.
- Remember that the quality of the data and statistics available will vary according to level. Pro sports have hard drives' worth of data available for each game. The amount of data that comes out of an NBA game will not be the same as that which comes from a Division III basketball game.
- Throughout this chapter, we'll use data and stats from the Sports Reference website.
- Know the benchmarks. Each stat we mention will include benchmarks for average players, good players, and superstars. This is one of the biggest roadblocks to sports fans and journalists using analytics. The benchmarks for traditional stats are embedded in our DNA as sports fans. If you hear a quarterback threw for 300 yards, or a basketball player averaged 23 points and 12 rebounds a game, you immediately know they were good. You know it without a second of hesitation. As Jay Jaffe wrote, "We learned that stars hit .300 and sepia-toned legends .400. Home run totals measured a player's strength. RBI's measured a player's ability to help his team" (2017, p. 9). If you're new to analytics and you hear that someone has a WAR of 7 . . . is that good? Bad? Seven sounds kind of low, but it could be good? If a pitcher has an ERA of 1.24, you know they are very good. But what if their WHIP is 1.24? Know the benchmarks. And more importantly, explain them to your readers. Which brings us to our final point.
- Context, context, context. When writing about analytics and statistics, context matters. This is something that sports fans instinctively know. That quarterback who threw for 300 yards? If 150 of them came in the fourth quarter when the team was down 30 points and playing against the second- and third-string defense, it's not as impressive. A player can average 23 points a game, but if they take 30 shots a game to score that many, it's probably hurting the team. The same holds true when you're using advanced analytics. It's necessary to contextualize this information for readers, to let them know what these numbers mean and why they are important.

If you find yourself still exasperatedly saying, "But I was told there would be no math!," you can relax. Take another deep breath. Remember, you are not calculating anything. You are looking up numbers, same as you would a batting average or shooting percentage. We're not doing math. We're looking at numbers and analyzing them. There's a difference.

Basketball

The free-flowing nature of basketball is embedded in the sport's DNA. As Kurtis Blow famously noted, they dribble up and down the court. As author Jim Carroll wrote, basketball is the sport where "you can correct your own mistakes, immediately and beautifully, in midair" (Mallon, 2010). Because of this, there aren't the dedicated individual matchups like in baseball or a clean breakdown of individual plays like in football. But there is still a deep analytics movement in basketball, from rating individual players in the NBA and the WNBA to ranking teams in advance of the NCAA tournament.

Card Stats: Points, rebounds, shooting percentage, blocks, steals, assists

Context: In basketball, we can call these the box score stats. These are the first statistics a basketball fan learns. In chapter 3, we used a basketball box score for your first game story assignment because it's the easiest from which to read and tell a story. That's because the statistics are easy to understand. It's the ultimate example of big numbers being good. Arguably the most iconic single-game performance in American sports came on March 2, 1962, when Wilt Chamberlain scored 100 points for the Philadelphia 76ers.

When we look at a player's season or career, we do so by taking the per-game average of all of the box score stats. These stats are all useful and valuable. But again, they often lack context. That's what the advanced metrics start to do.

Advanced stats: Box Plus/Minus, VORP, PER, Win Shares, Usage Rate, True Shooting Percentage, Effective Field Goal Percentage

Context: One of the most significant shortcomings of the basic box score stats is that they are raw numbers that don't take playing time or pace of play

Probabilistic Thinking and the Process

Imagine you're playing blackjack. You are dealt a pair of kings, giving you 20. "Hit me," you say. The dealer tosses you a card. The ace of spades. 21. Blackjack.

Was your decision to hit a smart one?

On the next hand, by a stroke of incredible coincidence, you are dealt a pair of queens, once again giving you 20. The dealer is showing 15, meaning they have to hit. "Stay," you say. The dealer flips over a card. An ace. They have 16, meaning they still have to hit. Only one card can help them. The dealer hits again. A 5. The only card that can help them. Twenty-one for the dealer, and you lose. Not only that, but if you had hit on 20, you would have gotten that ace, giving you 21.

Was your decision to stay a smart one?

It's pretty clear what the answers are to both of those questions. Hitting when you had 20 was not a smart decision. In fact, it was a galactically stupid decision. In an entire deck of cards, only four possible cards could have been useful (the four aces), which means you had a 93 percent chance of going bust. What happened wasn't a smart move. What happened was, you got lucky.

And in the second scenario—the one where you stayed on 20, only to see the dealer get the ace you would need en route to winning—you absolutely made the smart decision. In fact, you had a 93 percent chance that it would work out in your favor. You just suffered what card players call a bad beat. Put plainly, you just got unlucky.

This is a very basic example of **probabilistic thinking**.

One of the core ideas of probabilistic thinking is that the process matters more than the outcome. The decision and the process that got you to that decision are what is important.

You can see where the conflict comes from in the sports world. In fact, this is the fundamental conflict within the analytics movement.

Sports is, in many ways, an outcome-based world. It's a black-and-white world, in that at the end of the day, there is a winner and there is a loser. And the culture of sports is that winners did the right thing and losers did the wrong thing. If you make a decision, and you win the game, it was the right decision. No matter how you got there, no matter what kind of data you used, no matter why you made the decision you made. If you win the game, it was the right decision. More importantly, if you lost, it was the wrong decision.

Let's take our blackjack examples again but apply the traditional sports journalism mindset to them.

You hit on 20 and got the ace for 21. What a smart move that was! You're a winner, baby! You're a winning winner who wins. You are clutch! Forget those Ivy League eggheads and what their fancy numbers say. You went with your gut, and you won! You are Derek Jeter! You are Tim Tebow. You are a winner!

You stayed on 20, didn't get the ace, and got beat. You're an idiot! How could you stay? You blew it, baby! I don't care what the fancy numbers say! Don't give me that mumbo jumbo! Hello? Why do you play? You play to win the game!

We exaggerate. But not by much.

From Bill Belichick having his Patriots going for it on fourth-and-short in their own end of the field leading to a regular-season loss to the Colts, to Tampa Bay Rays manager Kevin Cash taking out an absolutely dealing Blake Snell midway through Game 6 of the 2020 World Series (a move that led to the Dodgers winning the game and the series), sports media traditionally view decisions through the prism of winning and losing.

But the analytics movement, as a whole, looks at process and probability, not outcomes. Often, outcomes in sports are out of the control of players and managers. The margin between a shot going in or bouncing off the rim, of a puck finding the net or hitting the post, of a swing yielding the game-winning base hit or a harmless pop-up, is often literally a fraction of an inch. Also, luck plays a much bigger role in sports than many of us are willing to admit.

A decision might be the right one nine times out of 10. But all it takes is that one time, that single loss, for it to feel like the wrong decision.

into consideration. A player on the famed "Seven Seconds or Less" Phoenix Suns of the mid-2000s would get a lot more possessions and chances to score than a player on the defensive-minded New York Knicks teams of the early 1990s. One way to level this playing field is to calculate our box score stats per 100 possessions rather than per game.

One of the stats that does this is **Box Plus/Minus (BPM)**. It's a box-score estimate of the points per 100 possessions a player contributed above a league-average player, translated to an average team. A score of 5 is better than average, and a score in double digits is an all-time great season. In 2023, Nikola Jokić led the NBA with a BPM of 13.00, ahead of league MVP Joel Embiid (9.2). Jokić's 2022 season yielded a 13.7 BPM, the best single-season mark ever. The WNBA's best BPM single season was recorded by Sheryl Swoopes in 2000, with a 12.9. The second highest came in 2019, when Elena Delle Donne recorded a BPM of 12.0 in her MVP season.

Statisticians use BPM to then calculate **Value Over Replacement Player (VORP)**. VORP "is an estimate of each player's overall contribution to the team. So basically, it tells us how valuable a player is versus replacing that player with someone else … a minimum salary player not in rotation" (Serrano, 2017, p. 5). The benchmarks are the same as for BPM, with a score of 10 or higher being an all-time season. Michael Jordan recorded a 12.47 VORP in 1988, the single best VORP season. VORP was not available for WNBA players as of this writing.

One of the primary advanced stats in basketball is the **Player Efficiency Rating (PER)**, developed by John Hollinger during his days at ESPN. PER takes into account all of the stats found in a box score, positive and negative (including things like missed shots, turnovers, and fouls), and measures a player's per-minute productivity.

> What PER can do, however, is summarize a player's statistical accomplishments in a single number. That allows us to unify the disparate data on each player we try to track in our heads (e.g., Corey Maggette: free-throw machine, good rebounder, decent shooter, poor passer, etc.) so that we can move on to evaluating what might be missing from the stats. (Hollinger, 2007, para. 7)

The WNBA and NBA average for PER is 15, with all-star players coming in around 20 and MVPs closer to 30. The highest recorded PER in pro basketball came in 2007, when Lauren Jackson of the Seattle Storm recorded a PER of 35.0 in her MVP season. In 2021-22, his second consecutive NBA MVP season, Jokić recorded the men's record PER of 32.85. The previous record, 32.08, was set by Wilt Chamberlain in 1962.

While PER helps to measure a player's individual performance, **Win Shares** helps quantify each player's impact on their team. Win Shares "attempt to divvy up credit for team success to the individuals on a team" (NBA Win Shares, n.d, para. 1) using individual, team, and league statistics. Offensive and defensive Win Shares are calculated and added together for a final total. Kareem Abdul-Jabbar's 1971-72 season yielded a record 25.4 Win Shares, which meant that he was responsible for 25 of Milwaukee's 63 wins that year. A'ja Wilson set the WNBA's single-season record with 10.36 Win Shares, meaning she was responsible for 10 of the Las Vegas Aces' 34 victories in 2023. Win Shares have also been calculated for men's college basketball since the 1995-96 season and women's basketball since the 2001-02 season. Kevin Love's 2008 season for UCLA resulted in a record 11.29 Win Shares on the men's side, while Brittney Griner recorded 15.68 Win Shares for Baylor in 2012.

Usage Rate is a stat that "calculates what percentage of team plays a player was involved in while he was on the floor" (Fromal, 2012). Basically, this looks at how often a player is involved in a team's plays. The average NBA or WNBA player would have a Usage Rate of 20. Russell Westbrook holds the single-season record with a Usage Rate of 41.65 in 2016-17, meaning he was involved in about 42 percent of all of Oklahoma City's plays that season. The career record is held by Michael Jordan (33.2), meaning he was involved in a third of all of the Chicago Bulls' and Washington Wizards' plays in his entire career. In the WNBA, Angel McCoughtry holds the three highest single-season Usage Rates in league history, including a record 35.48 percent in 2011. Through the 2022 season, her career Usage Rate was 31.70, meaning she was involved in nearly one-third of all of her team's plays in her 13 seasons.

Two advanced ways of evaluating a player's shooting are True Shooting Percentage and Effective Field Goal Percentage. **True Shooting Percentage** mathematically combines players' shooting percentages on two-pointers, three-pointers, and free throws to determine their shooting efficiency. Because of the way three-pointers are calculated in this stat, it's possible to have a True Shooting Percentage of greater than 100 percent. In the 2021-22 season, Rudy Gobert had an all-time NBA best .7324 True Shooting Percentage. In 2016, Nneka Ogwumike had a WNBA record .7371 True Shooting Percentage.

Angel McCoughtry holds multiple WNBA records.
Joshua Huston/NBAE via Getty Images

Similarly, **Effective Field Goal Percentage** calculates a player's shooting percentage while accounting for the fact that a three-point basket is worth more than a two-pointer. Adam Fromal (2012) uses the following explanation:

> Player A attempts 10 shots from the field, all from within the three-point arc, and drills five of them.
>
> Player B attempts 10 shots from the field, all from outside the three-point arc, and drills five of them.
>
> Player A, who was responsible for 10 points, has a FG% of 50 percent, just like Player B, who was responsible for 15 points, despite shooting the same number of times. However, Player A's eFG% was still 50 percent while Player B's was a much better 75 percent. (paras. 45–47)

College Basketball Team Rankings

An annual debate in the sports world every March revolves around the NCAA basketball tournament. Which teams deserved top seeds, which teams deserved berths in the field of 68, who was snubbed, who got in that shouldn't have?

This is a debate because, like in college football, teams play unbalanced schedules in very different conferences. How would a team that dominates a mid-major conference, like Gonzaga in the West Coast Conference, perform in a higher-profile conference like the Atlantic Coast Conference against Duke and North Carolina? Which men's team is better—a St. Bonaventure team that wins the Atlantic 10, or a Syracuse team that finishes in the middle of the ACC? Is a women's team from the SEC that finishes several games behind South Carolina really better than a mid-major team from Conference USA? If the University of Hartford women's team goes undefeated in a smaller conference like the Commonwealth Coast Conference, how good are they really?

A generation of metrics have been developed, used, and sometimes discarded to answer these questions. One of the most familiar is the **RPI (Ratings Percentage Index)**, which evaluates teams based not just on their record but on their strength of schedule. Seventy-five percent of the RPI rating comes from a team's strength of schedule. The idea behind the RPI was to gauge how good a team was based on their opponents. Were they beating up on the Colgates and St. Francises of the world, or were they playing and beating stronger teams?

In 2018, the NCAA announced the creation of the **NET rankings** (the NCAA Evaluation Tool) to replace the RPI as its primary evaluation tool for both men's and women's basketball. The NET rankings take five factors into account:

1. Team Value Index, which is an algorithm based on a team's results, game locations, and opponents set up to reward teams who beat other good teams
2. A team's net efficiency, which takes offensive and defensive efficiency into account
3. Winning percentage
4. Adjusted winning percentage (based on location and results)
5. Point differential

One other college team ranking system that is useful for reporters is the KenPom ratings. Created and maintained by Ken Pomeroy, the KenPom ratings rank all 357 Division I men's teams (KenPom does not rank women's teams) by an adjusted efficiency margin, determining by how many points a team would outscore an average D-I team. The site also shows offensive, defensive, and tempo stats per 100 possessions, a luck rating, and strength of schedule, and it provides a good analytic overview of how a team is playing in a given season (Gaudios, 2019).

Baseball

Few sports are as intertwined with advanced analytics as baseball. From the groundbreaking work of Bill James and his Baseball Prospectus to SABR to *Moneyball*, no sport has become as connected with analytics as baseball. There are several reasons for this. One is the individualized nature of a baseball game. Yes, it's a team sport. But one way of looking at a baseball game is as a series of isolated individual showdowns between hitters and pitchers. That makes it much easier to parse an individual's performance (and impact) in baseball than in football (where each play is complicated and interconnected) or in basketball and hockey (where play is much more free-flowing).

The other reason is the amount of data available from a Major League Baseball game. In 2006, Major League Baseball Advanced Media installed **PITCHf/x**, a system that uses multiple cameras to track the speed, location, and movement of every pitch thrown (Slowinski, 2010c). In 2015, in every ballpark MLB installed Statcast, which increases the amount of data available to teams and media members (MLB.com, n.d.-a). Writer Ben Lindbergh recalled working on a story about the length of leads that runners take off first base, using data from MLB Advanced Media that was accurate down to the millimeter. "If anything, we're overloaded with information. At the major-league level, every event is almost perfectly preserved" (Lindbergh & Miller, 2016, p. 30).

Card stats: Batting average, home runs, RBI, W-L record, ERA, saves, errors, putouts, assists, fielding percentage

Context: We discussed the issues with batting average earlier in this chapter. Fans think it tells us one thing (how successful a hitter is) when it actually tells us another (how many hits a batter gets in official at-bats, which do not include all plate appearances).

Home runs are a blunt number; there is nothing wrong with them, but they are by no means the be-all and end-all of a player's worth.

RBIs are completely context dependent. A player can only drive in runs if other players get on base before that player settles into the batter's box. The RBI stat doesn't really tell us as much about a player's skill as we think it does.

As for pitching stats like wins and saves, Keith Law (2017) devotes entire chapters of his book *Smart Baseball* to debunking their importance. Earlier in this chapter, we noted that the way in which a pitcher gets credit for a win is much more complicated than we think it is. But beyond that, as Law points out, it gives one player credit for an entire team's effort or blame for teammates' failings. A pitcher can pitch wonderfully, but if the teammates don't score runs, he's not going to earn a win. The current generation of New York Mets fans have seen this firsthand.

Law (2017) is even harsher on saves, a stat created in 1959 by former Chicago sports columnist Jerome Holtzman, calling it "an unholy mess of arbitrary conditions" that "doesn't actually measure anything" (p. 45). Like the pitcher's win, the save is a seemingly clear stat (a pitcher who closes out a game) but is actually incredibly complicated (MLB.com, n.d.-d).

> The conditions of the save rule create all sorts of internal paradoxes. The pitcher who throws a scoreless seventh inning and a scoreless eighth inning gets nothing, while the pitcher

who follows him, throws the ninth inning, and gives up a run but doesn't surrender the lead gets the SV in the box score. Which pitcher actually contributed more to his team winning the game? Yet which pitcher does Holtzman's Folly end up rewarding? (Law, 2017, p. 46)

Earned run average (ERA) is typically seen as a better evaluator of a pitcher's performance than win-loss record. As a baseball card stat, it's pretty good. But as Law points out, it still assigns full blame for a run scoring to the pitcher who allowed a runner on base, and it separates earned runs from "unearned runs," which occur when a batter reaches base by error (which, again, is determined by the official scorer in the press box).

Defense in baseball has long been one of the hardest things to statistically measure. Putouts measure how many times a defensive player completes an out, making the stat skewed toward first basemen who field groundouts. Assists are awarded to players who touch the ball before another player recorded the out—the shortstop who throws the ball to first base gets the assist. Errors are a part of every line score, but they're a bit problematic. The MLB rules determine that a player has committed an error when, "in the judgment of the official scorer, he fails to convert an out on a play that an average fielder should have made" (MLB.com, n.d.-b, para. 1), making the determination of an error almost 100 percent subjective. Also, the number of errors doesn't tell us much about how good a fielder is, because a player who gets to more batted balls and thus had more opportunities to make plays is likely to make more errors than players who didn't.

Fielding percentage takes a defender's putouts and assists and divides them by total chances. The limitation with fielding percentage is that it only takes into account plays a player makes without looking at plays a player should or could have made. A shortstop who can't get to a ball hit in the hole, or a center fielder who can't get to a ball in the gap, isn't penalized for not having the range of a better player

Advanced stats: OBP, Slugging, OPS+, Range Factor, WHIP, BABIP, DIPS ERA, WAR

Context: Let's start with the batting stats. On-Base Percentage (OBP), Slugging Percentage, and OPS+ became more accepted and common throughout the 2010s, to the point where television broadcasts now regularly include them in their graphics.

On-Base Percentage (OBP) was, in many ways, the start of the mainstream analytics revolution in baseball. This was one of the metrics that Billy Beane focused on when building the Oakland A's rosters that were the focus of *Moneyball*. On-Base Percentage measures how often a player reaches base. The statistic takes the sum of hits, walks, and times the batter was hit by pitches and divides that total by the number of plate appearances by the batter. This stat fills in some of the blanks left by batting average, as any kid who ever heard "a walk's as good as a hit" in Little League instinctively understands. The league average for On-Base Percentage in 2023 was .320. Generally speaking, an On-Base Percentage of .375 or higher is excellent. Barry Bonds holds the single-season record with a .609 On-Base Percentage in 2004, which means he got on base more than 60 percent of the time he came to bat.

Slugging Percentage measures a player's power beyond the raw numbers of home runs, taking the total number of bases reached and dividing it by the number of at-bats. As a benchmark, a Slugging Percentage of .450 is very good, and anything above .500 is outstanding. In 2001, the year he hit

Barry Bonds holds virtually every advanced metric record in baseball.

Michael Zito/WireImage

an MLB-record 73 home runs, Barry Bonds had a Slugging Percentage of .863.

Batting average, On-Base Percentage, and Slugging Percentage are combined to create a player's slash line (in that order). As an example, in his MVP season of 2023, Shohei Ohtani's slash line was .304/.412/.654.

Another stat used is **OPS**, which is the combination of On-Base Percentage with Slugging Percentage. According to FanGraphs, an average OPS is .710, and anything above 1.00 is excellent. Again, it was Barry Bonds who set the standard for this, with a record 1.422 OPS in 2004.

One aspect that baseball's raw numbers don't account for is variation between ballparks. Unlike all other major team sports, which have standard field measurements with few if any deviations between venues, baseball stadium dimensions and quirks vary from team to team. It's very different hitting in a stadium like Coors Field in the thin air of Denver than in a stadium closer to sea level like Petco Park in San Diego. A left-handed hitter could thrive with the short porch of Yankee Stadium but struggle in a park like the Oakland Coliseum, with roomy foul territory that turns harmless foul balls into easy outs.

To account for this, statisticians have started adjusting for players' ballparks. One stat that does that is **OPS+**. In addition to the stadium adjustment, OPS+ adjusts the score by 100 so that 100 is the league average. The higher you are above 100, the better your season is. Bonds once again holds the record, but this time from 2002 with his 268 OPS+.

In pitching, one of the more basic advanced statistics is **Walks and Hits per Inning Pitched (WHIP)**. As it says in the name, this is the sum of a player's walks and hits divided by total innings pitched. It measures how good a pitcher is at keeping runners off base, and it serves as a quick overview of a pitcher's season. Like ERA, lower numbers are better. A WHIP of 1.30 is considered league average, and a WHIP of 1.00 is excellent. Pedro Martinez holds the single-season record for WHIP with a 0.7373 mark in his Cy Young season of 2000.

In the late 1990s and early 2000s, statistician Voros McCracken developed a series of statistics under the umbrella term of **Defense Independent Pitching Stats (DIPS)**. The idea behind these is simple—separate how well a pitcher performs from how well (or poorly) his team plays behind him (Slowinski, 2011). One of the stats created here was **Fielding Independent Pitching (FIP)**, which measures a pitcher's effectiveness at striking batters out and preventing home runs, walks, and hit by pitches. "FIP does a better job of predicting the future than measuring the present, as there can be a lot of fluctuation in small samples. It is less effective in describing a pitcher's single game performance and is more appropriate in a season's worth of innings" (Slowinski, 2010a). Again, like ERA and WHIP, the lower the FIP number, the better. An average pitcher's FIP would be 4.20, and an excellent season is 3.20. Christy Mathewson's 1908 season is the single-best FIP, with a 1.287. In the more modern era, Pedro Martinez's 1999 season of 1.395 is the standard.

For fielding, Bill James invented the stat Range Factor to help better quantify a player's defensive range. **Range Factor** divides a player's putouts and assists by number of defensive games played. "Range Factor answers a pivotal question that went long unanswered when fielding percentage was used as the primary evaluative defensive metric: How many plays can a given fielder make? Or, put more simply, how much range does a fielder have?" (MLB.com, n.d.-c, para. 4).

Ultimate Zone Rating (UZR) is an advanced metric designed to determine a player's total defensive value by evaluating how many opposing runs they save. "UZR puts a run value to defense, attempting to quantify how many runs a player saved or gave up through their fielding prowess" (Slowinski, 2010b, para. 1). It's a complicated stat to compute but an easy one to interpret. A player's UZR is the number of runs relative to the average player at that position. Average is 0, so a player with a UZR of 5 is above average. A Gold Glove–level defender has a UZR of 15. Because defense is different at each position on the baseball field, it's always important to compare someone's UZR (or any defensive stat) to that of their position mates.

To determine a player's overall ability, **WAR (Wins Above Replacement)** is the most widely used and accepted stat. The point of WAR is to quantify how much better a player is than a replacement-level player, either a minor leaguer or a readily available free agent. There are slight differences in how WAR is calculated whether you are using FanGraphs, Baseball Prospectus, or Baseball Reference, but the overall picture is the same.

For a single season, a WAR above 2 means a player is at starter level, a WAR of 5 or higher is a player of all-star quality, and a WAR above 8 marks an MVP candidate. The single-season highest WAR for position players was Babe Ruth's 1923 season, where his WAR was 14.1. Career WAR is simply taken by adding up a player's individual seasons. Babe Ruth is the all-time WAR leader with 182.5.

American Football

No American sport has more moving parts on a given play than football. There are 22 players on the field for each play, which makes evaluating the result of a play difficult from a statistical point of view. The running back gets credit for a long touchdown run, but it could be due to a sensational block by the left guard or a missed tackle in the secondary. A quarterback throws an interception, and it counts against his stat total. The interception could be the result of a bad throw or a bad decision by the quarterback. But it could also be the result of a missed block up front, leading to pressure and the quarterback being uncomfortable while trying to throw. It could have been a bad route run by the receiver. Or it could have been a sensational play by the defender.

When football coaches say they "have to see the tape" before commenting on what happened, that is sometimes accurate. It's also sometimes an excuse.

All of this is to say that the basic card stats for football give us only a rough understanding of what happened in a game or in a player's performance.

Card stats: Yards, touchdowns, carries, completion percentage, catches, yards per play, interceptions, fumble recoveries, sacks, tackles, passer rating

Context: One way of viewing the card stats for football is to think of them as fantasy football stats. There is value in these stats. But given the complexity of football, these stats don't always provide a complete picture of a player's performance.

Football fans are familiar with players picking up yards and touchdowns in "garbage time," that is, in the late stages of a blowout. The value of a play or player is largely dependent on the situation. A five-yard run on fourth-and-4 is huge, while a five-yard run on third-and-23 is meaningless.

When you look at the NFL's official team stats, the top offenses and defenses are ranked by total yards achieved and allowed, respectively. This is an odd way of ranking teams, since games aren't decided by yards but by points.

Passer rating sure looks and feels like an advanced metric, but it's been used by the NFL since the 1970s. Passer rating takes into account pass attempts, completions, passing yards, touchdown passes, and interceptions, and it creates a score ranging from 0 to 158.3. The league average for the 2022 season was 89.1.

Advanced stats: DVOA, DYAR, QBR

Context: Two of the core principles of advanced football analytics are contextualizing an individual play (in terms of down, distance, and impact on a game) and contextualizing the play of an individual (e.g., separating a quarterback's throw from the receiver's route).

In the same way that Bill James pioneered work in baseball analytics, Aaron Schatz pioneered work in pro football analytics. Schatz is the founder of Football Outsiders, the leading website for advanced pro football analytics. The main stat used at Football Outsiders is **DVOA**, or **Defense-adjusted Value Over Average**.

> DVOA is a method of evaluating teams, units, or players. It takes every single play during the NFL season and compares each one to a league-average baseline based on situation. DVOA measures not just yardage, but yardage toward a first down: Five yards on third-and-4 are worth more than five yards on first-and-10 and much more than five yards on third-and-12. Red zone plays are worth more than other plays. Performance is also adjusted for the quality of the opponent. (Football Outsiders, n.d.-b, para. 2)

DVOA is calculated as a percentage, with positive numbers being better for the offense and negative numbers being better for the defense. There are rankings for teams (overall, offense, defense, and special teams) and for individual positions, and a team or individual's ranking is the best way to use the statistic.

As an example, the 2019 Super Bowl champion Kansas City Chiefs had the top offense that season via DVOA at 30.9 percent, which meant their offense (led by Patrick Mahomes) was nearly 31 percent better than the average NFL offense that season. The top defense in 2019 belonged to the New England Patriots at −25.2 percent, which meant offenses were nearly 25 percent worse against the Patriots than the league average. The second-best defense belonged to the San Francisco 49ers, which lost to the Chiefs in the Super Bowl.

This last nugget is an interesting case for using DVOA as a journalistic tool. The traditional sports journalism focus in football is often the starting quarterback, and for the Patriots in 2019 (Tom Brady's final season playing for them), it was easy to write a story about then-42-year-old Brady continuing his magic touch as the greatest quarterback of all time. Meanwhile, the 49ers' run in the NFC could be framed around the coming-of-age of Brady's onetime backup, Jimmy Garoppolo.

But the DVOA tells a different story. While the Patriots and 49ers had the top two defenses in the

NFL in 2019, offensively they were 23rd and 20th, respectively. Neither quarterback ranked among the top 10 in the NFL in either DVOA or **Defensive Yards Against Replacement (DYAR)**, which measures a player's performance against a replacement-level player, similar to WAR in baseball. Brady ranked in the middle of the league's quarterbacks, barely above average. Therefore, looking at these teams and writing and reporting on them from an analytics perspective would focus not on their quarterback play (which was, at best, OK) but instead on their league-leading defenses.

To go along with passer rating, DVOA, and the card stats, in 2011 ESPN developed **Total QBR** (Total Quarterback Rating) to evaluate a quarterback's play.

> Traditional box score stats distort the performances of (quarterbacks) because they (1) fail to account for all of the ways a quarterback can affect a game, (2) don't put plays into the proper context (a 5-yard gain on second-and-5 is very different from a 5-yard gain on third-and-10), and (3) don't acknowledge that a quarterback has teammates who affect each play and should also get credit for everything that happens on the field. (Katz & Burke, 2016, para. 6)

Total QBR is a proprietary ESPN stat that measures a quarterback's efficiency, measuring "all of a quarterback's contributions to winning, including how he impacts the game on passes, rushes, turnovers and penalties. Also, since Total QBR is built from the play level, it accounts for a team's level of success or failure on every play" (Katz & Burke, 2016, para. 7). It's on a scale of 0 to 100, with 50 being average and 75 being a Pro Bowl–caliber player. The single best season for a quarterback via Total QBR was Tom Brady in 2007 (the year the Patriots finished the regular season undefeated), with an 87.0.

College Football Team Rankings

Another area in which analytics have become more detailed and more useful to reporters is in ranking college football teams. Moving beyond the teams' records and standings in the Associated Press and ESPN/*USA Today* top-25 rankings and taking the unbalanced nature of college football schedules into account, these analytics seek to give us a better way to compare teams from different conferences. Two of the major stats are the **Fremeau Efficiency Index (FEI)** and **SP+**, both of which were developed for Football Outsiders in the first decade of the 2000s.

FEI "is a college football rating system based on opponent-adjusted possession efficiency, representing the per-possession scoring advantage a team would be expected to have on a neutral field against an average opponent" (Football Outsiders, n.d.-a, para. 1). In 2022, national champion Georgia finished the season ranked number one in the country with an FEI of 1.58.

SP+, which was developed by Bill Connolly, measures a team's overall efficiency. Connolly developed it to be a predictive ranking that was forward-facing rather than rewarding teams for what they had done in the past (Connolly, 2020). As with DVOA, the actual score is less important for a general audience than the overall ranking.

Soccer

Like basketball, soccer is a free-flowing game that doesn't lend itself as easily to advanced analytics as baseball and American football, and it doesn't have as many discrete data points as basketball. But starting in the mid-2000s, there was a growing analytics movement within soccer.

Card stats: Goals, assists, shots, shots on goal, saves
Context: The basic stats in soccer are the most basic kinds of counting stats. Goals and assists are self-explanatory, as are goalkeeper saves. Soccer stats include both shots and shots on goal. A shot is one that is taken toward the net but misses the net high or wide. A shot on goal is one that either results in a goal or a save or hits the post or crossbar.

Advanced stats: Expected Goals (For, Against, Goalie), Goals Saved Above Expected, Possession Value: Passes Per Defensive Action
Context: Advanced soccer analytics look at the quality of shots and scoring chances. **Expected Goals** (xG) attempts to quantify the quality of a shot. "A shot closer to the goal is obviously more valuable than a shot farther from goal" (Minkus, 2020). Shots are scored on a scale of 0.0 to 1.0, with numbers closer to 1 being more likely to be goals (so a shot with an xG of 0.5 has a 50 percent chance of being a goal). Expected Goals is calculated differently by different stat companies, but in general it includes "the distance from and angle to goal, and what sort of scenario the shot came from (a cross or a set piece, for example)" (Minkus, 2020). Teams with higher xGF (Expected Goals For) and lower xGA (Expected Goals Against) tend to win more games in the long run, even if their shots don't always go in. For goalkeepers, xG helps us to understand how difficult are the saves a keeper is making, and **Goals**

Saved Above Expected "measures shot stopping ability" (Minkus, 2020).

Minkus (2020) made an interesting point about soccer analytics:

> "Players that get many high quality shots tend to score lots of goals. A player's ability to get shots from good locations is actually a more important factor in scoring than his ability to finish chances from any location. Though analytics frequently confirm what people within soccer intuitively know, this is one example where statistics contradicts prevailing soccer wisdom."

Another analytic used in soccer is **Possession Value**, which measures the chance that a goal will be scored at any point while a team possesses the ball. This represents an attempt to better quantify the straight percentage possession stats. To measure defense, rather than using counting stats like tackles (which don't take into account how well a player defends off the ball), **Passes Per Defensive Action** is used to measure a team's defensive pressure.

Hockey

If basketball considers itself to be free-flowing, it's got nothing on the good old hockey game. Hockey is the most free-flowing and open of the four major North American sports, with teams constantly going back and forth from offense to defense, with frequent substitutions. This presents both a challenge and an opportunity for advanced analytics.

Card stats: Goals, assists, points, saves, goals-against average, penalty minutes, plus-minus, shots on goal

Context: The NHL is the only one of the four major U.S. sports leagues that automatically gives one of its major awards to a statistical leader. The Art Ross Trophy goes to the player who leads the league in points (goals plus assists, including second assists). Along with the basic counting stats, plus-minus is the most basic hockey metric. A player is credited with a plus if they're on the ice when their team scores a goal, a minus if they're on the ice when their opponent scores. Higher positive numbers are better. But as we've seen with so many stats, it's context dependent. "You can get pluses or minuses if you're nowhere near the puck, if you're heading to the bench or just coming on to the ice. You don't get them on power-play goals" (Harrington, 2014, para. 22).

Advanced stats: Corsi, Fenwick, Even-Strength Save Percentage

Context: In the same way that the analytics movement in baseball has focused on the importance of getting players on base and preventing outs, hockey analytics have focused on the importance of puck possession and shot attempts. **Corsi** and **Fenwick** are two stats that measure shot attempts, not just shots on goal (which only count if there's a goal or a save, but don't measure whether a shot goes wide or is blocked). Corsi takes into account shots on goal, shots that miss the goal, and shots blocked by a defender, while Fenwick does not count blocked shots (since they don't make it near the net). While the Stanley Cup playoffs are probably the most unpredictable postseason in professional sports, teams have tended to be among the leaders in Corsi and Fenwick when contending for the Cup. "The top 100 or so players in the league will be at the .520-and-above range" (Harrington, 2014, para. 27) in terms of attaining more shots for than shots against.

For goalies, wins/losses and goals against average are the traditional stats used. But save percentage—especially **Even-Strength Save Percentage**—is considered to be a better evaluation of a goalie's skill. Dominik Hasek's career save percentage of .9223 is the best in NHL history.

Golf

Card stats: Score, driving distance, greens-in-regulation, fairways hit

Context: The basic statistics in golf are fairly straightforward. A player's score is the number of shots it takes to complete 18 holes, with a plus or minus in relation to par (so on a par 72 course, shooting a 68 would be −4). Driving distance is the raw yardage a shot is hit off the tee. Fairways hit is the number of times a player's drive lands in the fairway, rather than in the rough, and greens-in-regulation is the number of times a player reaches the green allowing for two putts to reach par (so on a par 4 hole, they would reach the green in two shots).

But again, the raw numbers don't tell us everything. Driving distance doesn't tell us how accurate the player is. Fairways hit is a blunt instrument and doesn't tell us if the player missed the fairway by an inch or a mile.

Advanced stats: Strokes Gained

Context: Golf benefits from having one of the richest datasets and data tracking programs in all of sports—the **Shotlink** system (Shotlink.com, n.d.). Since the early 2000s, Shotlink has mapped every inch of every hole of every PGA golf course and, as of 2023, the U.S. Women's Open, which allows the system to calculate the exact distance of every shot, and the distance to the hole of every strike.

These data led to the creation of Strokes Gained. **Strokes Gained** compares a player's score to the average score of every other player in the field, giving more finely tuned detail than just the players' raw scores or other stats like greens-in-regulation and fairways hit. The PGA has also developed Strokes Gained specifically for tee shots, approach shots, shots around the green, and putting (PGATour.com, 2016). "Strokes gained recognizes that sinking a 20-foot putt represents a better performance than sinking a three-foot putt, even though they both count as a single stroke on the scorecard. Strokes gained assigns a number to this intuition" (Tremlett, 2019).

Databases and Other Online Resources

This chapter is just a way to get you started with analytics. For those who are interested, an enormous number of resources and articles are available. To learn more about any of the analytics we've discussed here or to find new ones as they are developed, Google (or your search engine of choice) is your best friend. ESPN has developed a robust analytics department over the years, and it is relatively easy to find past articles that explain stats (like QBR and PER). ESPN's stats pages are also the industry standard, and they include advanced analytics alongside the traditional statistics.

For sport-specific questions, the baseball analytics community is among the largest and most active online. Major League Baseball's official website has a fantastic stats glossary that defines how statistics (from the most basic to most advanced) are calculated, how to contextualize them, and even how to write or say them. FanGraphs and Baseball Prospectus are also wonderful sites to learn about advanced analytics. In football, Football Outsiders is the gold standard for advanced analytics.

And then there's Sports Reference (www.sports-reference.com). This site is a sports nerd's absolute dream come true. It has major league baseball stats dating back to 1871, minor league baseball stats dating back to 1877, and box scores for games back to 1904. Want to know how the Philadelphia A's did in their game on June 23, 1933, and how many strikeouts the pitcher of record had in that game? A few clicks gets you there (they beat Cleveland, 8-4. Roy Mahaffey struck out three in a complete-game win.) There are sites for pro and college football and basketball, including individual game results, year-by-year and career stat leaders (for both card stats and advanced analytics), and more. Their data is also available for download as a CSV file (for use in Excel or Google Sheets) or is embeddable in websites (with attribution), which makes it usable for reporters and journalists.

Time-Out

Using Sports Reference, find the box score for the first professional or major college game you ever attended. If you have never attended one, pick one at random. Using only the information available through the box score and that website, write a 500-word (maximum) story re-creating the game.

Summary

The ability to use nonhuman sources is a critical part of a sports journalist's job in the 2020s. The combination of money, teams, and players having the ability (and desire) to control their messages, plus restrictions introduced during the COVID-19 pandemic, has all worked to limit the access that sports journalists previously had to players and coaches. This means that reporters must be able to find story ideas and information from other sources.

Team websites are a starting place for sports journalists, providing basic roster and statistical information. The growing use of analytics in sports provides journalists with an opportunity to report on games and tell stories without relying solely on interviews and access.

It is critical to remember that just as good sports journalism does not rely merely on what sources say in interviews, good sports journalism also does not rely solely on nonhuman sources. Websites, databases, and statistical analysis are valuable tools for sports reporters, and this chapter has provided you with the basic tools to use these nonhuman sources in your work. However, they are just tools. Sports journalism is at its best when it combines the human reporting from chapter 3 and the nonhuman reporting in chapter 4. The two forms of reporting complement each other to enable us to make the best stories and help our readers understand what is happening with their favorite players and teams.

Discussion Questions

1. What are the strengths of using analytics and statistical analysis in sports reporting? What are the limitations of using this kind of analysis?
2. If sports journalists cannot cover a game in person and have no means of interviewing players and coaches, how could they use nonhuman sources to cover a game from outside of the stadium?

Applied Activity

Look up the most recent MVPs in the five major U.S. sports. This will give you six MVPs (one each for the NBA, WNBA, NFL, and NHL, and one each in the American League and National League for MLB). From a statistical, analytics point of view, did they deserve to win the award? Make a statistics-based case for your argument. Make sure you use both traditional and advanced analytics.

Digital Sports Media

Chapter Objectives

After completing this chapter, you will be able to do the following:

- Understand the historical role of backpack journalism, citizen journalism, and mobile journalism.
- Discuss the main four social media platforms, their benefits and drawbacks, and how they can be best employed in sports journalism.
- Understand how blogs and podcasts can be used by a sports journalist.
- Discuss the role and appropriate the use of artificial intelligence in sports journalism.

At the turn of the 21st century, there was widespread excitement in media circles about the Internet and the World Wide Web, the possibilities of new technology, and the ability to communicate across the globe for low costs and with ever-increasing speed. There was much speculation about what kind of communication would be possible in the future and what shapes and forms that communication might take.

As equipment for producing content for television became smaller and easier to manage, newsrooms were able to cut personnel, and television reporters became "one-man bands" (Gee, 2019). At the same time, every TV station, newspaper, and radio station was dabbling in creating a website to host content online and reach a larger audience. Broadcasters became writers, and—reluctantly—writers were learning to create broadcast content.

At that time, the ideal reporter had to lug around a notebook, audio recorder, and camera for still photos. Now a video camera could be added to the list of necessary items. Finally, a reporter couldn't very well be expected to drive back to the office with all that equipment to produce breaking news content on deadline, so an Internet-connected laptop with a FireWire to connect the camera(s) was needed to complete the package. And so was born **backpack journalism** (Gee, 2019; Rupprecht, 2020).

Legacy journalists assumed that backpack journalists' media content would fall short of the usual standards (Singer, 2011). Indeed, the idea of a backpack journalist, or a multimedia journalist in later years, led to some concern that such a person might have difficulty producing quality work in more than one or two media—that is, they would be a jack of all trades, master of none (Gee, 2019). Who could believe that a single person could be equally proficient in writing, editing, video, and still photography, and could use all those tools to tell an engaging and well-reported story?

Gee (2019) examined the phenomenon of backpack journalism in the context of how news consumers assessed it and found that viewers preferred content produced by more traditional news gathering in teams. Even so, budgets and technological advancements have combined to compel many newsrooms to lean heavily into using individual journalists to perform many tasks that were formerly handled by a small group, so there are still journalists who regularly lug around the equipment that is endemic to backpack journalism.

But the backpack in backpack journalism has been superseded by technology we now take for granted. Most of us have in our pockets or schoolbags all the tools of the trade in the form of a smartphone. This enables us to take notes, record interviews, take photos, capture video, and send all of these files to a newsroom or post them directly online. The smartphone's capacity to support all of these tasks has rendered backpack journalism mostly a thing of the past because we now consider it a bit unusual not to have a supercomputer in our pocket.

As backpack journalism fell by the wayside with the rapid advancement of technology, another early-2000s term found staying power—**citizen**

journalism. Thanks to the availability of technology, anyone could create media content around an event or simply express their viewpoint to a wide audience.

Journalists expressed concern about the rise of user-generated content, noting that their own training and experience—as well as their mandate to eliminate biases—would make mainstream outlets' coverage more reliable than that produced by citizens (Thomas & Sooknanan, 2019). Thus, with desktop publishing creating opportunities for the average person, a core aspect of a sports journalist's challenge is confronting the ongoing development of the media landscape. Competition from more people and multiemployee entities than ever before has blurred the lines between journalism and simply media content that is produced by random people.

This chapter offers a brief narrative about the transformation and adaptation of sports journalism in the digital age and highlights the use of various digital media tools (e.g., social media platforms, blogs, podcasts) in sports journalism. We discuss how these tools changed the way sports journalists create content and how fans consume this content, interacting with sports media entities. We also take a look at the emerging role of artificial intelligence and how it affects sports journalism.

Mobile Journalism

Mobile journalism has been a topic of discussion for decades, but it gained popularity more recently as technological advancements allowed for the creation and distribution of media content from remote locations (Cameron, 2009). In a profession that has long benefited from and depended upon the ability to send information over a distance, mobile journalism can seem like an ideal approach to journalism. What if there's no need for a sports journalist to return to the office in order to file a story and for the editing and design desks to receive it?

Sports reporting has lent itself to remote online work ever since reporters were filing stories by telephone from horse races a century ago while the clackity-clack-clackity-clack of teletype machines added to the soundtrack of the newsroom. For sports journalists on deadline and with no time to return to the newsroom, remote work previously meant typing a story during a sporting contest on a typewriter, and later a computer, then calling it in or sending it via phone line or WiFi (Buzzelli et al., 2022). Indeed, the authors of this book are familiar with plugging in a phone line to a laptop in a press box or a high school athletic office and sending the story on an Internet connection that could charitably be described as akin to molasses, speedwise. Still, that took less time than driving back to the office. Later, press boxes had wireless Internet, and sending stories became even faster.

As we have stated, mobile phones and tablets now have all the capabilities that a "backpack" previously offered (Cameron, 2009). While it might seem strange to type out a game report or story on a phone as opposed to a laptop, a tablet offers a larger and more convenient canvas. Traditional news gathering must also expand with new technologies. Online communities might provide insight into fan reactions and moods as well as useful information among the discussions (López González et al., 2014). Sports journalists must therefore add to their usual tasks monitoring such online spaces for potential breaking news.

Even before the advent of the smartphone and tablet, news organizations tried to incorporate

---

Time-Out

Rupprecht (2020) examined college students' use of backpack journalism over a period of six years. Interviews with the students revealed that they experienced a bond while traveling for assignments on which they engaged in documentary filmmaking. Although this is not the type of backpack journalism discussed in this chapter about sports journalism and technology, it does provide a similar experience.

In groups, discuss the following questions and record your answers in written form.

1. Think about what backpack journalism means to you. Is the definition put forth by Rupprecht (2020), regarding documentary filmmaking as a form of "backpacking" and becoming immersed in a community, more viable than the idea of a backpack containing various journalism tools?

2. Examine your smartphone. What types of sports stories can be told using its features? What types of elements could it include? Does it make the backpack obsolete? Are there stories that must be told with previous generation technology?

mobile journalism. In 2007, Reuters created a website to host news content created by Reuters journalists who were provided with a Nokia smartphone, a tripod, a wireless keyboard, a battery charger, and a microphone. Reuters reporters who covered the 2008 Beijing Summer Olympic Games used this setup (Cameron, 2009; Oliver, 2008).

As newsrooms tried to navigate both the present and the future of journalism, a new buzzword was created to address the then-uncomfortable merging of various media styles: **convergence**—a "convergence" of multiple types of media to create a whole that would provide the best possible coverage for news consumers. Today, it's difficult to think of a media outlet whose online presence does not feature multiple types of media—including writing, photos, video, and graphics. The emergence of smartphone technology and its use in news gathering was an indicator that journalism education would need to develop courses and laboratory (i.e., student media) opportunities for students to learn and hone the related skills (Cameron, 2009).

News Consumers

When was the last time you read a newspaper? When was the last time you purchased a newspaper, or even grabbed a free student-produced one off a campus newspaper rack? When you were growing up, did your household have a subscription to a newspaper, even if only for the Sunday advertising sections? What does a newspaper even look like these days?

Now think about radio. News stations have always captured a bit more of a niche audience than music-driven radio, so this book won't ask about your news radio consumption. But what about radio as a whole? Talk, music, etc.? Do you regularly listen to sports talk radio? Or do you more often choose podcasts and Spotify playlists?

This section addresses more than just readers and viewers. The term *news consumers* includes the audiences who will engage with sports journalism content produced for video or audio broadcast, more writing-based platforms, or a combination of these. Before the popularity of the smartphone, people who consumed news on the go were not a common sight except for commuters reading a newspaper on a bus or train. The notion that people would widely use a phone to watch video seemed strange. But the smartphone became ubiquitous, and news on the go has been a close cousin to news that is available on demand, all the time.

With that in mind, a new set of questions.

- How do you get your news? Links from social media? Which platforms?
- Do you read news on your phone?
- Have you observed others reading news on their phones, especially on public transportation?

Technology offers everyone more access to more information than ever before. And it has also given content creators the chance to reach a wider audience on more platforms than ever before. In a diversified and cluttered news environment, including multiple outlets and media, and thus multiple opportunities to disseminate information, it has become common to see print-based reporters on television or to hear them on the radio.

In such an environment, discussing a story becomes about more than just the basic facts. Journalists become commentators and known figures on social media. And news aggregators. And they get their names in breaking news chyrons. And they become part of a landscape that includes plenty of people who use technology to present themselves as media members, even when their main platform is a personal YouTube channel or a Twitter/X feed.

Time-Out

Take some time to think about the following questions:

1. How often do you search for news on your smartphone?
2. What outlets do you search?
3. How do you verify the truthfulness of trending topics?
4. In what ways can news outlets make the smartphone news experience more user-friendly?
5. In what ways can you improve your own searches for reliable sports news?

Content Creators

Technology has been a boon for journalists. Over the years, advancements have occurred in everything from writing tools to the printing press to photography to distribution. These have all produced benefits in reporting, content creation, and dissemination of news and information. With the Internet and digital tools, gathering and disseminating information has never been easier for anyone, including journalists.

It's likely that everyone reading this book has taken a photo or video on their smartphone, posted it online, and shared it with friends. And that leads us to the challenge posed in this chapter: The universal availability of technology to create and disseminate content online has increased potential competition for everything a journalist produces. For example, X's (formerly Twitter's) repost functionality offers quick dissemination of information across the platform (Kwak et al., 2010). As a result, scoops and newsworthy items can be posted by someone connected to the newsmakers who has access to that information, but who is not necessarily a journalist. In-game reports of injuries can be sent over social media by any attendee or TV viewer.

Journalists state their viewpoints, usually based on experience and interaction with coaches, athletes, and other stakeholders. Now those viewpoints compete in the marketplace of ideas with bloggers and podcasters who often have no locker room or clubhouse access, or any kind of inside information. But many independent media members are good writers and producers of interesting video who have considered and well-researched opinions. That type of compelling content, with or without an official media credential, can find a large audience that perceives their work to be equal to or superior to that of a trained journalist.

As user-generated content has gained prominence, sports journalists have had to reexamine their own worth in an increasingly crowded marketplace (McEnnis, 2013). Fans' perception of sports media often depends on whether they consider the coverage to be positive or negative. And the rise of bloggers, podcasters, and sport organizations' own in-house media provides additional competition. One effect is that while news and notes could previously be kept for a weekly print column, those tidbits must now be posted immediately on social media or the website to feed what has become a 25 hours a day, eight days a week news cycle. The immediacy also lends to the production of smaller and more easily understood news items among the longer forms that the online medium allows (Perreault & Bell, 2022). This need for immediacy can fly in the face of accuracy, especially when a story moves so quickly that details that might be accurate one moment change minutes later.

As random citizens with cameras participate in the information-gathering process (Watson, 2013), what once was a one- or few-to-many media communication model has become many-to-many. With so many potential sources of information, it is even more imperative that sports journalists master the use of technology and media platforms in order to reach the audience with true and informative stories and coverage. Sports journalists still play an important role in separating themselves from and sometimes rising above the flood of information that can fall anywhere on the spectrum from reliable reports to completely and deliberately made-up nonsense (McEnnis, 2013).

Disinformation and **misinformation** have become prominent issues in political reporting, both on traditional media platforms and in social media, but sports can have its share of deliberately false information too. Fake accounts that parody coaches or impersonate prominent sports journalists can proliferate and cause misinformation to go viral. During every free agency period in American professional sport, for instance, fake accounts for ESPN journalists such as NBA newsbreaker Adrian Wojnarowski proclaim that "(Star player) has signed with the Milwaukee Bucks!" often with details about how that player will fit in with his new team.

The desire and opportunity for readers and viewers to participate in the media process has risen, with the passive news consumer role being replaced by more active engagement. This can involve not only direct media content creation, but also the formation of online communities where events and stories about those events are discussed and dissected (López González, 2014). In this new world, a sport organization's public relations and social media team does not have the time to put out every single fire, and a media outlet cannot go around debunking every false report. Sometimes, respected mainstream reporters see an X handle with a recognizable profile photo and bio, making a statement about sports news, and they repost the statement without noticing the subtle difference in the screen name that indicates a fake account. Thus the journalists have amplified disinformation.

The takeaway is that the Internet has helped cause a blurring of media consumer perceptions of who is a journalist (Singer, 2011). This, then, is the major challenge facing sports journalists in terms of competition in an increasingly crowded marketplace for information and insight. How can sports journalists distinguish their work? In what ways can aspiring sports journalists develop skills that will help them stand out as reliable and dependable reporters whom readers and viewers will seek out?

Social Media

The nearly instantaneous cycle of news and information and the ability of anyone to create content facilitated the rise of social media. **Social media** is "forms of electronic communication (such as websites for social networking and microblogging)

Industry Profile

Scott Powers

Scott Powers

Scott Powers may not have seen it all, but he's certainly seen a lot. After completing college in the early 2000s, Powers worked for smaller newspapers, but he wanted to get home to Chicago. He created an online magazine to cover the thriving high school basketball scene in the Windy City.

"It probably would work now, considering what the Internet is," Powers said (via personal communication, February 2021). "Back then, it was a little bit more of a struggle in getting people to know about it and pay for it. And it wasn't a success in the fact that it didn't make much money, but it led to other opportunities."

Being a one-person band with that emagazine helped Powers hone his skills with visual elements and online media production, experience that soon proved beneficial.

"It was the video stuff and the photos that probably led to the opportunity at ESPN," Powers said. "I like to think I can write or report a little bit, but it was about being as diverse as I was."

At ESPN Chicago, Powers first covered local high school sports and then was assigned to cover the then-powerhouse Chicago Blackhawks of Patrick Kane and Jonathan Toews . . . in a sport for which Powers had very little enthusiasm.

Still, Powers immersed himself in the Blackhawks' world, including traveling with some players to Europe as they spent their day with the Stanley Cup. He was eventually caught in layoffs at ESPN Chicago and sought the next opportunity.

"I wasn't gonna let ESPN decide when my journalism career was over," Powers said. "I certainly had a lot of friends at that point who had been laid off, and had gone into PR and other places. And I decided I was gonna just grind it out for a while and see what could happen."

Soon, an email from an old ESPN colleague arrived, and Powers was one of the first hires made by online sports media outlet *The Athletic*. A startup based in Toronto and Chicago, *The Athletic* has since expanded coast to coast in the United States and added Premier League coverage in England.

"I never expected *The Athletic* to be what it is now," Powers said. "You were hopeful it might be something, at least within Chicago. And for it to be what it is nationally, and even somewhat worldwide now too, it's unexpected."

Powers is one of the outlet's Chicago-area sports reporters, focusing mainly on the Blackhawks and the NHL. Powers added a regular hockey podcast for *The Athletic* to his toolbox and noted that even with producing multiple types of media, there is always more to learn.

"I think of everything in a sports capacity, as a sports reporter," Powers said. "But if I had more of a knowledge of data, and visualization, and analytics, all those things that come into play now on the job . . . I think some of the greatest sports reporters are the ones that can tap into so many different areas and bring that to their beats."

Powers' two-decade journey in sports journalism has taken him from newspapers to his own startup and finally to two different online sports media sites that have each been juggernauts, though in a different way. He hasn't quite seen it all, but he's seen how much sports journalism has changed in a relatively short time period.

"And the fact that technology has advanced the way that it has, and there's a lot of things you can do with phones now," Powers said. "I was lugging around these cameras, and now the same thing can be done on the phone."

through which users create online communities to share information, ideas, personal messages, and other content (such as videos)" (Merriam-Webster, n.d.). Social media is an important place for sports journalists to display and share their work. The benefits of social media in terms of disseminating sports-related news have been proven and are also still being understood.

The moment when viral video and on-the-ground reports combined with social media to demonstrate that social media had come of age was the Arab Spring of early 2011. (Arab Spring was a wave of pro-democracy protests and uprisings in the Middle East and North Africa from 2010 to 2011.) Video, still visuals, and reports from the ground displayed the power of social media to bring information to a worldwide audience instantaneously (Frangonikolopoulos & Chapsos, 2012).

While that was a decidedly non-sports event, the power of social media had come to the fore. As it became clear that the general public was engaged on social media, the use of social media—especially Twitter (now known as X)—became an essential part of any journalist's toolbox. However, promoting articles on social media does not necessarily lead to a lengthy discussion or shelf life. Breaking news posted on X might receive a surge in attention at first, and then become just part of the clutter on the microblogging platform (Castillo et al., 2014).

By contrast, news stories that provide more in-depth coverage tend to receive more lasting conversation on social media (Castillo et al., 2014). In a sports journalism context, this has in a way justified the push since the early part of the century to move away from straight game stories. Instead, even daily newspapers followed the lead of online media in seeking to provide more insight and commentary about what a game means in the context of a season as opposed to standard play-by-play or game events with quotes.

The production of high-quality digital content is a time-consuming process, one that requires a full-time staff of people trained in sports journalism practices, but with added knowledge in digital media production. This effectively shifted the technical training requirements of those pursuing sports media careers. Now there is a growing need for people who can not only write a solid game piece, but can also shoot and edit video content, post dynamic content to a Facebook page, and then manage the engagement from fans who would leave comments on the various posts.

The use of social media to promote news articles has been found to increase traffic and readership (Castillo et al., 2014). The need to retain an unbiased approach and avoid becoming caught up in fans' viewpoints also remains important for sports journalists who work in the online medium (Perreault & Bell, 2022), including their social media approach.

The next sections focus on the four main social media platforms used in sports journalism—Facebook, X (Twitter), Instagram, and YouTube. (Other social media platforms are outlined in table 5.1.)

TABLE 5.1 Important Social Media Platforms

Platform	Demographics	Types of media	Best uses
Facebook	Largest percentage of overall users; greatest popularity among people 40+	Video, images, written pieces, stories	Major events posting, live video, community interaction
YouTube	Audience nearly as large as Facebook, all ages	Preproduced video, live-streaming video	Produced shows, exciting visual content
Instagram	Most popular among 18-34 demographic	Stories, images, candid video	Compelling visuals, graphics with information
Snapchat	Dominated by ages 12-23	Stories, video	Behind-the-scenes, youth-oriented content
X (Twitter)	Used by opinion leaders, brands, and journalists; use lower among "average" user; not popular in Europe	Short messages, links to other platforms	Breaking news, live game updates
Pinterest	Demographics vary; popular among women in USA	Images	Merchandise, visuals
WhatsApp / Facebook Messenger	Popular messaging app outside of USA	Links to content	Direct-to-fans messaging
TikTok	Most popular platform for Generation Z	Short-form videos	Viral video trends and direct-to-fans engagement

Adapted from Clavio (2021).

> ## Tips for Interacting With Audiences
>
> - *Be where the conversation is happening.* Use hashtags where appropriate to ensure your comments are seen. Interact with other sports media professionals covering your space to broaden the network of people who see you commenting.
> - *Invite audience interaction.* As a sports media member, you likely have a network of followers. Use a social media message to invite that group of followers to respond to a question or comment about the team or sport that you cover. Audience members enjoy being engaged in this way, and this can generate goodwill between you and the audience.
> - *Incentivize good behavior.* Once you start interacting with sports audience members, you will have many responses, some of them good and some of them bad. Don't give the bad responders any satisfaction. Choose to respond to the best questions and comments and leave the other ones unaddressed.
> - *Highlight and feature audience members.* When you are interacting with the audience, use the tools at your disposal to make them feel important. On X, use the "quote" function to repost your answer within your response. If you're using social media responses in another format such as a video or podcast, be sure to mention the audience member by her social media name.
>
> See *Social Media and Sports* (Clavio, 2021) for more tips on using social media.
>
> Reprinted by permission from G. Clavio, *Social Media and Sports* (Champaign, IL: Human Kinetics, 2021), 108.

While these platforms are discussed in the context of how sports journalists might use them, it should also be noted that the public nature of these platforms also means that anyone who either aspires to a media career or simply wants to comment on events or coverage of those events can do so.

Facebook

Facebook is an interesting platform with regard to the sports media landscape. Most readers of this book would probably say they "used to be on Facebook." Statistics indicate that the main audience for Facebook is people who are a few years post-college and older. However, it remains the most popular social media platform in terms of registered users worldwide, and it has gained a reputation for being a place where users will share news and media articles—sometimes for better or for worse (Beveridge, 2022). As of early 2024, Facebook boasted approximately 2.9 billion active users worldwide (Dixon, 2024).

Facebook is a high-traffic site on which major sports and media organizations have a presence, and where such organizations can engage users in conversation and provide information. Facebook's utility as a platform where multiple media types can be used to tell a story, coupled with its massive user base, ultimately keeps the platform in a prominent position when discussing locations for sports journalists to disseminate their work. However, rather than individual journalists' pages, story and information distribution on Facebook has tended to be through the outlet's main page. The focus on the use of individuals to engage discussion and form communities around shared interests places Facebook at the heart of most sport organizations' social media initiatives (ViaSport, 2020) due to the relationship-building capabilities.

Facebook has continued to add features and to increase the variety of content that can be posted to the platform. Functionality improvements allow users to provide feedback on content, including likes, comments, and shares, which measure **valence** and consumer attitudes. The functionality improvements and the variety of content, particularly the ability to provide behind the-scenes information, altered the experience between sport organizations and fans, giving sport organizations a direct touchpoint for relationship building.

Posting Basics

While Facebook has no character limit on posts, content tends to be much shorter. The optimum amount of text is between 40 and 80 characters, which typically earns 86 percent more engagement than longer posts (Jackson, 2020). Post length should be limited to three lines because Facebook cuts off the remaining content and requires users to click the See More button when viewing on mobile (Webb, 2019).

Industry Profile

Cody Sharrett

Cody Sharrett

Sports are supposed to be fun. Along those lines, it's OK for professionals who work in sports media roles to enjoy engaging with fans and readers. U.S. Soccer Senior Social Media Manager Cody Sharrett knows that, and lives it.

"I was at the Taylor Swift concert," Sharrett said (personal correspondence, July 2023). "And I posted a TikTok from there: 'Went to Eras Tour to scout our Gold Cup location,' because it was at Soldier Field, the men's team was playing at Soldier Field. So I had fun with that one."

While it predated the publicizing of the Travis Kelce and Taylor Swift One True Sportsperson and Celebrity Pairing, this bit of social media engagement by Sharrett also foreshadowed some fortuitous brand synergy. When U.S. Soccer created a video package to announce the team roster for the 2023 FIFA Women's World Cup (WWC), Swift was one of the celebrities in the announcement.

The megapopular singer and songwriter had done very little recent publicity outside her Eras Tour and Capitol One ads. But she took the time for the then two-time defending FIFA WWC champions.

"That's the influence of the women's national team: They're the most popular women's sports team in the world," Sharrett said. "There's no WNBA team that comes close, there's no NWSL team that comes close, there's no European team that comes close. The women's national team is the most popular, influential, women's sports team in the world."

A broadcasting major as an undergraduate, Sharrett joined U.S. Soccer in late 2021 and has had the opportunity to travel to work the organization's social media at the FIFA Men's World Cup in Qatar in 2022 and the FIFA Women's World Cup in 2023 in Australia and New Zealand. He notes that keeping up with social media engagement for the increasingly popular U.S. men's and women's national teams is indeed work that must be done, even if the travel is quite a perk.

Previously, Sharrett had worked for two NBA franchises, the Portland Trail Blazers and Minnesota Timberwolves, with the latter also including social media duties for Minnesota's WNBA team, the four-time champion Lynx. When he joined Minnesota, the Lynx had just appeared in the previous three WNBA finals, winning two titles and ensuring that Sharrett would gain experience engaging interested fans of both the NBA and WNBA.

"That has helped me mostly just be able to compartmentalize, and just manage my time between two teams," Sharrett said. "And make sure both are getting equal shine, and equal treatment, and equal content coverage. I think those past roles have been very useful in this current role."

Sharrett started to build a reputation for cleverly using social media platforms—including Facebook, Twitter, Instagram, and now TikTok—while with the Trail Blazers. Once, when a player was traded away for "cash considerations," Sharrett put together a short video featuring a bag sitting on the podium with a dollar sign on the bag, with a caption welcoming "Cash Considerations" to the team.

But going to U.S. Soccer was in a way returning to his roots, as Sharrett's first opportunity after college was creating digital content for MLS's Columbus Crew. The national team is a more unique sports experience, however.

"It's different from an NBA team; you're not around these people every day, you're around them for 10-day windows every six weeks, I'd say, on average," Sharrett said. "You try to get the most out of those 10 days. Where something like the World Cup, that's two months, six weeks, whatever, so you get to know them even better in those major tournaments."

As can be expected, Sharrett notes that reading the replies and mentions can hinder one's ability to continue creating quality social media engagement. It is also true that the job description of working social media for sport organizations continues to evolve as the role itself is still in its relative infancy.

"These roles didn't exist while I was still in college, and they were just being created as I graduated college," Sharrett said. "I've kind of grown with it. I'm that first wave of people in this career field."

Facebook Live is a way for journalists and athletes alike to share stories and interact with key publics.
Sye Williams/Golden Boy/Getty Images

From a structural standpoint, the platform includes a main page that contains a scroll of the most recent posts by the organization or individual. The main page also acts as a point of navigation to subpages containing additional information for events, photos, videos, information about the organization, and links to fan communities or groups.

Content posted to the main Facebook page can take many forms. From a technical standpoint, posts can include text, photos, videos, or linked articles, and they traditionally include a combination of elements in a single post. The information shared within these photos, videos, and articles can also vary, depending upon the policies of the organization; however, content typically includes player interviews, training sessions, competition itineraries, pregame preparations, press conferences, and organizational statements.

Some posts can have a more personal nature, which increases the connection between the fan, sport organization, and athletes. These posts can be conversational, highlighting interactions with fellow athletes, family, or friends. Along similar lines, posts can offer a glimpse behind the scenes and include candid interviews with athletes highlighting their favorite movies, shows, music, or extracurricular activities.

Contrasting posts are posts that are more constructed and promotional in nature. These posts include general promotion of upcoming matches, autograph sessions, or public appearances and promotion of sponsorships. These posts often contain a disclaimer identifying the post as "promoted" for transparency purposes, but they provide activation for the sponsor. In addition, contrasting posts can have a community building function and can include acknowledgments associated with community engagements and giveaways.

Video content can play a vital role in Facebook engagement, and although it represents a smaller percentage (around 12 percent) of content, it produces approximately 25 percent of engagements on the platform (Ellis, 2019), with video engagement becoming a driving factor in digital sports consumption (Nielsen Sports, 2022). While shorter videos aren't necessarily better in terms of engagement based on likes, comments, and shares, the average video on Facebook is between one and two minutes (Ellis, 2019). The sharing of such information via video content serves several purposes.

Practical Use of Facebook

Here are the best practices when employing Facebook for sports journalism.

- *Posting about major sporting events.* Facebook pages, whether employed by major sports news media organizations (e.g., ESPN) or by individual sport organizations themselves (e.g., individual Premier League teams), are great outlets for posting information about upcoming major events. Consider posting event information one to two weeks before a major event, depending upon the sport and frequency of games, to create a sense of anticipation. For example, posting about the College Football Playoff National Championship game can take place far in advance of the game because it is a one-off experience rather than a regular matchup. Similar strategies can be employed for major rivalry games as well. These can be static posts that contain pictures or behind-the-scenes information or even feature original illustrations.
- *Facilitating community interaction.* The features of Facebook, including likes, comments, and shares, as well as various content types, provides fans of a particular news outlet or sporting organization with a way to gather around their favorite sport, event, or team. Thus, people can connect through shared interests. One way sports journalists can capitalize on this community-building function is to pose questions about starting lineups or quizzes where fans have to answer questions about a memorable match.
- *Hosting live videos.* The proliferation of mobile phones allows for most sports journalists to incorporate video into their skill sets. In the context of Facebook, building on the community function, live video offers fans a way to immediately connect with content. Video content can include highlights of specific, memorable plays, behind-the-scenes content of training videos, athlete interviews, or charity functions.

Time-Out

Select your favorite sports team or league, find their official Facebook page, and follow the account.

1. Observe their Facebook posts for three days and make a spreadsheet to categorize the post content and multimedia elements.
2. Make note of the posts that you like and dislike, why, and their level of interactions (likes, comments, and shares).
3. Develop a weekly social media strategy for your team. Draft post content, multimedia elements, and a posting schedule. If using multimedia content, discuss how you would obtain or create the multimedia content and what your overarching strategy with the posts includes.

- The Facebook page is about connection to the organization and provides a place where fans can engage with the organization and each other.
- Connecting to content produced by the official media outlet of the sport organization reinforces the club as the main source of information, not a mainstream media outlet.

X (Twitter)

While Facebook provides connection and engagement with sport fans on a global scale, X (formerly known as Twitter) provides a more immediate, immersive function, and it is highly applicable for both sport organizations and sports journalists in the sports media landscape.

With more than three billion monthly active users worldwide as of 2024 (Dixon, 2024), X quickly followed in the footsteps of Facebook to become one of the most influential and game-changing platforms for sports journalism and digital media. X, by design, is a fast-moving, dynamic environment.

At its most basic level, X is a microblogging website that allows users to post small bursts of information in real time to followers. Users join X by creating accounts, which are connected to a username that is preceded by the @ symbol. Users can curate their X feeds in a way that provides news and information from a variety of organizational and individual sources, with breaking, up-to-date information delivered to them on their phones almost instantaneously by "following" other users (Kassing & Sanderson, 2010).

X's perceived utility as a platform for sports journalists has led to mixed results over the years. At first, it seemed like a location from which to easily distribute links and information. And it remains a popular tool for distributing links, especially following a somewhat recent technological upgrade. The platform's early days included needing to shorten links before posting, leading to another step when trying to avoid filling the original maximum 140-character count. As of this writing, X has increased its message capacity to allow 280 characters in each post, and the technology of the site has improved so that URLs no longer need to be shortened, so users have an opportunity for clearer messaging.

In addition, the open and public nature of X has meant that reporters not only post completed stories, but also score updates, breaking news, statistical items of interest, and often their own viewpoints. With Facebook, media and sport organizations might tend to "curate" their feeds, which is a diplomatic way of describing something some users might identify as a form of censorship. Facebook's functionality allows posts to be deleted by a page's owner, and it also allows for discussions to be locked.

On X, reporters might disseminate viewpoints about the teams they cover (e.g., the impact of player personnel moves, team performance, handicapping future games) and also reveal more personal information not only about their subjects but also about themselves. As with all public communication, X users' responses and reactions to sports journalists' more personal posts can feature multiple points on the online response spectrum, including congratulations on a new addition to the family, or a declaration that the reporters' political views are not welcome on X.

Elon Musk Era

In 2022, Elon Musk initiated the purchase of Twitter through public stock investments, eventually becoming the largest shareholder of the corporation. By October 2022, Musk had completed the purchase of Twitter for an estimated $44 billion, and he immediately began making changes to the platform and the organization. First, Musk engaged in a significant reduction of staff, both at a senior level, with CEO Parag Agrawal and policy director Vijaya Gadde being dismissed from their positions, and at the engineering staff level, which greatly inhibited the platform's ability to perform content moderation on posts.

Another major change that affected credibility on the platform was the removal of Twitter Blue, a free service that enabled the verification of certain accounts with a blue check mark following their account username. Account verification was the way in which people knew they were interacting with genuine accounts or organizations and not imposters. This required some form of identity verification (e.g., government-issued ID) and affiliation with certain organizations, such as government entities, news organizations, and the sports and entertainment industries, to name a few. Turning this into a paid service, Musk allowed for anyone, regardless of affiliation, to obtain a blue check mark in exchange for a monthly fee. This has resulted in increased difficulty in determining the credibility of information posted to certain accounts.

The end result of these changes has been a level of uncertainty surrounding the longevity of the X platform. With more users bearing blue check marks, determining what is credible content on the platform is more difficult and has resulted in reputable journalists being accused of providing "fake news." In addition, the decrease in content moderation capabilities has also resulted in a simultaneous increase in online abuse directed at sports journalists on the platform, particularly if they post content not directly related to sports. Some journalists have left the X platform to post content on similar platforms such as Threads (Instagram's version of X) or Substack. The limited global use of alternative platforms does mean that most sports journalists have maintained a presence on X, simply to disseminate breaking news or to provide live game updates, which aligns with the most common use of the platform by sports journalists.

Posting Basics

There is no single correct way to use X effectively as part of the journalistic process. Reporters should use it in whatever manner feels comfortable to them. X is best used for breaking news or live game updates (Clavio, 2021). There is a range of approaches to doing so; sports journalists can incorporate varying levels of personality as a way to establish their "personal brand" on the platform. Personal branding by sports journalists on the platform is becoming an increasingly relevant component to content on X, due to the amount of information posted to X every day. Establishing a personal voice while reporting on breaking news can be an effective way to build a following and make your X feed the preferred destination for sports news. Table 5.2 outlines the various approaches for using X for breaking news and conveying a personal brand.

TABLE 5.2 Approaches to Breaking News and Live Game Updates on X

Approach	Tone	Multimedia content	Sports journalist example	Example post
No personal branding, with straight delivery of news and updates	Neutral or occasionally humorous	Limited use of multimedia or external links to stories or still photos	Adrian Wojnarowski, Jeff Passan, Fabrizio Romano	"Tom Thibodeau—the leading candidate for the New York Knicks coaching job—had his formal interview with the organization today, sources tell ESPN" (Wojnarowski, 9 July 2020)
Light personal branding within news and updates	Light and playful with humor and sarcasm	Moderate use of multimedia or external links to affiliated content, photos, videos, podcasts, and memes	Adam Schefter, Meg Linehan, The late Grant Wahl	"EVEN MORE. @juhrman and @alexisohanian join me for a bonus episode of Full Time with Meg Linehan to discuss @weareangelcity. #NWSL" (embedded link to podcast) (Linehan, 21 July 2020)
Personal branding within news and updates	Informal, unique to the individual, humorous	High use of multimedia; video previews, interviews with athletes, highlight reels, external links to affiliated content	Darren Rovell, Roger Bennett, Katie Nolan	"PULISIC ON SINCE THE FIRST TIME IN JANUARY. AND HE SCORES. WITHIN MINUTES. BEST THING THAT HAS HAPPENED TO AMERICA IN FAR TOO LONG" (Bennett, 21 June 2020)

Time-Out

Select your favorite sports journalist or personality, find their official X feed, and follow the account.

1. Observe their posts for three days and make a spreadsheet to categorize the type of the post (e.g., straight news, promotion, humor, personality, commentary) and multimedia elements.
2. Make note of the posts that you like and dislike, why, and the tone of their content (likes, comments, and shares).
3. Develop a strategy for your sports journalist or personality that is consistent with their tone and personal brand. Draft post content, multimedia elements, and a posting schedule. If using multimedia content, discuss how you would obtain or create the multimedia content and what your overarching strategy with the posts includes.

To reiterate, there is no right or wrong way to use X as a sports journalist. Each journalist can choose to use the platform's tone and functionality in a way that best fits their needs and comfort levels. The challenge becomes how to best represent your brand and maintain journalistic standards.

Instagram and YouTube

The photo-sharing site Instagram and the video-based platform YouTube do not usually feature in traditional sports reporters' work. However, as this book has discussed professional paths to which sports journalism skills can apply, the use of Instagram and YouTube in public relations and marketing for sport organizations merits a spotlight here. We will begin with a discussion of Instagram and then transition to similarities with YouTube.

Instagram is the third most utilized platform globally in terms of average monthly users, with two billion people using the platform (Dixon, 2023). Additionally, Instagram is widely successful at garnering audience engagement, with more interactivity per post than Facebook, YouTube, X, and TikTok, ranging from 12,000 to 581,000 average engagements per post across various sport properties (Nielsen Sports, 2022).

As a site that primarily features photos and short videos, Instagram is an ideal location for highlights and quick interview bites, celebrations, and events that lend themselves to a visual presentation. Instagram's use for sports journalists is less clear. There is an opportunity for posting visual elements of game coverage. However, major sporting events have various rights-related rules for the use of video from their events. In addition, posting personal milestones on Instagram can lead to congratulations or harassment, similar to X.

A distinguishing feature of Instagram is that it focuses solely on photo and video content rather than text-based content through the posting of static photos, videos, live video, stories, and reels. Instagram lends itself to short-form video content, as noted above; however, the length requirements vary based on format:

- In-feed video: 3 seconds to 60 minutes
- Reels video: 15 seconds to 90 seconds
- Instagram Stories: 1 second to 60 seconds
- Live video: 1 second to 4 hours (although shorter is better)

Another useful feature is the sharing function on the platform, which increases the ability of accounts to repost user-generated content, content that is produced by sport fans, which can be repurposed and posted by teams and leagues on their official feeds.

Along similar lines, and perhaps surprisingly, YouTube is the second highest ranked platform, with 2.49 billion global monthly users (Dixon, 2023). YouTube is an exclusively video-based platform and works best for longer-form video content. The popularity of YouTube from a sports perspective is based on its use to stream live matches free of charge or to provide supplemental over-the-top sports content with commentary and graphics overlaid on the in-game match feeds. Typical sports content features on YouTube include highlight reels, sports shows, and even full games or matches. YouTube has slightly lower levels of engagement per post than Instagram, with average post engagement ranging from 300 to 28,000 views, but it can be used to build loyal fan followings through the subscription feature, which various sports properties can capitalize upon.

The use of Instagram and YouTube by sports journalists in their professions is minimal, although many may maintain a personal Instagram feed to share content unrelated to their profession to build their personal brand. Where Instagram and YouTube can become a key component of the sports journalists' toolkit is as part of the development of various forms of multimedia content. According to the Nielsen Sports *Year in Review* (Nielsen Sports, 2022), the growth of video consumption continues to be a driver of growth for various sport organizations and events. Instagram and YouTube's video-based formats are key drivers of these trends;

Practical Use of Instagram and YouTube

Instagram stories, images, and candid video content can be used to produce compelling visuals and graphics with information. The types of content that can be posted to Instagram in video format include the following:

- Behind-the-scenes information
- Candid interviews with players
- Promotional content for upcoming matches

Journalistic skills that can be built via posting on Instagram include the following:

- One-to-one interviews involving various lines of questioning
- On-camera training
- Shooting, recording, and editing video
- Supplemental content such as the use of audio in videos via the reels-based format

All of these skills improve the ability to produce short, yet engaging and informative news pieces for audiences while developing a personal voice and journalistic style.

These same skills can be developed by producing long video-based content on YouTube, with the addition of script writing-skills for preproduced videos and shows, on-air improvisation, and play-by-play skills for live-streaming video.

Time-Out

Select your favorite sports network or sport organization, find their official Instagram or YouTube accounts, and follow the feed.

1. Observe their Instagram or YouTube feeds for three days, and make a spreadsheet to categorize the type of the video content (e.g., short form, long form, game pieces, interviews, preproduced content) and document the multimedia elements (e.g., posts, stories, reels, live game broadcasts).
2. Make note of the posts that you like and dislike, why, and the tone of their content (likes, comments, and shares).
3. Outline the journalistic skill sets required to produce the content you like. What areas would you need to work on or build to produce this content? In terms of the content you dislike, what would you change to make it better?

thus, developing skills in multimedia forms of reporting, specifically video, will prove beneficial for sports journalists working in a sports team or network environment. This could be from a more journalistic perspective through the generation of news pieces for leagues and teams (e.g., sideline reporter for Fox Sports), or from a PR perspective such as behind-the-scenes clips shared via the organizational Instagram feed (e.g., Barcelona FC).

Blogs

Blogs (short for "weblog") are frequently updated forums that link to news and stories across the Internet (Cernohous, 2006) and facilitate commentary that allows an individual blogger's voice to be heard (Dart, 2009). Sport—a popular topic for blogs—generates large amounts of interest from readers, and in response, traditional sports media outlets began incorporating blogs as part of their content (Schultz & Sheffer, 2007). Online journalists have the opportunity to play a role in covering—and thus, promoting—sports that thus far had been seen as niche (Perreault & Bell, 2022). Stateside, probably no sport benefited more from the rise of the blogosphere and the opportunity for more voices to emerge and find an audience than soccer. eSports, including everything from more traditional sports games to video games featuring elaborate strategies to capture virtual cities or kingdoms, are the next frontier for invested online sports journalists to inform and educate the public (Perreault & Bell, 2022).

Despite their popularity with readers, sports journalists initially viewed blogs with disdain (Schultz & Sheffer, 2007). Buzz Bissinger, author of *Friday Night Lights* and former sports reporter for *Philadelphia Inquirer*, described blogs as follows during an appearance on the TV show *Costas Now*:

> "I think blogs are dedicated to cruelty, they're dedicated to dishonesty, they're dedicated to speed…. I care about the written word and I care about reporting. The writing on most blogs is terrible." (quoted in Sandomier, 2008)

While delivered as part of a heated exchange with then *Deadspin* editor-in-chief Will Leitch, Bissinger summed up what most journalists felt regarding blogs, which was that the traditional norms of journalism, including credentialed access to athletes and coaches pre- and post-game, limited the credibility of sports bloggers who did not employ these practices. This distinction between the normative practices for sports journalists and sports bloggers contributed to benefits and drawbacks for both.

Newspapers, magazines, and other traditional sources of print-based media provide sports journalists a platform to reach an audience. The various types of print journalism pieces outlined in chapter 3 offer variety, along with a process and a set of values associated with the sports journalism industry. If not explicitly written, these values fall within the realm of normative practices that most sports journalists adhere to, and they provide a journalist with a sense of structure.

One trade-off of traditional sports journalism is creative freedom. Imagine the opportunity to produce a sports piece with no space or word count limits. The type of sports piece is at your discretion as well. You can write a game piece, an opinion piece, a profile, or all three. If you want to write 5,000 words on your favorite sports teams or the nostalgia associated with attending games as a child, a sports blog works much better for this type of highly specialized sports journalism.

The technical aspects of starting and maintaining a sports blog involve learning a content management system (CMS) such as WordPress or Squarespace. For example, AirBnB, Spotify, and Disney all have WordPress-based websites. The advantage of using a CMS such as WordPress is that it provides website design templates, advanced tools for multimedia, and plug-ins that could enhance the reader's experience.

From a business perspective, in addition to writing and posting content, a sports blogger also must be able to employ marketing and advertising tactics to raise awareness of the available content. At the onset of any new business, costs are high while revenue is low due to low awareness of the new product. A new blogger might need to forgo making money for quite some time to successfully build a consistent following.

The benefit to digital media content was and is the fact that the Internet has no geographic bound-

Practical Use of Blogs

There are several ways in which sports blogs can be employed in sports journalism. Sports blogs offer the opportunity to maintain traditional journalistic standards while still providing different information for different audiences. Here are four ways that sports journalism students can use sport blogs to their advantage.

- *Source or provide different information for different audiences.* Obtain objective information on games and matches for the traditional sports fan who may need quick facts viewed on a mobile device, while also gathering more subjective information such as opinions or "color" information, all on one site.
- *Source or provide immediate, up-to-date information.* One of the primary benefits of live sport blogs is the immediacy of information provided, perhaps updated on a minute-by-minute basis. Blog information can be sourced from multiple channels—television, radio, social media posts (e.g., tweets, posts, YouTube clips), fan emails and texts—leading to additional sourcing.
- *Gain access to or build various sport communities for specific fan insights.* Many sport blogs, once established, represent an online community where fans can gather and share insights and opinions, or engage in debate, making sports blogs a unique repository for specific fan insights.
- *Access or provide unique information not found on traditional sports media websites.* Due to the autonomy of sports blogs in digital spaces, aspiring sports journalists can use blogs to access highly specific or niche information that might not be carried by traditional sports media outlets.

Time-Out

This activity helps you practice writing a blog post. Select your favorite athlete, team, or league for this exercise. Find the statistics and relevant information available on your athlete, team, or league to familiarize yourself with interesting themes or trends occurring with your selection. You can also incorporate any additional research you find relevant to your team and topic. Remember to employ the mechanics of writing a game story or opinion piece presented in chapter 3.

1. Using your statistics and relevant research, write a 500-word blog post incorporating your unique view and personal voice. You can also employ an inverted pyramid style into your blog post to make sure the reader sees your most important takes first.
2. Rewrite your blog post to reduce it to 300 to 350 words, keeping all important information necessary to your point. Readers tend to lose interest in longer stories, so practice presenting your story in as few words as possible.

aries, and thus awareness and readership have unlimited growth potential... as long as audiences are interested in the content. Thus, the shift in the sports media landscape within digital content was driven by reader interests, as opposed to the traditional media model of an organization sending messages it chooses to the reader.

In addition to the varied content available to consumers based on their interests, sports blogs also captured additional elements of consumer needs that had been unaddressed in traditional digital content—tone and humor. This shift from a neutral tone to one that was unapologetically biased, humorous, and at times tending toward gossip was illustrated best by the popular sports blog *Deadspin*. Since *Deadspin*'s founding in 2005, there has been a new legion of online sports content that has sought to display a harder edge, without worrying about access or, often, decorum.

Podcasts

Podcasts are another tool that sports journalists can use to provide information to listeners: coverage of sporting events, sports industry news, upcoming game or match predictions, discussions, behind-the-scenes information, interviews, and more. In some ways, podcasts have replaced written forms of online expression, such as sports blogs, as the preferred medium for fans to express their views about sporting events and discussions that stem directly from reporting by sports journalists. Podcasts are part of the evolution of news and views dissemination that started with blogs. They can be short- or long-form discussions featuring analysis and viewpoints. As mentioned in chapter 2, the increased popularity of podcasts helped sports and culture site The Ringer gain a massive following.

In terms of technology, while there are many audio tools in software as well as hardware that can be used by people looking to start a podcast, the use of recording software on a smartphone can also serve as a competent podcast medium. This may not lead to the best audio quality, but it is an excellent way for students to explore podcasting on their own and to hone their voices. Podcasts are also used by people who are not sports journalists to create content that engages a sizeable potential audience. For journalists and aspiring sports journalists, a core opportunity to separate from the morass of sports-related podcasts is to include interviews and similar reported content that could not be curated by the average person who does not have access to sports newsmakers. In addition, conducting deeper research in categories such as the effects of statistical analysis and sport-related business trends can separate sports journalists from most fan-related podcasts.

Practical Use of Podcasts

Here are several ways sports journalists can use podcasts to their advantage based on the content and focus of the podcast (Clavio & Moritz, 2022).

- *Conversational podcasts* provide in-depth conversations about a particular sport topic and the opportunity to source information on that topic.
- *Interview podcasts* are interviews with people who are involved with the podcast topic. This type of podcast offers sports journalists the opportunity to source quotes and gain expert insights, as well as the opportunity to pursue their own interviews with the experts.
- *Repurposed content podcasts* reuse previous content, such as interviews, existing material, and so on, to reach a different or wider audience. This type of podcast could be beneficial for sourcing a wide range of topical information.
- *Scripted podcasts* are prewritten podcasts on a particular topic. The specific focus of these podcasts make for excellent source material for niche topics.
- *Storytelling podcasts* are multiple-episode podcasts that employ a narrative format. This type of podcast requires a significant investment of time by the sports journalist but can be a great outlet for those who are looking to build on their long-form journalism skill set or who simply wish to present a longer narrative, which can be hard to find in today's fast-paced digital environment.

Hardware and Software Choices for Social Media Content Production

If you are . . .	Beginning hardware	Beginning software	Beginning training
Writing for digital	A smartphone, tablet, or lightweight computer	Native apps such as X (Twitter) or social media dashboards such as X-Pro	Writing drills and observation, followed by certification training such as Hootsuite Academy
Taking still photos	Most modern smartphones are capable; DSL-R camera	Free apps like Snapseed; paid software like Adobe Photoshop or Lightroom	Learning the basics of the "rule of thirds" and how to avoid backlighting subjects
Taking action photos	DSL-R camera with zoom lens	Free apps like Snapseed; paid software like Adobe Photoshop or Lightroom	On-the-job practice; training through courses
Recording podcasts	Standalone microphone with USB plug-in	Free software such as Audacity or GarageBand; also consider podcast-focused apps like Anchor	Basic audio editing training often can be found for free via YouTube
Recording video	Modern smartphone or standalone video camera	No special software needed for recording	Still photo training applies to video as well
Editing photos and graphics	A smartphone, tablet, or lightweight computer	Canva, Photoshop, or equivalent	Free YouTube training videos; paid training videos
Editing podcasts	A smartphone, tablet, or computer	Computer software like Adobe Audition or GarageBand; apps like Anchor	Free YouTube training videos; paid training videos
Editing video	A smartphone, tablet, or computer	Computer software like Final Cut Pro, iMovie, or Adobe Premiere Pro; apps like Splice or Quik	Free YouTube training videos; paid training videos

Reprinted by permission from G. Clavio, *Social Media and Sports* (Champaign, IL: Human Kinetics, 2021), 23.

Artificial Intelligence

The potential use of artificial intelligence (AI) in sports journalism—and journalism in general—has reached center stage at a time when there has been increased focus on the importance of reliable media. Notably, the on-going discussion about the positives and the potential challenges of AI does not lend itself to clear good-versus-evil conclusions (Jarvis, 2024). The continued development of new technologies is seen as supplementing and potentially surpassing the analytical abilities of humans (McLean et al., 2022). While journalists might be intrigued at the possibilities of AI in terms of assisting with analysis and with story production (for instance, the use of networked drones in news gathering is an ongoing consideration [Nwanakwaugwu et al., 2023]), implementing AI as part of a media approach has proven more challenging.

Observers have long understood that AI could create a sports game story based on a box score. If AI can write a competent (if not particularly enthralling) game story, how long before a media company looks to save money by asking computers to write previews, feature stories, personality profiles, analytics stories, and so on? Some media outlets have already embraced AI's potential to streamline news reporting Media giant Gannett experimented with using AI to write high school football stories, an idea that was not a hit with readers (Bauder, 2023). Both CNET and the Associated Press used AI to assist in writing stories about financial markets, and the AP also has used AI in writing sports game previews (Bauder, 2023).

AI's increased use has led to mistakes, to be sure. Following a shooting at Michigan State University in February 2023, Vanderbilt University officials found themselves needing to apologize for using the AI program ChatGPT to write a message to the VU community about the tragedy. It did not take someone savvy in AI programs to spot the issue, as the message ended with "Paraphrase from

Artificial Intelligence, Virtual Reality, and Augmented Reality

One of the most fluid conversations in sports is the effect of new technologies on how information is gathered and understood. These technologies include artificial intelligence (AI), virtual reality (VR), and augmented reality (AR) (Cossich et al., 2023). In addition, the term *Internet of Things (IOT)* has gained popularity as well. The IOT is defined as a network of physical objects (e.g., smartphones, wearables, automotive devices) that can network together for data gathering and performing tasks (Amazon Web Services, n.d.; IBM, n.d.). The IOT can also assist in developing better methods for sport training and injury management (Zhang & Zhao, 2023).

In the sports world, VR's utilization has been in creating realistic training environments for athletes. AR can be used to place digital information into a sport environment, which allows for real-time adjustments, and the technology has also been used for entertainment purposes (Cossich et al., 2023). AI has been put into use in analysis of data and has assisted in enhancing understanding of sport competitions in terms of statistics (Geissler et al., 2024), monitoring athlete performance, and predicting (and possibly preventing) injuries (McLean et al., 2022).

AI is also being used in sport officiating (Dowsett, 2024). An automated ball–strike system is being tested in minor league baseball (Passan, 2024). Professional tennis already employs AI technology to make line calls, with the ATP men's tour planning to completely phase out human line judges by 2025 (Associated Press, 2023). However, it must be noted that AI can falter. In December 2023 motion-capture AI calculated an NBA player's shot as a distance of 30 feet, which would have put him completely off the court when the shot was taken (Dowsett, 2024).

Augmented and mixed reality have become part of in-person game presentations and experiences, too. While the mid-2010s saw fans posting augmented reality screenshots of Pokemon Go characters they had "found" while attending sporting events, some organizations took that a bit further. The Baltimore Ravens featured a pregame scoreboard video depicting a large raven flying throughout the stadium in real time in a form of mixed reality. Just as Web 2.0 opened new doors to sports fans, the continued rise of AI and related tech should offer consumers the chance to individually curate their own sports media experience (Geissler et al., 2024).

Factors affecting the adoption of immersive technology and the desire to control from which medium individual users receive messages affect the utilization of AI, VR, AR, and mixed reality (Kang, 2020). The use of experiential media such as virtual reality in creating sports media messaging is also worthy of examination. Prior to both the 2018 and 2022 FIFA World Cup soccer tournaments, media content that incorporated virtual reality was produced by *Russia Today* and *Road to Qatar*, respectively. Scholars found that the content produced for these events was limited in interaction, featuring content such as stadium tours and placing the viewer as an observer of events rather than an active participant (Regret Iyer et al., 2022). Regret Iyer and colleagues (2022) pointed out the potential of VR: The immersive nature of VR could lend itself to more than mere tours of facilities, perhaps presenting more human stories such as athlete experiences.

OpenAI's ChatGPT AI language model, personal communication, February 15, 2023" (Mendoza, 2023). In late 2023, legacy magazine *Sports Illustrated* was found to have used AI-generated stories in its coverage. Content—including some writers' names—was removed after a third party exposed the use of AI to create that content. *SI*, for its part, blamed an outside contractor and announced an ending to its partnership with that contractor. *SI*'s union released a statement expressing its displeasure (Bauder, 2023).

Questions about the use of AI are not limited to storytelling through words. The ease of editing still photographs and videos also presents a potential ethical challenge for sports journalists (Moreland, 2024). Cameras have become easier to use than ever before, and with easily obtainable editing software, nonprofessionals can create visual images that are of top quality to the layperson's eye. In effect, sports journalists who want to use the AI features in these editing tools responsibly are playing catchup with the rest of society. And considering their ease of use, can sports journalists forgo the use of AI tools (Moreland, 2024)?

The use of AI certainly raises many ethical concerns, among them whether the use of AI to create sports stories might lead to job losses for writers (Latar, 2018; Segarra-Saavedra et al., 2019). Can AI create realistic human-sounding dialogue and writing? Can AI duplicate human intuition? What limitations remain, and at what rate will the list of AI's limitations get smaller? Anxiety related to technology has long affected journalists' viewpoints. This includes not only anxiety related to the need to learn new approaches but also worries that technology might streamline the job of a journalist and thus lead to automation taking the place of humans (Guiterrez Lopez et al., 2023). Other ethical concerns include who programs the AI? What instructions will be given to AI when creating news media content? Also, students and scholars must consider the outsized influence of social media platforms like Facebook and Google on the dissemination of news stories (Baaseed, 2023).

Human decision-making and journalistic ethics remain important even with these new methodologies (Guiterrez Lopez et al., 2023), and the people and groups tasked with charting media's course through new technologies have taken notice of the increasing use of AI. In early 2023, the Society of Professional Journalists released a report focusing on ethical issues related to the use of AI. It noted the importance of the human element in media and the need to continue to strive for honesty with news consumers regarding all practices in journalism, including the use of AI (Society of Professional Journalists, 2023). Later in 2023, the Public Relations Society of America

Practical Use of Artificial Intelligence

The use of AI in sports journalism will undoubtedly continue to evolve. Here are some tips for ensuring AI is used ethically and correctly.

- *Be ethical and transparent.* When deciding to use AI, sports journalists should keep the Society of Professional Journalists (SPJ) code of ethics in mind, including being ethical and transparent. Sports journalists should take responsibility for their work (Society of Professional Journalists, 2023). To follow the SPJ code of ethics, sport journalists should clearly acknowledge the use of AI (Bostwick, n.d.).
- *Prioritize fact-checking.* Before using any material generated by AI tools, validate the sources of information and fact-check data. It is the responsibility of the sports journalist—not the AI system—to verify that content is not infringing another's work. Sports journalists must prioritize fact-checking. Otherwise, they become part of the problem by lending credibility to inaccurate information (Bostwick, n.d.; PRSA, 2023).
- *Act independently.* Sports journalists who use AI tools may not fully understand how those tools work, and they may not be aware of potential biases within the algorithms. This can prevent them from being fully independent (Bostwick, n.d.). Thus, sports journalists should take the time to learn how AI tools work.
- *Recognize the limits of technology.* Understand that there are limits to AI software and know what those limits are. AI is not a substitute for human judgment, and it cannot replicate human experience (PRSA, 2023).

also released guidelines regarding best practices for the use of AI. Titled "Promises and Pitfalls," the report urged verification of AI-generated information and a continued ethical approach (Staley et al., 2023).

In response to the evolving use of AI and other technologies such as augmented reality, virtual reality, and Internet of Things in sports and sports journalism, it is advisable that young reporters learn about these technologies and their potential effects to the same level as a sports journalist might learn everything they can about the upcoming free-agency period or about how analytics have affected shot selection in basketball. Going forward, part of a sports journalist's role will be to interpret how this technology influences sport, every bit as much as a sports journalist must be able to explain to readers why what looked like a catch was not a catch. And remember: Human journalists' skill and experience will complement emerging technology and vice versa (Torrijos, 2019). Humans can use technology to help them to produce interesting stories; AI cannot do the same to the same level (Latar, 2018).

Summary

As media have evolved with the development of new technologies, previous norms have also faded away and given way to new paradigms. Online opportunities give sports journalists the chance to quickly post news and stories without a thought to space restrictions. Social media platforms offer the chance for instantaneous news distribution, both for journalists and for those who connect with them on these platforms. As the technology has evolved, so too have news-gathering and dissemination techniques. A newer challenge is the use of artificial intelligence in sports journalism. This has involved the creation of game stories as well as photo editing, among other uses. The importance of preserving traditional journalism ethics when using technology will and should apply to the use of AI.

Discussion Questions

1. What do you think are the most obvious effects of the emergence of social media use in sports journalism?
2. What do you think is the most effective online platform or platforms for disseminating trustworthy sports media content? Why do you feel this way? Please give examples.

Applied Activity

Working with a group of four or five other students, establish either an Instagram feed or a YouTube channel. The social media feed should cover a sport-related topic of your choice. Every two weeks, report on what kinds of posts you make (e.g., informative, fandom, entertainment, game highlights) and which posts receive the highest levels of engagement in terms of likes and comments.

Sports Journalism and Public Relations

Chapter Objectives

After completing this chapter, you will be able to do the following:

- Define public relations.
- Distinguish between sport public relations, sport marketing, and sport communication and sports journalism.
- Outline the various functions within sport public relations and media channels.
- Highlight, through case studies and examples, the benefits of public relations.
- Identify career pathways for sports journalism students within sport organizational public relations.

The first rule of public relations is that no one actually talks about the importance of public relations until you have to deal with a tremendous amount of negative press. In that case you are actually referring to crisis communications, a highly specialized area of expertise within the field of public relations. Crisis scenarios, such as the scandal within the United States Gymnastics Association involving widespread allegations of abuse by former coaches and staff (Simko-Bednarski & Vera, 2021), often provide the rationale for sport organizations to hire a public relations staff.

However, many public relations functions involve day-to-day tasks. These include, but are not limited to, working on corporate communications and community relations, managing media access and public relations for athletes and coaches, engaging **key publics** through various communication channels, and managing the sport organization–media relationship. While these functions would appear to be unrelated to sports journalism, more and more formally trained sports journalists are being hired away from traditional newspaper, magazine, online, or television organizations to work in a public relations capacity for a sport organization. The tools for effective public relations practices, such as writing and creating video and other visual elements for clients, are the same as those used by sports journalists working in traditional media. And the primary functions of public relations are communication and relationship building—often with members of the media who share their skill set.

This chapter will define exactly what we mean when we say "public relations," describe the emphasis on relationship building, and examine the public relations functions at a sport organization that align with sports journalism skills.

Public Relations

If you ask people to define public relations, you will probably get a description of communication driven by an agenda. Common words associated with public relations are *spin* and *deception*, and possibly even *lying*. For this reason, the field is widely considered one of the most misunderstood and underappreciated, yet most significant and valued areas of sport communication (Hopwood, 2010). The global sports industry grew by more than $25 billion from 2022 to 2023, and the market is predicted to exceed $620 billion by 2027 (Business Research Company, 2023). Given the level of attention devoted to sports and the financial impact of the sports industry, strategic communication and **relationship building** with key publics is vital for viable, competitive sports businesses.

Public relations is the management and relationship functions between organizations and their publics (Harlow, 1976). More specifically, the Public Relations Society of America (PRSA) employs the following definition: "Public relations is a strategic communication process that builds mutually beneficial relationships between organizations and their publics" (Public Relations Society of America, 2021). According to the PRSA, public relations functions include examining public opinion or attitudes and protecting the reputation of the organization. This places public relations within the dynamic framework of managing relationships and reputation through communication.

An organization's reputation can have a significant impact on its business. Reputation is a by-product of organizational action and public perception (Hopwood, 2010). It is an intangible asset that is not easily established but is very easily destroyed. Thus, when performed properly, public relations protects the hard-earned reputation of the organization by promoting positive public perceptions.

There are two basic models for creating and maintaining the relationships that are essential to effective public relations strategies. Both highlight the importance of communication practices.

- Jefkins (1994) created the public relations transfer process (figure 6.1). This focuses on converting negative emotions such as hostility and apathy to sympathy and interest through knowledge sharing by communicating with key publics.
- Dozier and colleagues (1995) introduced the new model of symmetry as two-way practices, which emphasizes a two-way model of communication in which the organization and the public can both benefit from the relationship. If either the organization or the key publics dominate communication, the communication becomes asymmetric, but when two-way communication is nurtured, a win–win zone is created that produces mutually beneficial outcomes.

Despite the importance of public relations to sport organizations, there is still a lack of understanding about the profession, and sport organizations tend to presume that fans and other key stakeholders will remain loyal indefinitely. To be competitively viable, sport organizations should have an active public relations function to maintain, and even enhance, the reputation of the brand. This is where skilled sports journalists can fit into the equation. Relationship and reputation management are achieved through communication with key publics, and sports journalism students are trained in effective communications. The difference is in how they apply those skills.

Sport Public Relations

Sport public relations emerged largely from the public relations functions that were performed within sport marketing departments (Hopwood, 2010). Sport marketing is focused on functions that increase revenue, while sport public relations focuses on relationship building with key publics through communication. According to Stoldt et al. (2020), **sport public relations** "is a brand-centric communication function designed to manage and advance relationships between a sport organization and its key publics" (p. 28).

The relationship management role is highlighted, but the communications component is also integral to successful public relations within sport. Additionally, the communications component represents a transferable skill set between sports journalism and sport public relations. Sport communication includes the skill sets and media (i.e., technical

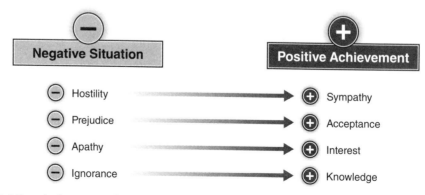

FIGURE 6.1 Public relations transfer process.

aspects) used in the sport communication process (Hopwood, 2010). Sports journalism students are trained to produce content for and communicate through various media. In moving from sports journalism to sport public relations, sports journalism students use the same skill sets, but with the strategic objective of facilitating relationship building.

Building and Maintaining Relationships With Key Publics

When they are focused on goals that emphasize positive image or reputation, public relations activities can easily fall into the area of spin. This is a traditional approach to public relations (Ledingham & Bruning, 2000). But the emphasis has shifted toward a more strategic and behavioral relationship form of public relations that achieves true value (Grunig, 1993).

Sports journalism students are well versed in producing content that is designed to inform and engage an audience. The one-way and mediated nature of sports journalism, however, dictates that the audience for a particular news piece is predefined. For example, when working for a news organization covering a team or teams in a geographic area, your audience consists of the sports fans who support those teams. Conversely, in public relations, many audiences or key publics may exist simultaneously, and they must be identified in order to build a relationship.

Publics are groups that can affect an organization in some way (Stoldt et al., 2020). Within a sport organization, publics can include fans, single-game or season ticket holders, sponsors, and TV broadcast partners, and they can be subdivided based on how the organization wishes to target a key public because different people in these groups will have different needs (Grunig & Repper, 1992). For example, within the stakeholder group of sponsors, you could have a local community organization that chooses to place a single-page advertisement in the game program, and you could also have a large national sponsor that spends millions of dollars per season for in-game signage to be displayed on

Mascots help to build relationships with key publics.
Emilee Chinn/Cincinnati Reds/Getty Images

the electronic advertising boards. While both are sponsors, these are two very different key publics that require a different level of communication to maintain a mutually beneficial relationship with the sport organization.

Key publics can be identified using a typology described by Grunig and Hunt (1984) that includes nonpublics, latent publics, aware publics, and active publics.

- A **nonpublic** has little impact on the organization, and a relationship is never established.
- With a **latent public**, there is a problem or issue that connects the public to the organization, but the public is unaware that this issue exists.
- A latent public becomes an **aware public** when awareness of the issues is established, but they do not take action.
- An **active public** is one that has awareness and establishes communication with the organization (Shilbury & Rowe, 2010).

To reach key publics, Grunig and Hunt (1984) developed four foundational models (figure 6.2):

1. Press Agency Model
2. Public Information Model
3. Two-Way Asymmetrical Model
4. Two-Way Symmetrical Model

Once key publics have been identified and classified into typologies, and strategic communication tactics have been employed to build relationships, the issue then becomes how to maintain these relationships to build a proactive public relations philosophy. One strategy for maintaining these relationships is for the organization to perform stewardship practices.

Stewardship prompts organizations to consider the impact of their decision-making on key publics and to employ the two-way symmetric model of public relations rather than taking a press-agency approach and focusing solely on generating positive press (Kelly, 2001). Stewardship is comprised of reciprocity, responsibility, reporting, and relationship nurturing.

- *Reciprocity* involves saying thank you to key publics for their support through acknowledgment and actions. Reciprocity promotes positive feelings about the organization through positive interactions.
- *Responsibility* refers to social responsibility and is based on codes of conduct to uphold standards.
- *Reporting* is the process by which organizations communicate key information to relevant publics.
- *Relationship nurturing* is an ongoing effort to maintain relationships with key publics.

Press Agency Model
- A one-directional, asymmetrical model of communication in which the organization develops communication without interaction with key publics
- Seeks to change the behavior of key publics with no behavioral change from the organization
- Goal is to generate positive publicity

Public Information Model
- Focuses on one-directional communication designed to inform key publics
- Emphasizes objective information rather than positive publicity

Two-Way Asymmetrical Model
- Identifies the attitudes and options of key publics
- Develops messaging to alter or change behaviors of key publics

Two-Way Symmetrical Model
- Solicits input from key publics
- Compromise between the organization and key publics in terms of behavioral change
- Creates a win–win scenario for both parties

FIGURE 6.2 Foundational models of reaching key publics.

Now that we have established a working definition of public relations, explained how it applies to sport organizations, illustrated how to determine key publics, and described how to effectively build and maintain relationships with these publics, we will move to the communication tools, or media, employed to reach these key publics. These media include news media (e.g., news releases, media guides, match-day programs, corporate communications), organizational media (e.g., media guides, games notes), social media (e.g., Facebook, Twitter, Instagram, TikTok), and digital media (e.g., websites, podcasts, blogs), and we will describe how they can be used during a crisis scenario.

Communicating to Key Publics Through News Media

While social media and digital media have revolutionized how sport organizations communicate with key publics, and while they offer the advantages of lower cost and ease of distribution, sport public relations are still based largely on communicating through traditional news media and sports journalists. News releases, visual PR elements, media pitches, interviews, stadium tours, and media days are all tools that sport public relations offices use to connect with media organizations in order to communicate their messages.

Most of these tools are based on written or visual production skills that sports journalists gain through their journalistic training; the skills are simply being applied on behalf of a sport organization instead of a news media outlet. The relationship between the sport organization and the news outlet is mutually beneficial. What the public relations office gains from working with the media in terms of credibility and increased reach, the media organizations gains in a never-ending supply of content that fans readily consume.

Before we describe the tools that are used to communicate with the news media, we will discuss some guidelines sport public relations departments should establish for the relationship, including a media policy with an organizational spokesperson and guidelines for coach and athlete availability.

Media Policy and Organizational Spokesperson

Sport organizations generally do not have a problem generating interest in sports stories; the public demand for sport-related content is high. It is important to establish an organizational media policy that clearly outlines who speaks to the media, how media requests are handled, and how and when to request access to coaches and athletes. This provides clear direction and equal treatment for everyone involved in the process.

Part of developing a media policy is identifying the organizational spokesperson. The **organizational spokesperson** acts as the voice of the organization and answers questions from the media. This enables the sport organization to establish a touchpoint for directing questions and also to control the organizational messaging so that it is clear and consistent. The spokesperson is usually a high-ranking member of the organization, such as the CEO, COO, general manager, or head of the sport public relations department. Their perceived credibility is based on their in-depth knowledge of the organization and their years of experience. The spokesperson traditionally handles questions of a significant nature (e.g., coaching changes, crisis scenarios, major player trades), while day-to-day operational activities, such as who to contact for a pre-game quote, can be handled by the public relations teams.

Coach and Athlete Availability

Most public relations practices can be translated from nonsport to sport settings. Coordinating media access to high-ranking employees of the organization is a traditional function of public relations. In addition to high-ranking employees such as the owner or general manager, access to coaches and athletes also requires public relations management. The primary focus for athletes and coaches is training and preparation for competitions, and while audiences often have an interest in the thoughts and views of these people, some feel media requests are intrusive or disruptive. To establish clear expectations for both the players and the media, public relations offices in sport organizations set aside specific times for coaches and athletes to be available to the media. Most general availability (i.e., weekly press conferences, pregame player availability) can be established in advance in the media guide, and changes to availability can be communicated through news releases.

During general media availability times, sports journalists should schedule interviews with coaches and athletes in advance. In addition to press conferences and interviews, the most common form of availability is pre- and postgame interviews, which typically provide the quotes that are a key part of sports journalism. After competition, access to coaches and athletes usually occurs in the locker room. The atmosphere can sometimes be contentious if the competition was especially heated, so a postcompetition cooling-off period may be applied. Because of the importance of these sessions, players and coaches must be available for specific amounts of time, and they could be fined by the team or the league for failing to appear.

Fines for failing to appear before the media can vary based on the event and type of offense. A standard example is Venus Williams' fine of $5,000 for failing to appear after a loss in the 2016 Australian Open (Venus Williams hit with $5,000 fine, 2016). Heftier media fines include Marshawn Lynch's infamous $75,000 fine from the NFL for failing to appear in 2015 after the NFC title game (Sharp, 2015) and Brooklyn Nets guard Kyrie Irving's $25,000 fine from the NBA for failing to appear during media week (Maloney & Kaskey-Blomain, 2020).

News Releases

Even with all the available forms of communication that exist today, the **news release** or press release is one of the most widely used and accepted forms of communication available to public relations professionals in the sports industry (Stoldt et al., 2020). The news release works as an awareness-generating tool for the organization to communicate newsworthy information to a key public, most notably the media, while positioning the organization in a positive way. News value, or newsworthiness, is the most important element of the news release. Because it is produced by the sport organization, any information they deem of value can be labeled as newsworthy.

News releases can be written to highlight competitions or to announce coaching or staff changes, sponsorship deals, or other activities deemed worthy of coverage. Writing a news release is similar to writing a news article. One key difference, however, is that while news releases are distributed to the news media, the media are not the only key public of value to the organization. Consider the announcement of a minor sponsorship deal, for example. The media may not consider this very newsworthy and may not give it much coverage, but a news release should still be published because it is communicating for another stakeholder in the organization.

When writing a news release, the writer should think about how the information has value to a key public. The acronym TIPCUP (timeliness, impact, prominence, conflict, unusualness, and proximity) from the framework provided by Thompson (1996) can be applied.

- *Timeliness* usually refers to breaking or new information, but it can also apply to the timing of an event in the context of seasonal play or to its timing in relation to competition from other sport organizations in the media coverage area.
- *Impact* is determined from the perspective of the audience. News organizations that regard the information as impactful will pick it up for coverage.
- *Prominence* is the concept that if the information is delivered by the spokesperson, then it is newsworthy.
- *Conflict* in day-to-day sports competition may not be deemed newsworthy, but a business-related conflict between a sport organization and a sponsor, for example, may be newsworthy and deserving of coverage.
- *Unusualness* refers to news that does not occur often, such as the Chicago Cubs' World Series win in 2016, which broke a 108-year postseason "curse" (Martin, 2016).
- *Proximity* applies to coverage within the geographic area where the sport organization resides due to its local impact.

News Release Structure

The press release is structured so that its newsworthy elements can be quickly determined and transferred into a news piece (Treadwell & Treadwell, 2000). The elements of a news release are the header, the body, and the ending, which comprise the boilerplate format recognizable to sports journalists. A standard template for a press release is shown in figure 6.3. Consistent with media writing guidelines and to increase ease of use, press releases follow AP (Associated Press) style.

The header is arguably the most important element of the news release. It contains the organization's name, media contact and phone number, the release date and time, and the dateline as well as the headline. Standard information such as the organization's physical address can be included, but the media contact information is key—should the media contact be unavailable when a reporter calls for more information, the news release may not receive coverage.

The release date and time tell the media when information can be released; most are written "for immediate release." The dateline provides locational information, such as the city, and is placed in all caps, followed by a hyphen. Finally, the headline is placed before the first paragraph, or lead, and should draw attention to the newsworthy element of the release. If a news release is being distributed by email, the headline is often placed in the subject line. A headline can make the difference between getting media coverage or not. A good headline should be catchy to grab the journalist's attention and should highlight the news element that makes the release worthy of coverage.

The body of the news release should adhere to the inverted pyramid style of writing, placing the most important information (i.e., who, what, where, when, why, and how) at the beginning of the release. Ideally, this information should be contained within the lead. Information placed further down in the release should provide explanatory and contextual information about the newsworthy elements. A news release is meant to be brief—traditionally not more than a page long—with short paragraphs consisting of one or two sentences.

The ending of a news release can contain information about the organization, such as historical information, the mission, or the vision. To signal the formal end of the release, three hashtags are placed, centered, to indicate no further information.

Large sport organizations can often rely on the news media to provide regular coverage of their events, but smaller organizations may need to develop stories to pitch to the media to gain regular attention in the news cycle. Media pitches are story ideas that a PR representative of the sport organization suggests to a sports journalist to gauge interest. A pitch, which can be performed through email, should always be followed by a formal news release and possibly a phone call to a sports journalist.

Sports journalists who move on to jobs in sport public relations can easily adapt their writing skills to the requirements for writing news releases. The key element to take from your sports journalism training is the ability to identify what is newsworthy and to present this information as a viable story.

Date: Month/Day/Year
For Immediate Release

For further information contact:
[Name]
[Title]
[Cell Phone]
[Email Address]

Interesting and Newsworthy Headline

A subhead that adds context and information

[Dateline/City]

Lead – 11111111111111111111111111111111111111111111111111111111111111111111

2222222222222222222222222222222222222222222222222222222222222222222222 2222222222222222222222222222222222222222222222222222222222222

3333333333333333333333333333333333333333333333333333333333333333333333 3333333333333333333333333333333333333333333333333333333333333333

4444444444444444444444444444444444444444444444444444444444444444444444 4444444444444444444444444444444444444444444444444444444444444444 444444444

5555555555555555555555555555555555555555555555555555555555555555555555

[signals end]

(If you go to a second page, put the word –more- at the bottom of page one. Then put the first two words of the headline on page two and the words, Add 1. Then put the ### at the end of your release.)

FIGURE 6.3 *(a)* Press release template.

///

Sport Organization Logo
Date: 01/05/2024
For Immediate Release

For further information contact:
Jane Doe
Director of Public Relations
812-123-4567
jane.doe@intermiamicf.com

Inter Miami CF Sign Legendary Forward

Luis Suarez Joins Through the 2024 MLS Season

MIAMI – Legendary forward Luis Suarez has signed for Inter Miami FC on a one-year contract from Brazilian side Gremio. Suarez will join for the upcoming 2024 MLS season.

A prolific forward for such teams as AFC Ajax, Liverpool FC, FC Barcelona, and Atletico Madrid, as well as the Uruguay national team, Suarez's prolific career has included more than 500 goals for club and country. He has won the UEFA Champions League, FIFA Club World Club, the CONMEBOL Copa America, and five La Liga titles, among other personal accomplishments.

"Suarez brings a wealth of experience in top competitions and will be a valuable asset to our team in the 2024 season," said Inter Miami co-founder David Beckham. "We're excited to have him join and reconnect with his former teammates, producing the same style and substance he was known for in previous seasons."

"Inter Miami is building a world-class team and I'm thrilled to be joining this project," Suarez said. "It is especially meaningful to me as I will be playing with individuals who know my style and how we can connect to score goals. I look forward to stepping out on the field and representing Inter Miami, playing with joy and happiness, and winning trophies along the way."

Suarez will make his debut at the beginning of the 2024 MLS season.

###

///

FIGURE 6.3 *(b)* An example press release.

Visuals

An often-overlooked area of public relations that is now gaining more and more prominence is visuals. While public relations is viewed as an extension or parallel to sports journalism due to its emphasis on writing, its visual aspects are becoming increasingly important as storytelling shifts to more digital platforms, particularly in digital and social media. Specifically, B-roll video footage and photos are helpful in this function.

B-Roll

B-roll is pretaped video provided by a sport organization to broadcasters that features standard shots of the stadium, a local town or city for background information, and pretaped quotes or sound bites related to a particular game or rivalry. B-roll is typically unedited; it is provided because it gives the organization a level of control over the messaging. Although B-roll is traditionally offered free of charge, it has benefits for the sport organization because a media outlet can not only include it in broadcast footage but can also edit and distribute it on digital and social media platforms for additional coverage and reach.

Video News Release

A video news release is a preproduced packaged story that is provided to news organizations. These are short clips, between 60 and 90 seconds long, and while they are more expensive to produce than B-roll, they are the preferred length for distribution on digital and social media channels for news organizations to build awareness and engagement for a story. If they are not used by news organizations, these packages can be distributed across the sport organizations' own digital platforms to create significant engagement.

Industry Profile

John Koluder

John Koluder

Today, John Koluder is, as he says on his LinkedIn page, "Helping to grow the Beautiful Game in the Hoosier State" as the Special Member Benefits Director with the Indiana Soccer Association and U.S. Open Cup Communication Consultant for U.S. Soccer Federation.

It's a far cry from a couple of decades ago, when after graduating from college in the early 2000s, Koluder was far from his native Indiana. He was on an unpaid internship with Major League Soccer club D.C. United. To cover expenses, he was working the front desk at a Holiday Inn for 35 hours a week while putting in a similar number of hours working for the dominant team in MLS' early days, less than a decade after the league launched.

"From playing two games a week on a Wednesday and a Saturday, you're probably putting in 40 hours," Koluder said (personal communication). "You know, that includes showing up at the stadium at 9 a.m. to put flags on the roof of RFK stadium. Great view to the Capitol, but not a great view down, if you're afraid of heights."

Koluder had covered the Indiana University men's soccer program as an undergrad, working games on student radio and for the student newspaper. Attempting to break into working in MLS in the early part of the 21st century was tricky. The league had folded both Florida teams (Miami Fusion and Tampa Bay Mutiny) after the 2001 season.

But Koluder found himself accepting the unpaid position with D.C. United, writing articles for official team materials. Soon, his boss asked whether he had ever considered public relations.

"Well, I can write, I can travel, that's pretty much two of the things I really want to do and if I can get paid for them, that'd be fantastic," Koluder said of his mindset. "Obviously, PR and journalism are very similar, but also can be on opposite ends of spectrums in regards to philosophy. It's going from wanting to make everything transparent, to making sure you're controlling messaging that gets out."

Following the internship, Koluder moved to Chicago for a full-time PR role with the Chicago Fire. The move came just as the league had become more stable and online technology had begun to change PR and media approaches.

"Both PR and journalism were figuring it out on the fly," Koluder said. "I think once the teams realized they had to become their own media outlets—that's around that time, the early 2000s—that teams figured out not only did they want to do it. But they kinda started to need to do it, because they couldn't rely on the resources of traditional media newsrooms to tell their stories."

Following his time in Chicago, Koluder moved to expansion club Real Salt Lake in 2007. As someone working PR for a still-growing soccer league, Koluder found that the mission—and the workload—were quite different than with a more established sports operation.

"MLS staffs aren't the size of Major League Baseball, or NFL, or NBA staffs," Koluder said. "You've got probably half the staff, if not even in some leagues or some clubs, a third of the staff or a quarter of the staff of what teams in these other leagues would have. But you're expected to have the same output and fight for media coverage and have better placement."

The development of social media platforms also led to Koluder and his colleagues needing to create messaging while learning new techniques on the fly. Following his MLS days, Koluder's career led him back home again to Indiana, leading the PR team for the 2013-2014 launch of United Soccer League team Indy Eleven.

He spent most of the next decade at Indy Eleven, with two intervening years working PR for the Indianapolis Ballet Company before returning to Indy Eleven. Since summer 2023, Koluder has been with the Indiana Soccer Association, and he noted that his willingness to move away from familiar surroundings in the early days was key to finding his career path.

"For better or worse, I think I'm much the better for getting around the country for 10 years," Koluder said. "And not just living in those places, but being in a position that did a lot of travel. Probably . . . 10 to 20 trips a year around the country to different markets. So, I got exposed to parts of the country I never thought I'd go to before, never thought I'd live in before."

Photos

Photos are widely used by sport organizations as the primary form of visual storytelling. Action shots, which portray the dynamic nature of sports, are used to represent games in news media accounts. When a member of the PR staff photographs behind-the-scenes footage such as training sessions in addition to athletic events, the organization owns the images, and they are not subject to copyright laws. Event photos can then be provided to the news media as part of the sport organization–media relationship or distributed by the organization through its digital and social media channels.

Visual journalism skills are now taught in most multimedia journalism courses. These skills are highly applicable and transferable to sport public relations.

Interviews

Although it is one of the most basic ways reporters gather information to produce stories, an interview can be a delicate process involving multiple steps. Chapter 3 highlighted the various elements to consider when conducting an interview, but the interview is essentially a balance between the journalist's goal to provide readers with pertinent information and the organization's desire to reinforce a positive image.

A trained sports journalist will be well versed in developing the questions to produce high-quality content. It is the job of the PR representative to get additional information from the sports journalist about the deadline and storyline angles to facilitate the production of the story, generate interest, and prepare the interview subject for questions. The idea is that if the PR representative knows some of the questions beforehand, they can provide better responses for quotes. Also, if there is one best person to answer a specific question, it may take time to make that person available. From the sport organization's perspective, preparing the interviewee allows for the development of key messages that align with organizational messages.

Media Days and News Conferences

Media days and news conferences represent two structured events organized by the sport organization in which multiple members of the media from various outlets are invited to attend. A media day is a one-day session where many interviews can be conducted with in-demand players and coaches in a back-to-back format. The overarching goal of the media day is to provide as much access to players and coaches as possible in a casual atmosphere to minimize future demands for interviews.

Media days provide access to players in a more casual atmosphere.
Keith Birmingham/MediaNews Group/Pasadena Star-News via Getty Images

News conferences are similar to media days, but they are held regularly either to provide news media with scheduled access to the head coach and selected athletes, or to address major news events such as charges of violent conduct, season-ending injuries, or other emergencies. If a news conference is convened for a major news event, the organizational spokesperson or key executive-level staff person may need to be involved. The decision to hold a news conference depends on whether the information could be communicated in a news release or through other standard channels. Holding a news conference is time intensive and may not always result in positive coverage for the organization. There are also logistics to be considered.

News conferences can be held either on-site at the stadium or off-site at another location. On-site locations for news conferences allow for the organization to announce a conference quickly and to easily accommodate members of the media who are familiar with the stadium and location. Off-site news conferences are more difficult to organize, but a hotel presents a viable option for a news conference if a sport organization cannot accommodate the event due to its size, and hotels also can provide services such as food, parking, and a designated room to hold the conference.

From the organization's standpoint, it is important to schedule the news conference for major announcements as quickly as possible; keeping major, breaking information a secret is nearly impossible in today's digital environment. It is common practice to hold news conferences in the early afternoon so journalists and producers can make 5:00 p.m. broadcast news deadlines, and also to account for late writing deadlines the previous evening.

To formally notify the media of a news conference, a news advisory, which is similar to a news release but does not provide enough information to cover the story, is issued. Once the media have been formally notified of the date and time of the news conference, planning a news conference will involve the development of a press kit, room and setup considerations, and even teleconferencing elements. Press kits should be distributed to the media in advance; they should list the time of the press conference and identify who will be speaking to the media. Any background information on the spokesperson or individual addressing the media should also be included, such as title, any accomplishments, and correct spellings of names. Lastly, and especially since the 2020-21 COVID-19 pandemic, teleconferences have become a viable news conference delivery option if an in-person news conference cannot be conducted. Most people can join a teleconference through a phone or personal laptop computer, and the teleconference minimizes costs associated with travel or time zone differences.

For the sport PR staff, preparation for a news conference is similar to the preparation required for interview requests. Good PR representatives will prepare the spokesperson for potential lines of questioning and story angles based on their previous journalistic training. In terms of managing the sport public relations and news media relationship, ask yourself what information you would like or need to have as a sports journalist, and provide that information to the news media in advance. From an event planning point of view, which may be unfamiliar to you, again ask yourself how a well-run news conference should be conducted, and imitate that structure.

Time-Out

Let's examine the skills needed to be successful in sports journalism and sport public relations. Refer to the mechanics of writing a game story or opinion piece described in chapter 3, and consider additional skills from outside your journalistic training.

1. Write down the top 10 skills used in sports journalism on a daily basis. This can include research, story ideation, writing, and skills needed to communicate with people to produce a story.
2. Write down the top 10 skills used in sport public relations on a daily basis. This can include media preparation, event planning, writing, and skills needed to communicate with various publics and to develop relationships.
3. Identify how the skill sets of sports journalism and sport public relations overlap. You could visually map the skill sets and then draw connecting lines to similar functions or transferable skills.

Communicating to Key Publics Through Organizational Media

Working hand in hand with the news media is an essential function for sport public relations departments. There are also supplemental materials, produced without any involvement of the mass media, that are designed to secure positive coverage for the organization. These types of materials are referred to as **organizational media**, and while they are geared toward the news media, they are often made available to the key publics through various organizational channels (Smith, 2017). The two most-used pieces of organizational media are media guides and game notes. Other options include newsletters, programs, and brochures, as well as electronic organizational media such as video and audio.

Media Guides

Producing media guides is a key task for public relations professionals in sport organizations. They are usually published each year before the competitive season begins so that members of the media can have additional factual information about the organization and the team (Helitzer, 2000). In collegiate athletics, media guides may be published for each sport, making the production a time-intensive and potentially expensive process. Sport organizations should compare the costs of printed media guides with the potential cost savings of distributing them in electronic PDF format. Professional sport organizations and organizations with larger budgets will traditionally print their media guides, while smaller organizations will rely on electronic distribution.

The media guide strengthens the public relations–mass media relationship by reducing the amount of research sports journalists must conduct, making their job easier. Due to this mutually beneficial relationship, production of the media guide is significant, particularly the distribution to well-known journalists who regularly cover the team.

Media guides traditionally feature the following information (Stoldt et al., 2020):

- General information
- Team and event information
- Season reviews
- Historical information
- Governing body information

The general information includes staff contact information, media guidelines for press credentials and interview requests, organizational structure, and biographical information on high-ranking employees.

Information in the media guide about teams and events should include a roster of the players with name and numeric information, as well as profiles of the coaching staff and players. Season-specific information could also be outlined in a preview format and could contain information on opponents, storylines about rivalries, and background on opposing teams. A previous season review and historical information about the team may also be included, with the goal to being to strengthen the relationship between the news media and the sport organization.

The final section in a media guide traditionally includes information on a governing body, including historical facts about the league and its leaders. In professional sports, this is typically focused on leagues, such as the National Football League (NFL) or the Premier League (PL), while collegiate sport governing body information will include the conference and national associations such as the National Collegiate Athletic Association (NCAA). For international events, governing bodies could include organizations such as the International Olympic Committee (IOC).

To properly plan for the production of the media guide, one approach is to work backward from the date of publication. In addition to scheduling time to write the content, time is also needed to perform background research, interviews, and statistical updates from the previous season, and to obtain copyright permissions. Time is also needed for copyediting, review by key members of the organizations' staff, and print and digital layout. If an organization succeeds in making it to postseason competition, then a postseason media guide can be produced to supplement the information in the media guide.

The media guide contains a great deal of factual information about the sport organization and the team that could also have value for other key publics such as fans or advertisers. Taking advantage of economies of scale to reduce the per-unit cost of production, sport organizations may want to produce additional copies of media guides that they can then sell to key publics not in the media. Additional sources of revenue for the media guide include selling advertising space to local community organizations or allowing the media guide to be included as part of a season ticket package to incentivize sales.

Game Notes

Another important element of organizational communications is game notes or advances. Very similar to the media guide, game notes are previews of each upcoming game provided to members of the media in advance to help broadcast and news media organizations with coverage. Game notes include a header with the team logo, event information such as time, location, date, and stadium, and records for both the sport organization and opponents. Information for the media broadcasts will highlight the radio, television, and streaming information as well as commentator information and contact information for the sport organization. Game statistics are often included to help broadcast commentators, particularly the color commentator, to fill in gaps during breaks in play, such as win-loss records when leading at certain intervals or other facts that can be provided as bite-sized bits of information during broadcasts.

Newsletters, Programs, Schedule Cards, and Brochures

Newsletters can be very beneficial for sport public relations practitioners because they provide wide communication to a key public. Newsletters resemble magazines or newspapers, but they contain information that is produced solely by the organization for positive publicity. The frequency of newsletter publication (e.g., monthly, quarterly, semiannually, annually) is an organizational decision that may depend on the number of key publics, the organization's size and budget, and preferred delivery options. Newsletters can also have an internal or external focus. Internal newsletters address the organization's employees and alumni, and external newsletters address fans, community members, and sponsors.

Game programs are traditional organizational media that are produced for specific events on the days when they occur and are sold by the organization hosting the event. Traditionally, the game program contains information on both teams, such as lineups and rosters, plus one or two feature stories from players or coaches from the home organization. The game program is produced in-house by the public relations department, which handles all writing, editing, and design responsibilities. Game programs are important to fans; they can become collector's items and even gain in value for historically significant games.

Also specific to sport organizations are posters, schedule cards, and brochures. Posters and schedule cards are common at the collegiate sports level and are sport-specific, but they can also be as important as the game program to fans. The content of these items focuses on the season schedule, and they also offer sponsorship opportunities for local businesses to display their support, another relationship management tactic with a key public. Brochures are traditionally trifold pamphlets that can be produced in both print and digital versions and used for advertising purposes, such as for promoting youth camps, and they can be offered to key publics such as the local community.

Communicating to Key Publics Through Digital and Social Media

Communicating with the news media either directly or indirectly is still mainly done through traditional media channels, based largely on written content. In today's media environment, however, digital and social media have expanded the available channels. These channels offer new and creative opportunities for sports journalism students to translate their multimedia skills and training into careers in sport public relations.

The Internet has transformed the way organizations provide information and communicate with key publics. News organizations now use the sport organizations' websites to gather information for their reporting (Stoldt et al., 2020), which gives sport organizations more control over their messaging and provides a fundamental asset in the toolbox of public relations efforts. Digital content includes organizational media such as the website, blogs, podcasts, vlogs or video content, and digital communities that all enable communication with key publics, largely in a one-directional manner. Social media, while it also delivers content digitally, is typically considered a separate type of content because of its two-way nature.

Organizational Websites

The primary benefit of a website is that it can serve most key publics through a single platform; it provides

- global access to information,
- immediacy of information and content choices for users,
- a wide variety of content types,
- conversions for e-commerce and revenue generation,

- behavioral and demographic analysis,
- interactivity and connection, and
- adaptable and customizable features (Stoldt et al., 2020).

The website should be designed not only to meet organizational goals but also to meet the needs of key publics. For example, if your key public of fans wants frequently updated or new, interactive content, then you must design a website that enables the quick creation of this content.

Most professional sport organizations have access to a centralized, in-house website development team employed by their leagues (e.g., MLB Advanced Media, LP) to create a consistent look and feel for all websites (Stoldt et al., 2020). A properly designed, well-functioning website enhances the relationship between an organization and its key publics. On the other hand, a poorly designed website can have the opposite effect and can harm efforts to achieve the organization's public relations goals. Website design can take different approaches; minimalism, organization, conversion, mobile accessible, and efficiency of loading times are all valid considerations.

Providing key publics with various ways they can engage with the organization through the website—such as through community partnerships or volunteer efforts—helps maintain a strong connection, and it has been found that text facilitates a greater connection with an organization (Stoldt et al., 2020). Words on a page carry meaning, and with the correct tone and voice and with the ability to update information in real time, the website conveys authenticity and credibility while strengthening the loyalty of key publics.

There are specific ways in which an organizational website can be used to serve each key public. These key publics can include the news media, community organizations, consumers and fans, donors, and business partners and sponsors. In the creation of organizational public relations objectives, fans may take precedence because they are a potential source of direct revenue, but the mass media is one of the most important relationships for any sport organization due to their ability to generate continued awareness and interest from fans.

The most important thing a website can provide for the news media is information. Reporters need information from sport organizations to help them generate their coverage. To serve this need, websites can include repositories of information specifically designed for members of the media. For example, the National Football League has a communications website that includes schedules, standings, the most current rulebook, a fact book, and the latest news releases (NFL Communications, 2021). The type of media outlet will determine what form of information will be most useful in each case, but ultimately the public relations task is to identify the information they need, provide it in the forms they want, and make it accessible when they need it.

Information dissemination is not the only function a website can serve. Promotion is another key goal for the website. Promoting the sport organization's public service work and its partnerships with local organizations is vitally important for maintaining a good standing in the community. Entire sections of the website are often associated with this function, and they can be cross-linked with the promotion of charitable associations and the volunteer work of coaches and athletes, generating a wealth of positive publicity for the organization. For large sport organizations with global brand recognition or with speakers who are in high demand, the website can serve as a connection point for receiving charitable requests, directing users to charitable donation policies, and fielding requests for public appearances.

Another key public that can be served through the sport organization's website, but with a slightly different focus than community relations, is donors. Fundraising efforts are built on the establishment of long-term relationships, and the website can nurture these relationships through continued communications. Most donors are happy to provide funds, but they also want to know how their money is being spent, and this is a part of maintaining the relationship between the donor and the sport organization. The public relations department can produce a donor newsletter, disseminated by email, to provide monthly, quarterly, semiannual, or annual updates to donors about how their donated funds are being used. Donor newsletters with regular updates establish an open communication channel between the organization and donors, and they can also be highlighted on the website to generate positive publicity.

Videos, Blogs, and Podcasts

Video has become increasingly important as a standard content offering. The ability of websites to provide quick and easy access to video content and to stream live video increases the reach and visibility of this content with key publics. Video production can have significant costs, but the development of "backpack" journalism and the multimedia training sports journalism students receive nowadays makes this a viable option for sport organizations going forward.

Blogs are websites in and of themselves and can be implemented either from within or outside of the sport organization. Internal blogs can be used to provide key publics, such as former members of the news media or fans, the opportunity to connect with the organization. Chelsea FC, a football (soccer) organization based in the United Kingdom with a global fan base, has a website link to a blog called The Shed (The Shed, 2021), on which fans can contribute content around a number of different topics. External blogs, while a valuable form of community building for the organization, are not controlled by the public relations staff and thus are not subject to the organization's messaging strategy. However, monitoring such blogs, especially if they play a prominent role in an online community, can help the organization to gauge not only the quality of its content, but also consumer attitudes and opinions.

Along similar lines, podcasts are a rapidly growing addition to website content. Podcasts are audio files that can be downloaded or streamed from mobile devices and listened to from any location. From a production standpoint, podcasts can be recorded with a few microphones and can be edited with software available on most personal laptop computers. Internally produced podcasts from the organization can provide insider and behind-the-scenes access to players and others in the organization, engaging key publics in a more personalized way. Equally valuable are externally produced podcasts created by media outlets, big-name sports journalists, or social media influencers with preestablished followings, which generate additional interest and engagement at no cost to the sport organization.

Social media directors provide valuable content for organizations to use to interact with key publics.
Ethan Miller/Getty Images

Social Media

Sports journalists have adapted their practices to use social media platforms to increase awareness of news stories and organizational content and even to enhance their own personal brand reputations. How are these communication tools used with the same journalistic skill set in a sport public relations context? Social media networks provide sport organizations with a tool that facilitates information sharing and relationship management through two-way communication, effectively increasing the reach and engagement capabilities of the sport organization with key publics (Stoldt et al., 2020).

A key to the success of sport public relations practices on social media is understanding the **two-way symmetrical model of communication** (Grunig & Hunt, 1984). Two-way communication is built into social media platforms because fans and other key publics can interact with the sport organization through comments. This built-in functionality, when used for monitoring and engagement, allows the organization to identify and interact with key publics. They can solicit opinions in order to identify the issues that are relevant to key publics, and they can facilitate relationship building through continued dialogue and engagement. The speed at which information is generated and published on social media, combined with the need to produce content for news and organizational media functions, calls for a strategic social media management process that creates, schedules, analyzes, and engages with social media content (Cawley, 2021). This is where sports journalism students can use their professional skills to create social media content to achieve public relations objectives.

Sport organizational content on social media can take many forms, such as text, photos, videos, graphics, and more. It is important that it effectively engage a key public by promoting thought, emotional reactions, and action (Stoldt et al., 2020). These goals can be achieved through a day-to-day, strategic process of content creation on social media and should focus first on planning.

Although the daily news cycle of in-season competition dictates the content produced by sports journalists, the goal-oriented communications focus of sport public relations dictates that games are just one element to be considered when planning content. Additional considerations include both short-term and long-term communication objectives, as well as the organically occurring opportunities to engage with key publics on social media.

Planning content in the short term—days, weeks, or months—for social media can be dictated largely by the immediate nature of the platforms. Based on trending topics or themes, posts and content can be generated and uploaded to social media quickly with functional features such as hashtags or fan contests designed to facilitate awareness of short-term campaigns or to generate excitement for big games.

Long-term promotional objectives—spanning over a season or a calendar year—have a more strategic orientation, and this is when the sport organization's competitive calendar becomes an invaluable planning tool for social media content. Public relations practitioners can effectively build a social media calendar that maps to the competitive calendar. Planning can begin with the dates and times for competitive matches and then can be supplemented with promotional events, additional information, and stories that can be developed throughout the season.

A prime example of an opportunity to pursue long-term promotional objectives is the rivalry match, with promotional efforts and creative story lines helping to build anticipation and excitement mapped out in advance. Key player matchups within these rivalries can be highlighted, with other story ideas added as they occur. Thus, the calendar serves a brainstorming or storyboarding function to generate ideas while also providing a way to record all promotional efforts that can be tracked back to the goals and objectives.

There is no formal framework for building a social media planning calendar, and a number of software programs can be used to facilitate this process, but it should include all social media platforms the organization operates. For each platform, further tracking can include specific promotional elements such as content type (e.g., photo, video), subject of content (e.g., game or player promotion, training updates), and day of week and time of post (e.g., Monday morning, 7:00 a.m.). To further align content with organizational goals, metrics can also be included to link content with objectives for each key public, and the employees responsible for content can be listed. Additional content will need to be created to address unforeseen issues such as injuries or changes in game times, but a primary calendar is a great public relations tool to ensure that all efforts are strategic and implemented with goals in mind and not on an ad hoc basis.

Content planning should align with overall organizational objectives. If the organization has an overarching goal to increase revenue by increasing the number of season ticket holders, then social media content can be produced to highlight the benefits of season tickets. Not only will this public relations initiative increase awareness and hopefully improve perceptions of season ticket benefits, but with proper social media monitoring, this will also generate leads for the ticketing and marketing office. Organizational branding objectives can also be pursued through social media efforts. Every sport organization has a brand identity. While the marketing department generates this brand identity, the public relations department communicates it to key publics by positioning it in the mind of the consumer in a certain way.

Building on the concept of alignment and branding is the strategic consideration of voice and tone in content as it applies to brand identity. Everyone on the public relations team will have a preferred style of writing and tone, but it is important that they come to a consensus on the tone and voice of the branded content they produce, so that it not only provides stylistic consistency but also aligns with, supports, and promotes the brand identity of the organization. Without this alignment, content could appear haphazard, inconsistent, and ultimately ineffective in achieving the desired public relations outcomes. Balancing the need for consistent tone and voice is the need to preserve some flexibility in order to align with specific key publics in areas such as demographics and psychographics.

Demographics are related to the physical characteristics of people and include variables such as gender, age, location, household income, and sometimes educational level. Psychographics are somewhat subjective and harder to capture because they involve individual feelings or behaviors. They can provide insights into what people like or why they engage with certain content. In today's information-driven communications environment, tools to measure and report demographic and psychographic components are built into social media platforms in varying degrees.

The administrative access feature connected with a business Facebook account, which is different from an individual or personal Facebook account, provides an organization with demographic information through Facebook Insights. Facebook Insights contains information such as the age, gender, and geographic location, such as the city and country, of individuals following the page (Facebook for Business, 2021). Facebook Insights can also provide psychographic information such as when a post is viewed (i.e., time of day, day of week), the number of likes, comments, and shares (i.e., engagement), how long content is viewed if it is interactive (such as a video), and entry sources into the content (e.g., direct login, search engine redirect, link from other social media platforms).

Instagram analytics provide insights similar to those of Facebook, with information about when users are actively viewing page content and the time of day and day of week that garner the most audience engagement. Similarly, X provides analytical insights on demographic information, including gender and location, while age is not reported because it is not a required element when filling out a profile for the platform (Twitter Analytics, 2021). Further demographic analysis can be conducted by the organization using a survey sent to users to gather household income and education level. Psychographic information from X can be collected on different metrics, such as follower interests as derived from likes and retweets of data, and consumer purchases through links.

Obtaining demographic and psychographic information on key publics also facilitates the development of brand authenticity; the tone and voice of social media content should represent the perceived authentic image of the brand. Authenticity combines real and constructed attributes to characterize a brand (Beverland, 2005). Authenticity also refers to how genuine social media content appears to be because key publics tend to be skeptical about overt public relations tactics and selling strategies (Charlton & Cornwell, 2019). While it might seem beneficial to follow the trends of other sport organizations' social media posts, especially if they produce significant audience engagement in terms of likes, comments, and shares, the audience will not respond well if this feels inauthentic for your organization. In fact, posts that are overtly advertising-based or feel inauthentic to fans will elicit negative responses and potentially damage the relationship with your key publics.

Obtaining information about your key publics—particularly fans—will help you to build long-term relationships because you can gain a better understanding of their perception of the organization's identity. Transparency is key in situations where content is being communicated solely for business purposes, such as activating sponsorships or promotional efforts. Simply placing hashtags such as #ad or #sponsored tells the audience that this is a promotional message, which is acceptable practice in social media. If advertising is coming from the verified account of a player or coach, then it is even more important to be transparent about the message's promotional intent. (Verified accounts are those that have been validated with email and phone contact information to prove the identity of the organization; they carry an additional level of authenticity.)

To successfully create engaging social media content across various platforms and to coordinate these efforts throughout a sports season can be a daunting task. Sports journalism students are well versed in creating and delivering digital media content on multiple platforms. This is a skill set that makes a trained sports journalist an attractive asset to a sport organization's public relations department. Today's sports journalism students are formally trained not only in story generation but also potentially in graphic design and video production and editing, and they are often familiar with the software programs for producing and disseminating multimedia content.

For producing content, available software programs include Adobe Spark, a web-based version of the Adobe InDesign and Photoshop products. These are industry standard programs in advertising and public relations, as well as multimedia journalism, that allow for the creation of news releases, advertisements, infographics, social media graphics, and even videos through built-in templates. For content planning and delivery, sports journalism students may also be familiar with X-Pro (formally known as TweetDeck), a social media tool specific to X that allows for content creation across multiple accounts, as well as social monitoring of various accounts for direct mentions. X-Pro also allows users to schedule X posts in advance, saving time and energy on content creation. These are by no means representative of all of the software tools available to help you create social media content and monitor the results across channels, but they illustrate the capabilities that exist and that sports journalism students can apply in a sport public relations framework.

Public relations efforts on social media platforms are often criticized because they cannot be linked to a direct measurement of financial impact for the organization, known as return on investment (ROI). Social media analytics provided by Facebook, Instagram, and X can, however, provide metrics to assess the effectiveness of social media content. For example, categories such as activity, reach, engagement, acquisition, conversion, and retention (Seiter, 2015) can be used to measure the varied aspects of the content's impact.

- Activity can be measured by the amount and type (e.g., photo, video, infographic) of content produced across various platforms in a given time frame and then compared with the time required to produce the content to determine cost of production.
- Reach can be measured in terms of views, which are representative of individuals who see the content, while impressions represent individuals who could potentially view the content.
- Engagement refers to how individuals interact with content and can be measured in overall terms (e.g., the number of likes a post receives) or averaged across all followers of the network to return a percentage figure.
- Acquisition efforts relate to content that is designed to obtain new traffic and build new relationships with key publics. Increased acquisition demonstrates valuable return on public relations efforts. One key acquisition metric that can be measured is website acquisition channels—provided by Google Analytics—which outlines the various ways in which users enter a website. Social media content can be one channel to direct fans to the website.
- Conversion or conversion rate measures how often content contributes to an organizational action, such as a subscription, download, or sale.
- Retention metrics report satisfaction of users with content or experiences.

While digital and social media can provide a wealth of opportunities for additional channels of engagement with key publics, they have increased the need to monitor all channels outside the organization to ensure message control when possible. Additionally, with the advent of mobile devices that record high-quality audio and video, public relations practitioners must be aware of content that could prove damaging to their organizations. The bottom line is that technology has created a rapidly changing environment that provides new tools for public relations practitioners to engage with key publics. Keeping up to date on advances in technology will help public relations practitioners to stay at the forefront of new and innovative ways to engage with key publics and to maintain the relationships necessary to successful public relations.

Crisis Communications

At the beginning of the chapter we noted how **crisis communications** is the most well known and most high-profile form of public relations practice. When handled poorly, crisis situations can have a lasting impact on the brand and reputation of the sport organization. Thus, these situations carry great importance for the organization, but what distinguishes day-to-day incidents from a crisis?

Any organization will experience incidents during day-to-day operations. Sport organizations, with their added level of event planning, will often experience emergency situations, whether that be a player injury during practice, a fan requiring medical attention during a game, or even a venue-related security threat before an event. A crisis can also develop not as a result of an in-the-moment action, but from long-standing organizational practices that are suddenly made public in the news—revelations of organizational gender discrimination or sexual harassment, for example. A crisis is defined as an incident that seriously affects an organization's financial standing, reputation, or brand (Stoldt et al., 2020).

Preparing and Identifying Types of Crisis Plans

The potential damage to a brand or to an organization's reputation that can be wrought when a crisis is poorly handled calls for a crisis plan. An emergency plan, while necessary to address unforeseen events, is not the same as a crisis communications plan. The **crisis communications plan** offers a clear, directed, step-by-step plan of action for people to follow in a crisis situation. There are both internal plans and external plans.

- Internal crisis communication plans outline the roles of the individuals within the organization, communication lines directly above and below, and what actions to take.
- External crisis communications plans deal with the messaging strategy and who speaks on behalf of the organization, when, and in what format.

Crisis communications plans are not foolproof, and they are sometimes difficult to implement because events are often unforeseen. However, most crises arise not from spur-of-the-moment happenings, but from major issues in an industry that have been known for some time, such as corruption, player or coach misbehavior, or drug use, which makes it possible to plan for them.

When there are known areas where a crisis may occur, preventive measures can be taken. Possible issues within sports include security threats, natural disasters, construction issues, in-event incidents such as player or fan injuries and fan violence, off-field incidents such as legal problems, violations, or player scandals, personnel decisions such as player trades or coach firings, and other issues such as financial or political difficulties (Favorito, 2007). Each potential scenario can be evaluated based on its impact on the organization and the likelihood that it will occur and then planned for.

Because forecasting cannot cover all possible scenarios, an organization prepares for crises by developing an action plan that describes employee responsibilities and communications. This crisis plan then becomes a functional template for the organization to implement when something happens. Crises typically occur in three stages—precrisis, crisis, and postcrisis—and plans can therefore be divided accordingly.

The Crisis Communications Plan

There are several steps to developing a crisis communications plan.

1. The first step is to obtain senior leadership buy-in; otherwise you run the risk that others within the organization will see no value in the plan.
2. The second step is to identify key individuals for input because they will have the information needed to shape the plan.
3. The third step is to make the plan available to everyone so that they are informed about it and are aware of their roles and responsibilities.
4. The fourth step is to test the plan to identify potential omissions and to determine that it can be run smoothly if implemented.
5. The fifth step is to actually employ the crisis communications plan during a crisis. This does not occur often.

Steps in a Crisis Communication Plan

1. Obtain senior leadership buy-in.
2. Identify key individuals for input.
3. Make the plan available to internal staff.
4. Test the plan.
5. Employ the crisis communications plan.

If a crisis occurs, then the plan must be implemented as soon as possible. This is typically done by a senior member of the PR team, who then notifies management and puts the plan into action. The key issue is when to determine if an event reaches crisis status. One approach would be to let an issue sit within the news cycle for a day to see if it gains traction. The downside to this approach is that if a crisis warrants action after the first day, it is too late to implement the plan because the news is already in the media. Monitoring the news cycle can help to provide clarity about when to act on a crisis communications plan, but identifying a critical point in the cycle is challenging. In any case, once the crisis plan is implemented, the response team takes action.

The response team for a crisis communications plan will include public relations staff as well as members of senior management and possibly human resources, who possess valuable organizational knowledge. Internal communication is a high priority, and a call tree, which contains names, numbers, and organizational order, can be helpful to clearly outline the chain of communication. When external communications with the media are begun, they can take many forms, but most communication will come first through a news release or statement, and then through organizational channels such as the website or social media platforms. Initial statements will address the situation, express a willingness to provide additional information, and, when applicable, offer sympathies or condolences. Following a statement, an organizational spokesperson can address the media directly at a quickly arranged news conference. The spokesperson is typically not a member of the PR staff; there are many reasons for this, but the PR staff will have other responsibilities in the crisis plan, and another senior staff person would be perceived as more credible.

Managing a Crisis Situation

When managing a crisis, there are specific strategies that can be used, and choosing a strategy is a critical decision. This decision depends largely upon whether the crisis was a result of organizational action.

- *Denial posture* is traditionally used when the organization feels no responsibility and is accused of false or misleading actions. To combat this type of crisis situation, the organization can go on the attack and respond harshly to the allegations, they can deny the allegations, or they can place the blame elsewhere.
- *Diminishment strategy* is used when the organization faces an accident or something that was largely out of their control.
  - One approach in this scenario is an excuse-based strategy to minimize involvement with the crisis.
  - Another approach is a justification strategy to minimize perceived responsibility in the event there was damage or injury.
  - The rebuilding strategy is employed when the organization bears some responsibility for what is seen as a preventable crisis. In this situation, the approach is apology with acknowledgment of responsibility and compensation.
- *Bolstering strategy* occurs in conjunction with the other strategies to remind key publics of the past good that an organization has accomplished, to praise individuals for their continued support, and to illustrate how the organization has been affected as well.

Effective Communication

To communicate the organization's position during a crisis, key considerations include messaging, channels of dissemination, and how to deal with media requests for information.

- In order to effectively control the information during a crisis, key messages need to be identified and reiterated consistently. Key messages should be targeted toward the affected publics, not just the media, but they should also be presented in a way that can provide quotes for media coverage.
- The selected distribution channel or channels for key messages vary based on your goals. Personal communication carries the greatest impact but lacks speed, especially when dealing with breaking news. Having your designated spokesperson ready to address a crisis with follow-up live interviews available helps alleviate time constraints. The Internet can be a viable option to facilitate information dissemination, but it can make the organization appear cold or uncaring when faced with crises that involve injuries.
- The role of the mass media in a time of crisis cannot be downplayed because they can deliver information quickly and with credibility to key publics.

The final element, which is not always considered, is for an organization to formally state an end to a crisis because it brings definitive closure to an event.

Assessing a Crisis Response

It may be tempting to move on from a crisis after it has occurred, but the time for learning and reflection is immediately after a crisis. Key questions to ask to gauge the effectiveness of the crisis response include the following:

- Was the plan activated correctly and in a timely manner?
- Did the correct communication channels function as planned?
- Did we employ the correct mitigation strategy?
- How effective were the channels of communication?

Summary

In this chapter, we identified the need for public relations, identified the theory and principles that separate public relations from marketing and promotional efforts, and outlined various key functions of public relations in regard to social, digital, and news media. Finally, we addressed how crisis scenarios—the most visible area of public relations—can be planned for so that they do not become dangerous to the brand or reputation of the organization. Sports journalists should be able to see how their skills and abilities in journalism would translate effectively into the world of public relations.

Discussion Questions

1. What are the benefits of using social media platforms for sport organization public relations? What are the potential drawbacks?
2. How would you set about building and implementing a crisis communications plan? How many people would be involved? Should you develop different crisis communication plans based on perceived impact?

Applied Activity

In this exercise, you will develop a preliminary sport public relations campaign built around an upcoming rivalry game with another sport organization. For teams, select a prominent sports rivalry in any professional or collegiate sport of your choosing. Find the date and location of the game. Also, take the position of working for the sport organization hosting the rivalry match at their venue.

Identify the key pieces of news media, organizational media, and digital and social media that will be used to promote the rivalry. Additionally, outline the key publics intended for your content.

Working backward from the date of the competition, develop a tentative calendar for production and delivery of content. This should include various distribution channels across all platforms and take into consideration time for research and scheduling athlete and coach availability for content creation.

Create a news release highlighting a newsworthy element of the rivalry, as well as two pieces of digital and social media content to support the campaign.

Media Ethics and Law

Kelsey Slater, PhD
North Dakota State University

Chapter Objectives

After completing this chapter, you will be able to do the following:

- Understand basic ethical concepts and how they relate to the sport and journalism industries.
- Emphasize the value of ethical practices related to selecting sources, reporting, and framing of stories.
- Demonstrate the ethical issues sports journalists must confront when it comes to bias and relationships with sources.
- Describe best practices for dealing with ethical and legal issues in sports journalism.
- Recognize the laws that govern journalism as they relate to the sports media field.

In April 1992, former world number-one tennis player and three-time Grand Slam champion Arthur Ashe reluctantly held a press conference to announce that he had contracted the AIDS virus from a blood transfusion that he had received during heart surgery nine years before. Ashe would have preferred that his medical status remain private, and he only called a press conference after a reporter from *USA Today* asked for confirmation that he had contracted the disease.

While *USA Today* was only investigating a report that it had received, some questioned whether Ashe had a **right to privacy** related to his medical status or whether his position as a public, albeit retired, figure, combined with the prominence of the AIDS crisis at the time, made this story important information the public needed to know (Jones, 1992). While there is no direct mention of the right of privacy in the U.S. Constitution, there is judicial precedent that establishes a reasonable right to privacy when it comes to sensitive information like Ashe's medical status. The challenge for journalists is to determine if the information is of paramount public interest and whether that interest then outweighs the person's right to protect their information. Ashe's status as a public figure greatly weakened his argument against publishing information about his AIDS diagnosis and keeping his medical status private.

Although given that the report was true and that the constitutional right of the **freedom of the press** gave *USA Today* the legal right to publish, that does not guarantee that the choice was ethical. In the United States, the First Amendment to the U.S. Constitution guarantees an individual the right to free speech as well as recognizing the press's right to publicize and disseminate information. However, this right is not completely without limit, both legally and ethically. The question of whether to publish sensitive information like Ashe's AIDS diagnosis is not the only type of ethical or legal issue that sports journalists face, nor is it the only ethical or legal issue that is common to sports. In this chapter, we examine ethical and legal concepts that are fundamental to sports journalism.

Sport is a ubiquitous part of human culture, and when one examines sport, it is not difficult to find ethical controversy (Twietmeyer, 2019). For example, sport scholars and practitioners have long debated the ethics of athletes' use of performance-enhancing drugs (e.g., Devine, 2019; Lavin, 1987). While student journalists are taught the value of objectivity, it applies more to the quality of the reporting than to the subject matter of the reports. Placing value on objectivity in reporting is not the same as teaching student journalists to avoid taking a position on ethical issues.

On the issue of steroid use in sport, sports journalists do not avoid making value judgments on whether or not the use of performance-enhancing drugs harms sports or athletes. In fact, sports journalists debate this hot-button topic each year when members of the Baseball Writers' Association of

America (BBWAA) cast their ballots for entry into the Baseball Hall of Fame.

After 10 years on the ballot, seven-time National League MVP and career home run leader Barry Bonds failed to reach the 75 percent of all votes threshold for entrance into the Baseball Hall of Fame. While Bonds' résumé is comparable to those of other players who received entry into the prestigious and exclusive club, many believe that he was kept out because of his alleged steroid use during his Major League career (Bissada, 2022), despite never having tested positive for performance-enhancing drug use. In many cases, including deciding whether or not to vote for Bonds, some members of the BBWAA made the value judgment that PED use is harmful to the sport, and baseball players proven to have taken—or even suspected to have used—performance-enhancing drugs during their careers should be excluded from the Hall of Fame.

Understanding ethics is key for sports journalists because they are charged with navigating ethical controversies in sport, including steroid use, and they should be knowledgeable about these subjects so that they can accurately report their thoughts to the public. Sports journalists must also deal with ethical issues related to language, biases, and sources, as well as newer ethical issues that have arisen due to technology like social media. Sports journalists have the power to influence their audiences. Therefore, they must promote good ethical behavior that will not cause harm to subjects or to the audience (Weedon et al., 2018).

Defining Ethics

Ethics is a branch of philosophy that helps people to understand two main issues. The first is concerned with the concept of trying to understand what is "good." The second issue that ethics seeks to examine is the relationships and behaviors between people, and how people should treat others (Twietmeyer, 2019). Understanding what is good and how people should treat one another is a complex subject, and there are many schools of thought that try to explain how to determine what is truly good.

Utilitarianism

One school of ethical reasoning is **utilitarianism**, which is a consequentialist ethic. According to this school of thought, it is the outcome rather than the action that determines what is the good. For a utilitarian, the ends will justify the means (Twietmeyer, 2019). English philosopher Jeremy Bentham is considered the founder of utilitarianism, and he argued that humankind is governed by two masters: pleasure and pain. He believed that through maximizing pleasures and minimizing pain one could find the best outcome. Furthermore, Bentham placed no value judgment on individual actions or on the consequences of those actions. He argued the best way to determine the good is for people to seek to maximize pleasure for the greatest number of people.

> Now, pleasure is in itself a good: nay, even setting aside immunity from pain, the only good: pain is in itself an evil; and, indeed, without exception, the only evil; or else the words good and evil have no meaning. And this is alike true of every sort of pain, and of every sort of pleasure. It follows, therefore, immediately and incontestably, that there is no such thing as any sort of motive that is in itself a bad one. (Bentham, 1781, p. 83)

Therefore, from a utilitarian's perspective, there are no good or bad actions, only good or bad consequences. It is easy to see why many people follow this ethical philosophy because there is something intuitive about choosing to do good things because people want good results. However, this can become more complicated because it is often difficult to know the true consequences of specific actions until after the fact (Twietmeyer, 2019).

Thinking back to the first example, the reporters at *USA Today* who were following information on Ashe may not have realized the consequences of their investigation until it was too late. Revealing Ashe's status was not something that could be taken back; once any story is out in the world, it cannot be unshared. Considering the power of social media to spread information, that is even more true today than it was in 1992 when people first learned of Ashe's diagnosis. Following a consequentialist ethic could be dangerous for sports journalists. For example, one could use unethical practices to gather information and then justify those practices because the resulting stories led to an increase in readership or in social media following, which is a desirable outcome for many sports journalists. Although utilitarianism is a logical way to examine and quantify the good, it may not promote the best ethical practices for sports journalists.

Deontology

Another school of ethical reasoning is **deontology**, which unlike utilitarianism is not concerned with outcomes but rather with duties. A deontologist believes that duties or the rules guide how people ought to behave (Twietmeyer, 2019). Deontological ethics were promoted by 18th-century German philosopher Immanuel Kant, who argued that people have categorical duties that they are always obligated to follow, regardless of the outcome.

> So the action's moral value doesn't depend on whether what is aimed at in it is actually achieved, but solely on the principle of the will from which the action is done, irrespective of anything the faculty of desire may be aiming at. (Kant, 1785, p. 10)

As a result, Kant would argue that if people have an obligation or a duty to be honest, then it follows that one should always tell the truth without a concern for the consequences. While respecting duties or obligations makes logical sense, it is a challenge because rigid adherence to the rules without exception is often impractical in real life. For example, many people would consider it justifiable to tell a small lie in order to protect the feelings of a friend, even if being honest is a Kantian obligation (Twietmeyer, 2019).

Related to the *USA Today* inquiry into Ashe's medical status, deontologists would argue that *USA Today* had a duty to its readers not to withhold information—therefore, sharing the story was ethically good. However, deontology provides sports journalists with no option to use their own judgment to determine if sharing information that might have negative consequences is a real good.

Sports journalists may have additional challenges if they adhere to deontological ethics because the number of written ethical standards in the field is limited, and the standards that exist can differ between organizations (Kian et al., 2018). While encouraging people to fulfill their obligations to others seems like a sound way to understand the good and to guide ethical behavior, deontology may be too inflexible for sports journalists and may even prevent them from making decisions that are best for them, their readers, and their organizations.

Virtue Ethics

The final ethical philosophy that has implications for how people try to understand the good is **virtue ethics**. Greek philosopher Aristotle is often cited as the most important name in virtue ethics. Aristotle argued that good is not concerned with actions or outcomes; instead, people should be focused on *being* good. Aristotle claimed that being good has intrinsic value, meaning that people should not be good because it will lead to good results or will be good for them, but because goodness should be an intrinsic part of one's character (Twietmeyer, 2019). Aristotle recognized that being good is challenging, but that it is better to work at being good than to shy away from a virtuous life. He said, "the good has rightly been declared to be that at which all things aim" (Aristotle, 1999, p. 3).

Therefore, being good is something that requires constant practice. Just like in journalism, where it takes practice to become a good writer, or in softball, where it takes practice to become a great hitter, being good requires a constant effort. Critics of virtue ethics argue that being good creates an unreasonable standard that human beings cannot hope to attain. However, people do not hope for mediocrity, and sports teams do not start the year hoping to win only a quarter of their games. While striving to be good all the time is a challenge and one that may lead to failure, it does not mean that people should not try to be good even when it is difficult (Twietmeyer, 2019).

Was it ethical for *USA Today* to publish the story about Arthur Ashe?

Robin Platzer/Getty Images

Related to the Ashe example, did the journalist at *USA Today* strive to be good, or was there a greater concern for the outcome, that is, breaking a major story? Journalists have a responsibility to report the news, but they should be wary of reporting news that can cause irreparable harm. While most journalists and editors said that had they received the tip about Ashe's AIDS diagnosis, they also would have run with the story, others felt that Ashe deserved the right to cope with dying in private (Olesker, 1992).

Whether or not to reveal Ashe's medical status was a complex ethical dilemma for *USA Today*, and whether it should be considered good journalism is still debated. However, the Ashe case sheds light on the importance of ethical decision-making for journalists as they select and pursue stories (Laucella, 2009). Ultimately, virtue ethics can serve as a sound basis for helping sports journalists to practice ethical behavior. While it is challenging to continuously be good, there is value in striving to be good, and it should be a guiding impulse for sports journalists as they do their work.

Understanding these ethical theories can help sports journalists navigate the plethora of ethical issues that they will face during their careers. One major challenge for sports journalists is the lack of universal and practical ethical standards for the entire field (Kian et al., 2018). The Associated Press Sports Editors (APSE) maintains a short set of seven ethical guidelines, including issues related to the responsibility of a news organizations to pay for a journalist's travel, preventing conflicts of interest, and assigning stories to journalists based on merit rather than race or gender (Associated Press Sports Editors, n.d.). However, the most telling part of these guidelines is the last line, where the APSE states, "Guidelines can't cover everything. Use common sense and good judgment in applying these guidelines in adopting local codes" (Associated Press Sports Editors, n.d., para. 8).

Therefore, while the APSE does offer some guidance, they put the onus on individual sports journalists or their organizations to maintain and encourage good ethical behavior. The next section of this chapter examines how to deal with ethical dilemmas related directly to writing and how sports journalists handle issues such as framing and bias.

Ethics, Law, and Writing

In chapter 3, you learned about *how* to write a story as well as *what* to write about, and both of these important aspects of sports journalism have ethical implications. When it comes to *how* to write a story, two of the biggest ethical violations that a journalist can commit are **plagiarism** and **fabrication**. Not providing proper credit to a source or providing false information are never acceptable, and they can have significant legal implications.

Plagiarism and Intellectual Property

Unlike other ethical issues where gray areas may exist, journalists are obligated never to steal the work of another and to verify information before they release it to the public. The Society of Professional Journalists (SPJ) leaves no room for error in their assertion that journalists never plagiarize. "Whether inadvertent or deliberate, there is no excuse for plagiarism" (Bartlett, n.d., para. 6). In the light of all of the ethical theories previously discussed, there is universal acknowledgment that plagiarism is unethical. Not only does it break every rule of professional journalism and disregard the efforts of the author whose work was stolen, but it will also end badly for the plagiarist; the offense is easy to uncover, and the sports journalist will often be fired.

While it may seem like an obvious no-no that is hammered into journalism students in their classes and in university honor codes, plagiarism remains a problem in the sports journalism industry. Not

---

Time-Out

Select a national news outlet (e.g., *New York Times*, *Wall Street Journal*) and find their ethical standards or guidelines.

1. Examine the ethical guidelines. Determine what the outlet feels are the most important ethical principles for their writers.

2. Read the 10 most recent sports articles. From the articles, could you tell if the sports journalists followed the publication's ethical guidelines?

3. Based on your observation and examination of a national news outlet, develop a set of ethical guidelines for yourself and a set that could be used by your institution's newspaper. How do these sets of guidelines differ? In what ways are they the same?

Industry Profile

Gregg Twietmeyer

Gregg Twietmeyer

In 2002, Gregg Twietmeyer was working on a one-year contract as an assistant sport information director at Albion College, an NCAA Division III program, in Albion, Michigan. About halfway through his contract, it became clear that the opportunity to renew was unlikely, so he reached out to his former master's program adviser at the University of Michigan to discuss doctoral programs. This pivot in his career put Twietmeyer on the path to academia, where he now conducts research and teaches sport philosophy and sport ethics in the Sport Administration Division at Mississippi State University.

Sport philosophy and ethics are not the most common areas of emphasis for doctoral students in sport management, but ethical issues surround sports media and the sports industry. Dr. Twietmeyer credits his initial interest in sport ethics to a business ethics class he took for his master's program taught by Dr. Timothy Fort at Michigan. When he decided to pursue a doctoral degree, he knew he wanted to work on the humanities side of sport. His interest in sport philosophy continued to flourish through his doctoral studies, where he worked under Dr. Scott Kretchmar at Pennsylvania State University.

With 15 years of faculty experience under his belt, he has spoken at conferences all over the world, published numerous journal articles on sport philosophy, and written the book *Fundamentals of Sport Ethics*, which is used by countless sport management programs across the country. His work on sport ethics is guiding the next generation of sport professionals, and that includes budding sports journalists who will be faced with many ethical dilemmas during their careers.

Media ethics are particularly important for sports journalists, who must be trustworthy and accurate in their reporting and storytelling. "When the public loses trust, then society suffers," Twietmeyer said (personal correspondence, April 2024). "Because the facts—not just the issues/policy—become matters of debate."

This is explicitly linked to accuracy, as the public will lose trust in the media if they feel they are being fed propaganda or that the information they are receiving is inaccurate. "There is nothing wrong with opinion journalism per se, op-eds and editorial pieces have an important place," Twietmeyer said. "But when advocacy seeps into what is supposed to be a straight news piece, then accuracy suffers and trust disappears."

This leads to some of the biggest ethical challenges that face sports journalists today. Twietmeyer mentioned that media consolidation and league-owned media have created ethical changes for sports journalists. Twietmeyer expressed concern that consolidation of the media has limited the number of diverse voices and thus the diversity of topics that are discussed.

"Consolidation also leads to a corporate mindset that focuses on how media can generate revenue," Twietmeyer said. "Rather than having revenue support the mission of good journalism."

The macro issues that can affect journalistic integrity and independence are considerable threats to sports journalists. However, Twietmeyer also advises future sports journalists to be wary of potential conflicts of interest and to understand ethical practices for dealing with sources. While building positive relationships with sources is key to being a successful sports journalist, it is important not to be so close that you lose objectivity. Twietmeyer observes that friendships with sources can create situations where a journalist is acting as PR for the team rather than as an independent outlet.

"A baseball writer too close to an owner—as a key source—may simply parrot the ownership talking points," Twietmeyer said. Therefore, it is essential for sports journalists to understand the responsibilities they have both to their sources and to their readers.

properly citing sources is a common type of plagiarism that may not always be intentional. But there are also more egregious examples of plagiarism in modern sports journalism.

In 2014, Neil Harman, former tennis reporter for the *Times of London*, admitted to plagiarizing 52 different sources for the official Wimbledon yearbook. Harman stole writings from many prominent newspapers, including the *New York Times*, the *Guardian*, and *Sports Illustrated*, and passed off the works as his own within the Wimbledon publication (Soong, 2014).

Not only is the theft or misattribution of another's work inherently unethical, but it could violate laws regarding **intellectual property**. The sports industry has capitalized on the value of broadcasting rights, which stem from **copyright** laws (Hylton, 2011). Copyright protects the creator's or owner's exclusive legal right to copy, disseminate, and distribute their work. Major media organizations have paid billions of dollars for the broadcast rights for major sporting events like the Olympic Games and the FIFA World Cup, and therefore television broadcasts are not allowed outside of the official television or streaming feed (Kian et al., 2018). However, with current digital technology, fans can now live-blog and record and share video at sporting events in real time, which makes it easier to get around the rules. Sports journalists need to understand the guidelines for their particular context because some sport leagues and organizations have stringent policies about intellectual property.

Fabrication and Defamation

Although stealing the work of others is the ultimate unethical practice in sports journalism, fabricating stories, quotes, or sources is also unethical. The problem of misinformation is not limited to political reporting but has reached the world of sports as well (Curtis, 2017). The SPJ states that "Journalists should be honest and courageous in gathering, reporting and interpreting information" (Society of Professional Journalists, 2014). While it may seem to budding sports journalists that promoting honesty and providing true information to the public are an obvious necessity rather than an ethical dilemma, there are still examples of sports journalists fabricating information.

In 2011, Fox Sports claimed that there were multiple headlines across Chicago newspapers that were questioning the leadership of then Chicago Bears quarterback Jay Cutler. However, upon investigation, the *Chicago Tribune* found that the headlines Fox Sports used were entirely made up (Rosenthal, 2011). Fox Sports wanted to frame Jay Cutler in a certain way, and when the outlet could not find actual sources to back up this viewpoint, Fox Sports employees decided to make up some of their own in order to push their desired narrative.

NFL sideline reporter Charissa Thompson came under fire in 2023 after she admitted to fabricating reports during games when coaches were too late coming out after halftime or did not appear at all. Instead of saying nothing, she would attribute general statements like "we need to stop hurting ourselves" to coaches (Brito, 2023). After the backlash for her unethical claims, she walked back her statement, saying that when coaches did not provide quotations, she would use information based on her own personal observations and make sure not to attribute it to any individual coach or player (Church, 2023). Thompson's actions are a clear violation of the ethics of journalism and are a disservice to players, coaches, and fans, who rely on journalists to make accurate reports before, during, and after sporting events.

Not only is the fabrication of quotes and sources unethical, but it can also have legal repercussions for journalists in the form of defamation. **Defamation** is communication that harms the reputation of an individual. Defamatory statements can come in different forms, including libel and slander.

- **Libel** occurs when a false statement is made in a written form (e.g., blog, newspaper article, social media post) and harms the victim.
- **Slander** occurs when a false statement takes a verbal form (Bieber, 2022).

As in Ashe's case regarding privacy rights, the status of athletes as public figures raises the burden of proof in defamation cases. For public figures, not only must the statements be false and cause harm to the person's reputation, but it must also be proven that the defamation was done with malicious intent. Although defamation is difficult to prove in court, it has not stopped many athletes from claiming libel or slander against members of the media.

Brett Favre sued Shannon Sharpe, Pat McAfee, and Mississippi Auditor Shad White for defamation for making false statements about him related to the misuse of funds through the Temporary Assistance for Needy Families program, a program designed to help low-income families in Mississippi. The state of Mississippi claimed that up to $5 million of welfare money was improperly used for a volleyball area at the University of Southern Mississippi, Favre's alma mater, where his daughter was also a collegiate volleyball athlete. Favre ended his lawsuit with McAfee after McAfee apologized for his on-air statements, and a judge dismissed the case against Sharpe because using colorful language that is an obvious exaggeration is federally protected free speech regardless of the potential harm (Pettus, 2023). Sharpe's defense was based on the lack of malicious intent and the contention that he was exaggerating about Favre stealing from underprivileged families. However, the greatest defense against defamation is the truth, so just as sports journalists should avoid fabricating information, the truth also protects them from defaming teams, athletes, or coaches.

Ethics of Ignoring Information

Before examining ethical issues related to the work of sports journalists, let's take a look at the ethics surrounding what you don't write or prepare for air. We previously discussed the fact that members of the BBWAA make a value judgment each year on the use of performance-enhancing drugs in baseball when they are voting on which players to elect to the Hall of Fame. However, sports journalists who were covering baseball during what is now termed the "Steroid Era" have acknowledged that they knew about the likely prevalence of performance-enhancing drugs but chose not to investigate the issue. Even during the home run race between Mark McGwire and Sammy Sosa in 1998, when both big-league hitters were chasing Roger Maris' single season home run record, there was little to no mention of possible steroid use that was aiding players' ability to hit the ball out of the park (Jurkowitz, 2006; Strupp, 2006).

With the exclusion of players like home run king Bonds and seven-time Cy Young winner Roger Clemens, both accused of steroid use, from the Hall of Fame, it seems now that sports journalists are taking the ethical dilemma of steroids more seriously. But that may not make up for ignoring the issue for decades. Choosing to ignore an issue is making an ethical judgment. For sports journalists, it is important to remember that sometimes what you purposefully leave out or choose not to investigate is just as important as what you highlight.

Interviewing and Sources

In chapter 3 you learned about conducting interviews and how to integrate quotes into your story. As previously mentioned, quotes need to be clear and void of technical jargon that might confuse your audience. From an ethical standpoint it is also important to make sure that quotes you use are taken in the context that the source intended. When a journalist uses a quote, the audience has faith "that words portrayed as a direct quotation constitute not only a verbatim replication of the source's comments, but also faithfully represent the source's beliefs and attitudes" (McGlone, 2005, p. 520).

Therefore, it is unethical to take pieces of a quote or to use a quote out of context in order to frame your article a desired way or to achieve a particular goal through your story. Using quotes out of context may fit the ethical theory that some ends justify the means, but it is a poor example of being good by treating people the way you would want to be treated.

There are many examples of sports journalists purposefully taking quotes out of context. For example, in 2021, Golden State Warriors head coach Steve Kerr went on a podcast and mentioned that he had enjoyed the previous season, when the Warriors went 15-50, more than the 2018-19 season when the team went 57-20 and lost in the National Basketball Association (NBA) finals. Former NBC Sports Bay Area sports reporter Drew Shiller took that quote and cited the idea that former Warrior Kevin Durant was the reason for Kerr's feelings, even though Kerr never mentioned Durant as part of the challenges of the 2018-19 season. Kerr, who has a reputation for being one of the more media-friendly coaches in professional sports, was upset about the manipulation of his words and claimed that it was ethically wrong to use his quotes out of context (Traina, 2021).

Manipulating quotes to create a frame or to create controversy could fall into the category of fabrication, which we already discussed as unethical. However, it is clear that in the age of clickbait, more journalists succumb to the temptation to use quotes out of context, especially on social media, to get more eyes on their stories.

While it is important to explore methods to increase readership, it should not come at the cost of ethical behavior, especially with regard to a serious practice like fabrication or manipulating quotes. In fact, misquoting sources or deliberately taking their words out of context could also have harmful consequences for relationships with sources and access to sport organizations.

Sports journalists often rely on high-level access to athletes, coaches, and sport organizations to do their jobs. Therefore, compared to other desks in the newsroom, sports journalists are often more connected to their sources (Suggs, 2016). Sports journalists must find a balance as Anderson (2001) commented, "Sports journalists who wanted to gain and maintain professional credibility had to do so while sustaining a close relationship with the source of information" (p. 364). As many sports journalists cover a beat, including an individual sport, team, or organization, they become not only highly connected to their sources but also dependent on them (Rowe, 2005).

This can cause ethical dilemmas for journalists who want to maintain positive relationships with teams, athletes, and coaches but also want to provide unbiased reports. This can be especially challenging for sports journalists who write for more locally based papers and cover a high school beat. Researchers found that high school sports beat writers were more likely to favor hometown teams than professional sports beat writers. Perhaps this was due to the likelihood that high school beat writers have less experience and are more likely to be fans of the local team (Hardin & Zhong, 2010). However, it is not just high school sports reporters who are concerned about preserving relationships with their sources.

Think back to the example of the Steroid Era. Many sports journalists who were covering baseball during that time acknowledged that they had, at the bare minimum, a suspicion related to steroid use in baseball, but they chose not to pursue the story (Jurkowitz, 2006; Strupp, 2006). For some, it was the lack of hard evidence. But for others, they knew that if they angered the players they would be cut off from their sources, which would make it almost impossible for them to do the job (Jurkowitz, 2006).

There are also legal implications for sports journalists related to interviewing and sources. Journalists doing investigative work want to protect their confidential sources, and most states have **shield laws** that protect reporters from having to reveal confidential sources. Currently there is no federal shield law, and the amount of protection granted to journalists varies by state.

During the Steroid Era, *San Francisco Chronicle* reporters Mark Fainaru-Wada and Lance Williams were threatened with jail after they refused to reveal a confidential source for their investigative report on the Bay Area Laboratory Co-Operative (BALCO) steroids investigation. The reporters received confidential information about the federal grand jury testimony from defense attorney Troy Ellerman, and they refused to testify, citing their responsibility to their sources (Eliason, 2007). Ellerman later pled guilty, which led to the subpoena against Fainaru-Wada and Williams being dropped, but this case highlights the need for journalists to understand shield laws in their state and how they handle confidential sources.

Managing Bias

Bias is showing prejudice or favor to one person or group over another. Bias in the media can take many forms, and it is something that journalists need to be able to manage well to preserve good media ethics. While media bias is often connected to political journalism, it has ramifications for sports journalists as well. Before discussing some of the specific types of bias that sports journalists must manage, we will look at how readers perceive bias.

Reader and viewer perceptions of media bias can often be based largely on whether the story confirms those news consumers' preexisting viewpoints (Gentzkow & Shapiro, 2006). When applied to sports journalism, a column or game report's perceived quality or worthiness often has little to do with the information presented, but rather hinges on whether the reader or viewer likes what is being reported. For example, scholars found that fans of particular football teams view sports reporting as biased when their team is accused of wrongdoing, even if they find the news source credible (Mirer et al., 2018). Research has also shown that the source of a game report can influence perceptions, with the local reporter or outlet being more accepted by local fans than a report from an outlet based in the home of the opponent (Kim & Billings, 2017).

For sports reporters and outlets even in traditional media, trust can be built over a period of time,

---

Time-Out

1. Examine the shield laws or court-recognized privileges in your state. What challenges or protections do these laws offer? How might they affect the practice of journalism in your state?

2. Compare your state's shield laws with those of a neighboring state. What differences or similarities do you notice? Are there any surprising aspects?

3. Compare your state's shield laws to those of another country. What differences or similarities do you notice?

and the reader or viewer forms a relationship with the media outlet similar to one formed with a team. While fan perceptions of your reporting may be out of your control, there are types of biases that you must be aware of and manage well.

Racial Bias

The first type of bias that sports journalists must manage is racial bias. Sport leagues across the United States and the world have a diverse population of athletes (Lapchick, 2020). Therefore, in order to accurately portray different athletes, coaches, and executives, sports journalists must be aware of the language they use to report on them. Merullo et. al. (2019) examined more than 1,400 football sports broadcasts seeking evidence of individual broadcaster bias and found that White athletes were more commonly mentioned by their last names than non-White athletes. Also, White players in their examined sample were more often described in terms of intelligence and personality, while the broadcasters' terms for non-White athletes often included nods to their physical ability.

Similar results were found when examining intercollegiate basketball. Scholars found that Black athletes were more often described as successful due to their natural athletic abilities, compared to White players who were more often characterized as successful because of hard work (Eastman & Billings, 2001). These patterns are not uncommon in the research; Rada and Wulfemeyer (2005) also found that commentary about African American athletes concentrated on physical and natural ability, while commentary about White athletes mainly focused on their intelligence or hard work.

This presents an issue of media ethics, and of sports media ethics specifically, about how players from differing backgrounds are described. The three studies just mentioned are only a few of many that have identified this tendency for members of the sports media to describe athletes with a certain amount of racial bias. While this is not to say that sports media members are inherently prejudiced, it has also been proven that certain tropes have survived through the years, even in a field that prides itself on avoiding the appearance of impropriety. Although most research on how sports media frame athletes of different races examine basketball and football due to their high populations of diverse athletes, racial bias can be found in the coverage of countless sports. However, one of the most well-known and common occurrences of racial bias in sports is related to quarterbacks in the National Football League (NFL).

In the NFL, questions remain about whether Black quarterbacks are still perceived by coaches and scouts as not being at the same level as their White counterparts (Trotter, 2021). There have, in fact, been many cases at all levels of the sport where an African American quarterback has been encouraged by team personnel or scouts to switch positions to running back or defensive back. From 2015 to 2019, three of the five NFL Most Valuable Player award winners were quarterbacks who were African American. Yet, to illustrate how ingrained the bias has become, 2019 MVP Lamar Jackson, who had won the Heisman Trophy playing quarterback at the University of Louisville in 2016, was encouraged to switch positions for his professional career by the NFL TV analyst and Hall of Fame general manager Bill Polian.

Inevitably, the sources and power brokers who have such ideas often influence media members who cover the various franchises and leagues, not just in football, but in all sports at all levels. These race-based narratives thus find their way into the media ecosystem, and this creates an ethical dilemma in terms of providing fair coverage regardless of subjects' racial background.

> ### Time-Out
>
> Select a national sports broadcast for this exercise.
>
> 1. Select a few athletes—preferably starters or players who will get a large amount of playing time—who represent diverse backgrounds to focus on during the broadcast.
> 2. Listen to the commentary and write down words that the commentators use to describe your selected players (e.g., smart, physical, talented, hard-working, attractive)
> 3. Identify any trends that you noticed. Did the commentators have any tendencies related to the racial backgrounds of the players?

Gender Bias

Another way in which identity-based biases can manifest is in how gender affects sports coverage. While there have been advances in terms of an increase in the amount of women's sports airing on television, those advances have occurred in the wake of decades of media content that favored coverage of men's sports (Eastman & Billings, 2000).

Gender bias in sports reporting is often subject to **bias by omission** or **bias by story selection,** where female sports are either not covered at all or there are a relatively small number of female-focused stories written by a publication. Another common bias that is often associated with gender is **bias by placement**. An example for a traditional paper would be burying stories about women's sporting events below the fold or not giving them a major headline. In television or online media it might mean relegating headlines about women's sports to the bottom ticker or placing headlines off the outlet's main page.

Additional gender bias in sports journalism occurs with how female athletes are framed. Often they are sexualized or discussed based on their physical appearance rather than their athletic ability (Harris & Clayton, 2002; Ponterotto, 2014). This reinforces stereotypical gender roles and can also negatively affect how the public views female athletes and sports.

Another common frame that we see applied to female athletes is discussing them not for their individual merits but for their connection to prominent male athletes or celebrities. For example, professional soccer player Kealia Ohai, who previously played for the Houston Dash in the National Women's Soccer League, was traded in 2020 to the

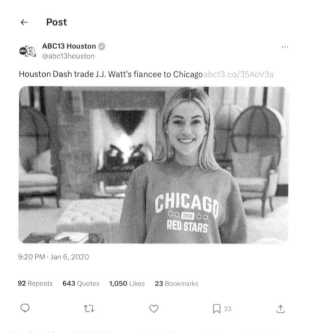

Reprinted from ABC 13 Houston [@abc13houston]. (January 6, 2020). https://twitter.com/abc13houston/status/1214386381180588032?s=12

Chicago Red Stars. Houston's ABC affiliate tweeted the news but instead of referring to Ohai by name or discussing her athletic achievements, they highlighted her connection to NFL star J.J. Watt; the post read, "Houston Dash trade J.J. Watt's fiancée to Chicago" (ABC13 Houston, 2020).

This is a problem because it gives the impression that the female athlete is only newsworthy because of the relationship to a male athlete. In this case, it wasn't a matter of having to fit the headline within Twitter's 280-character limit; it would have taken fewer characters to have the headline read, "Houston Dash trade Kealia Ohai to Chicago."

This was obviously a conscious choice made by the sports journalist to highlight Ohai's connection to then-fiancée and now husband Watt. The outlet may have written the headline this way because they believed that a story about Watt, who was playing for the Houston Texans at the time, was more likely to drive clicks and views to their website than a reference to Ohai by name. While this was not a fabricated statement—Ohai was Watt's fiancée—it definitely skirts the lines of ethics where journalists are manipulating frames in order to increase their social media presence.

Watt himself took to social media to call out Houston's ABC affiliate for their bias, calling the headline "trash" while encouraging journalists to "be better than this" (Watt, 2020). While this is just one example, there are countless female athletes who have been reduced to their connections to male athletes, coaches, and celebrities rather than written about for their own achievements.

The sports media have a large impact on the public's perception of athletes, sports, and leagues. Therefore, how sports journalists talk about female athletes and women's sports can greatly affect women's ability to make further strides in athletics. Combined with the growth of sport participation by women and girls around the world, the growth in television, streaming services, and social media has enhanced opportunities for the media to showcase female athletes. It may seem that female sports and athletes have been able to make big strides, but research shows that they have not come as far as many would suggest (Fink, 2013).

Discrimination

In addition to racial and gender bias in sports reporting, sports journalists may also face discrimination in the workplace. **Discrimination** is the unfair treatment of an individual or group based on personal characteristics such as gender identity, race, age, sexual identity, or ethnicity. It was only in 1978 that *Sports Illustrated*, on behalf of sports journalist Melissa Ludtke, sued the New York Yankees to allow female sportswriters access to locker rooms. The court ruled that the Yankees had violated Ludtke's guaranteed rights of equal protection under the 14th Amendment, particularly because Yankee Stadium was owned by the city of New York and was thus a state actor (Brennan, 1979). Although female sports journalists are now given the same locker room privileges as their male counterparts, there is still a wider discussion about equity within sports journalism.

There are concerns in the sports industry about discrimination, particularly related to gender and sexual identities as well as race, and the field of sports journalism is no different. In The Institute for Diversity and Ethics in Sport's "2021 Sports Media Racial and Gender Report Card: APSE," scholars found that there had been an improvement in the racial diversity of sports journalists, but both racial and gender disparities continued to exist (Lapchick, 2021).

Time-Out

Select a sports media outlet (e.g., ESPN, Fox Sports, *Sports Illustrated*)

1. Collect the 10 most recent stories on women's sports and the 10 most recent stories on men's sports.
2. Identify the gender of the author of each of the articles and make notes about trends related to the byline distribution.

In a study on Black sports journalists, researchers found that Black television sports journalists feel there is a lack of diverse perspectives within the media, hindering and often limiting the coverage of Black athletes. Hiring practices are limiting the number of minority voices, specifically Black voices, in the newsroom, with many Black sports journalists commenting that television stations will only hire one Black sports journalist (Hull et al., 2022). Potential discriminatory hiring practices have also been examined with regard to women. Previous research found that sports departments often struggled to retain female sports journalists, and this has created a lasting problem with a lack of diversity in the newsroom (Boczek et al., 2023; Hardin & Shain, 2005). In addition, because female sports journalists are more likely to cover women's sports, which are often considered less prestigious than men's sports, it may make it difficult for female sports journalists to rise in the ranks to cover the most significant beats or to become editors (Boczek et al., 2023).

Researchers examined association football (soccer) articles in German newspapers from 2006 to 2020 and found that women authors reported significantly more often on women's association football than on men's association football. Female authors were responsible for 49 percent of articles written about women's association football compared to only 8 percent of all articles written about association football (Boczek et al., 2023). This is not to suggest that sports journalists are inherently prejudiced against women and women's sports, but that gender bias and potential discrimination against female sports journalists still cause ethical and potential legal issues in the field that we must strive to correct.

Team-Run Media and Bias

Although many of the ethical issues that confront sports journalists involve bias related to racial or gender identity, there is also a bias that comes from the media source. As discussed in chapter 5, the rise of the Internet and social media changed the sports journalism landscape. One result was growth in the number of sport organizations that took control of their own messaging through team-owned and -operated media.

Managing team-operated media can mean maintaining a team's website or running a college's sports information department. But team-operated media can also include television networks like the Yankee Entertainment and Sports Network, whose largest shareholder is Yankee Global Enterprises, which owns the New York Yankees and also a 20 percent stake in the New York City FC Major League Soccer team. This can create complications for sports journalists in these organizations who must toe the line between their employers and their ethical responsibilities.

As the Internet grew in popularity as a place where fans could find information about their favorite sports and teams, sport organizations began to use the World Wide Web as a conduit to those fans. In the 1990s, this included posting statistics, player pages, and game results. As online technology advanced, teams began to incorporate video and written features on team and player activities. After years of traditional sports media dominance, teams were now developing their own content. As public interest and employment in traditional print media waned, teams and sport organizations found more

> **Time-Out**
>
> Select your favorite sports team or league. Find their official website and the major regional newspaper that covers this team.
>
> 1. Collect the 10 most recent stories on the team website, and then the 10 most recent stories about the team featured in the closest regional newspaper.
> 2. Make notes about the tone of the articles and the information in both sources.
> 3. Compare and contrast the similarities and differences presented by the news outlet and the team. Think about what you like and dislike about the articles.

trained journalists to hire who could create stories for their official sites.

In terms of media ethics, this presents some interesting challenges and potentially awkward situations. Even the best and most disciplined sport organization will sometimes experience an event that a team and its fan base might consider negative. Anything from a loss to an off-the-field incident would be fair game for a traditional media outlet or a blogger to cover. However, the reporter for Rivals.com's Tennessee Volunteers site would not cover the 2009 incident in which Vols players were arrested for armed robbery (Low, 2009), even though coverage of sport-related topics were appropriate and expected.

Fans now have had more than two decades of consuming and enjoying news from official online sites and social media feeds. These platforms offer the chance for fans to receive their news directly from the teams. Fans have also been able to discuss—and usually, defend—their favorite teams on platforms such as popular microblogging site X (formerly Twitter) (Brown & Billings, 2013). Yet many readers still find traditional media outlets to be worthy of their respect and attention. A study in 2018 found that consumers of sports news regard legacy media outlets as more respectable than their online official team counterparts, though the researchers also noted that this viewpoint may continue to evolve (Mirer et al., 2018).

From an ethical standpoint, employment that affiliated a journalist with a team—say, by hosting a radio show on a station owned by the local professional sport organization—was usually forbidden in the legacy sports media industry. Any kind of paid affiliation, or even accepting gifts from a team a journalist was covering, was looked down upon. Some news organizations even banned their beat reporters from accepting giveaways on promotional nights held by teams they were covering. So the opportunity for reporters to serve as official representatives and storytellers for individual teams has marked quite a change in media ethics.

However, while the skills used and the presentation format resemble traditional sports media, journalism practitioners who work for team websites are probably best compared to public relations practitioners. As Mirer et al. (2018) acknowledged, people may change their opinion on the role of team-run media in sport as it becomes a larger part of the sports journalism landscape.

Social Media and Ethics

Sports journalists often use social media to keep their followers up to date on current sports stories. Shortening the news cycle is one of the biggest effects social media has had on sports journalism, and this change has had a few ethical implications.

Before the Internet and social media, sports journalists had some time to think about their stories before they went off to press for the next day's edition. In most cases, they at least had a few hours before the package needed to be ready to go on air on television. Now with social media the news cycle is counted in the seconds it takes to send a tweet or post to Facebook, which gives sports journalists very little time to think before they post.

With this shortened news cycle comes additional pressure for sports journalists to break the story first before another writer has that chance. This has caused some lapses in judgment that breach good ethical principles.

The tragic passing of retired NBA star Kobe Bryant, his daughter, and seven others after a helicopter crash was first reported by gossip news site TMZ. The report was released so quickly that many on social media believed it could be a hoax. In their rush to publish, TMZ broadcast the report of the death of Bryant and the other victims before the authorities were able to contact the families (Tracy, 2020).

After the initial report rumors were rampant on social media and during ABC's broadcast of the NFL Pro Bowl, ABC News' Matt Gutman falsely reported that all of Bryant's children were killed in the crash. In addition, a social media rumor spread claiming that a former teammate of Bryant's, Rick Fox, also perished in the crash (Tracy, 2020). People all over social media, including journalists, were in such a rush to confirm the story and to provide details on the accident that they shared false stories before receiving confirmation.

Therefore, sports journalists have to ask themselves, how fast is too fast when dealing with sensitive information? Sports journalists rarely have to deal with releasing sensitive information like Bryant's helicopter crash, but it is important to know when not to rush information regardless of the topic.

Many players have mentioned that they first learned that they had been traded from scrolling through social media (Arnold, 2020). While players have expressed some irritation about this, sports journalists are just reporting on tips that they receive about team personnel. Ethics would only be a factor in these cases if sports journalists reported false information because they did not take the time or care to check their facts before rushing to publish it.

Another ethical issue that affects sports journalists is the abundance of false information that is reported online. Research shows that fake news on X will reach 1,500 people six times faster than truthful tweets. The researchers suggested that tweets containing false news often had more new information that users had not seen before, which was more likely to trigger an emotional response and result in more retweets (Langin, 2018). Therefore, if sports journalists rely on social media reports, they have to make sure that they check their sources thoroughly and report accurate information.

The immense pressure on sports journalists to report quickly, sometimes before they have the chance to confirm their facts, not only leaves them open to accidental fabrications, but also can hurt their credibility and cause them to lose their audience. Although social media have opened the door for sports journalists to connect with readers all over the world, they must take care not to let journalistic and ethical principles go out the window.

Sports Gambling and Ethics

Like steroids, the ethics of sports gambling has been debated many times over the years. Famously, Pete Rose received a lifetime ban from Major League Baseball in 1989 amid allegations that he bet on baseball games during his time as a player and a manager for the Cincinnati Reds. Just as Bonds and McGwire have been kept out of the Hall of Fame, Rose has also been excluded because of his misconduct (Reed, 2021).

Interestingly, while many fans of the game have labeled steroid users as cheaters, the public is typically not as harsh when it comes to the morality of gambling in sport. A survey of 1,000 Americans found that 64 percent believed that it is not immoral to bet on sports (Green, 2016). The perceived immorality of sports betting may have declined because it has become normalized as a hobby within U.S. culture (Petrotta, 2023). But what is ethical for the general population may not fit the standards for sports journalists, and the situation has only become more complicated as sports gambling has become more pervasive.

May 14, 2018, was a red-letter date for sports in the United States, and by extension, sports media. On that day, the U.S. Supreme Court struck down the Professional and Amateur Sports Protection Act, which effectively made gambling on sporting events illegal in every state except Nevada (Liptak & Draper, 2018). That ruling opened the door for exponential growth of the sports gambling industry. In just one month—October 2021—gamblers wagered more than $7 billion on sports (O'Brien & He, 2021).

Sports gambling in the United States is big business for sports leagues, teams, and media. Nearly every major national sports media outlet—ESPN, NBC, ABC, CBS, Turner Sports, *The Athletic*, *The Hockey News*, The Ringer, SB Nation—has partnered with at least one of the four major sports betting companies (O'Brien & He, 2021). In 2022, most sports news outlets, from TV networks like ESPN to newspapers like *USA Today* and others owned by Gannett, had sections on their websites that linked to gambling news.

The language of sports has always been infused with the language of gambling. From the very notion of the underdog to the NFL's weekly injury report to the popularity of March Madness and fantasy sports to the daily line of odds for every major sporting event on a newspaper's agate page, sports and gambling have always been intertwined (Moritz, 2022). The legalization merely removes the taboo. Instead of using euphemisms to describe gambling ("for amusement purposes only"), gambling news can be discussed openly.

But the rise in gambling creates some potential ethical quandaries for sports journalists. As a part of their job, reporters know information before it is made public—information such as player injuries, free-agent signings, players leaving the team, or coaches taking new jobs. This information could be useful to gamblers or could allow journalists to place bets themselves.

This would be the sports journalism version of insider trading, where journalists use information they learn and place a bet based on that information before reporting the news. This is especially dangerous because sports gambling is mostly conducted using mobile apps—the temptation to place a bet is literally at your fingertips.

Where things get interesting is that there are no regulations that address this. Unlike professional and college sports, where league and NCAA rules prohibit gambling by players, coaches, and other team personnel, there are no such industry-wide prohibitions in sports journalism. As we discussed at the beginning of this chapter, the codes of ethics—those of the SPJ and the APSE—are better seen as guidelines rather than rules the way that ethical codes are in law and medicine.

Also, there is no language in those other codes that directly addresses sports journalism and gambling. The SPJ's Code of Ethics urges reporters to "avoid conflicts of interest, real or perceived," and to "refuse gifts, favors, fees, free travel and special treatment, and avoid political and other outside activities that may compromise integrity or impartiality, or may damage" (Society of Professional Journalists, 2014), but that language is vague and open-ended.

In the APSE ethical guidelines, there is an entire paragraph about the sharing of notes and quotes, but nothing about betting with information reporters receive while doing their jobs (Associated Press Sports Editors, n.d.).

Beyond the insider trading aspect, gambling on a team they cover could also influence sports journalists' coverage in subtler ways. Take the following hypothetical example: A reporter is covering, say, the University of Houston football team. Houston is playing the University of Memphis and is favored to win the game by 17 points. The reporter, in this hypothetical, places a bet on Memphis to cover the spread (meaning Houston either loses or wins by fewer than 17 points).

Houston wins the game comfortably, but it keeps its starters in the game and scores a late touchdown to push the margin of victory to 20 points, meaning the reporter loses the bet.

If the reporter writes a story the next day that is critical of Houston's decision to leave the starters in the game, risking injury, was that story written from an honest journalism perspective? Or was it written because the reporter lost money on the game?

Interviews with sports journalists (Funt, 2021; Moritz, 2022) suggest that this kind of insider trading is frowned upon by those in the industry. The *Las Vegas Review-Journal* has a staff policy that prohibits reporters from gambling on teams they cover. Doing so, an editor was told, "compromises the integrity of your beat" (Moritz, 2022). The reason for this is that it creates a potential conflict of interest for a journalist's coverage. Reporters' work should be to inform the public, not to produce a direct financial benefit.

Sports journalists can participate in a family fantasy football league or in a March Madness Bracket Challenge with friends and still practice good ethical behavior. However, if you think there is a chance that your actions are creating a real or perceived conflict of interest, it is better to err on the side of caution and avoid betting on sports.

Workshop Ethical and Legal Dilemmas

You might be new to thinking about the ethical and legal ramifications of being a sports journalist. The following questions help you workshop various ethical and legal dilemmas. Read each scenario and then answer the questions. There's not necessarily a right or wrong answer.

1. As a sports journalist, you are eager to enhance a story's drama, so you include a fabricated quote from a star athlete. While this might make the story more engaging, it raises ethical concerns about journalistic integrity and the potential harm caused by spreading false information.
    - How can the sports journalist balance the need for an engaging story with the ethical responsibility to report accurate information?
    - What steps should be taken to verify quotes and information before publication?

2. A sports photographer captures a compelling image during a game and sells it to a news outlet without obtaining the necessary permissions from the sport league, violating copyright laws and potentially leading to legal consequences.
    - What measures should sports photographers and media outlets take to ensure they have the legal right to use and distribute sports-related images?

- Why are copyright laws important for protecting the intellectual property of others?

3. After receiving an anonymous tip, you publish an article, without sufficient evidence, that accuses a tennis coach of match-fixing. This not only damages the coach's reputation but also opens the door to legal action for defamation because you failed to adequately verify the source.
   - What ethical obligations do sports journalists have to verify the accuracy of potentially damaging information before publishing?
   - What steps should you take to verify information from different sources?
   - How can media organizations avoid legal repercussions while still uncovering and reporting on important stories?

4. A sports journalist who is also a die-hard fan of a particular team struggles to maintain objectivity when reporting on that team. The journalist often provides positive press to the favored team and downplays any negative qualities of the athletes on the team.
   - How can sports journalists manage their personal biases, especially when reporting on teams or athletes they support?
   - How do you balance the dual identities of being a fan and being a journalist?

5. A sports journalist convinces an athlete to share a personal story of hardship, promising to shed light on an important issue. However, the journalist exploits the athlete's vulnerability to sensationalize the story for personal financial gain, raising ethical questions about the treatment of sources in pursuit of a compelling narrative.
   - How can journalists ensure that the stories they tell are not exploiting the vulnerabilities of their sources?
   - What ethical guidelines should be established to protect sources and maintain the integrity of journalism?

6. A sports media outlet decides to cover only stories about men's professional sports leagues, ignoring female athletes. This compromises the outlet's journalistic integrity and transparency.
   - What responsibility do media outlets have to report about men's and women's sports?
   - What can journalists do to prevent gender bias, particularly the oversexualization of female athletes?

Summary

Ethics is the branch of philosophy that tries to help us understand what is the good and how people should treat each other. In sports, we can see ethical dilemmas all the time—steroid use, for instance—so it is not surprising that sports journalism has to address these ethical dilemmas. While there are limited ethical guidelines from major news organizations that offer some guidance on how to behave ethically, sports journalists are generally expected to understand the good and treat other people well.

Different ethical theories seek to answer the question about what is the good. Utilitarians are concerned with consequences; they contend that there are no good actions, only good outcomes. Deontologists argue that people are obligated by certain duties and must adhere to them regardless of the outcome. Virtue ethicists do not emphasize either good actions or good outcomes but rather argue that people should focus on *being* good. An understanding of ethics is important for sports journalists because it can help them to navigate complex issues that they will face throughout their careers.

Sports journalists must avoid ethical missteps in their writing. They must never commit plagiarism or fabrication. Stealing another's work or falsifying information, either intentionally or by accident, will never be ethical no matter what lens you look through, so it is important to act honestly when you write your stories. Not only are fabrication and plagiarism unethical, but they can also have important legal implications related to intellectual property and defamation.

Bias is another ethical issue that sports journalists must manage. They must be aware of how they portray athletes, coaches, and other sports personalities of different racial and gender identities. Racial and gender biases still find their way into sports journalism and broadcasts, which creates an ethical dilemma for journalists who aim to provide fair, just, and equitable coverage to teams and athletes regardless of race or gender. An awareness of areas where discrimination may occur is also important because women and people of color are often subjected to negative hiring practices within sports journalism. Ensuring a diversity of voices in the newsroom is important, and it is work that we can do together to grow the field in a positive way.

The rise of technology in connection with both sports gambling and social media have also created ethical challenges for sports journalists. Gambling has been entrenched within sports for years, but when sports gambling was made legal across the country in 2018 it became even more relevant for sports journalists. The biggest risk is that gambling can create conflicts of interest. Not only can sports journalists use their inside knowledge for monetary gain, but they may also become biased if the emotional effects of their gambling outcomes creep into their reporting.

The ethical impacts of social media are seen especially in the way they have shortened the news cycle. Sports journalists now more than ever feel the pressure to publish quickly, and that can create problems because there is less time to check facts before the story is posted online. This can lead to accidental fabrication, which is not only unethical but can also be harmful to a sports journalist's credibility.

In addition to the ethical challenges just described, there are also important legal ramifications for members of the sports media. Sports journalists must understand important laws regarding privacy, intellectual property, free speech, and reporter's privilege. Shield laws may vary by state, and different sport leagues may have different policies on infringement of intellectual property. Sports journalists are obligated to be educated in their specific contexts to avoid legal missteps.

Discussion Questions

1. Why should sports journalists care about ethics?
2. Should there be limits on freedom of the press?

Applied Activity

A prominent college football player, known for exceptional talent on the field, is caught in a controversy involving alleged academic misconduct. The athlete's academic records, including potential disciplinary actions, have become a subject of public interest. A sports journalist has been granted access to these records and is faced with the decision of whether to report on the player's academic troubles, potentially jeopardizing their academic and athletic career.

1. What ethical principles are at stake in this scenario? Consider issues such as privacy, the public's right to know, and the potential impact on the athlete's personal and professional life.
2. What legal considerations should the sports journalist take into account before reporting on the athlete's academic misconduct? Are there laws or regulations governing the disclosure of academic records?
3. How can the journalist balance the public's interest in knowing about the athlete's academic issues with the athlete's right to privacy? What factors should be considered in making this ethical decision?
4. Identify potential harms that may result from reporting on the athlete's academic misconduct. Consider the impact on the athlete's reputation, mental well-being, and future opportunities.
5. Are there alternative approaches the journalist could take that would still inform the public while minimizing harm to the athlete? What other angles or aspects of the story could be explored ethically?

Career Paths in Sports Journalism

Chapter Objectives

After completing this chapter, you will be able to do the following:

- Identify the traditional path of a sports journalism career.
- Describe the economic challenges facing the newspaper and journalism industries as a whole and sports journalism in particular and how those challenges have disrupted career paths for aspiring sports reporters.
- Understand the new potential career paths and opportunities that digital and social media are providing sports journalists.

In many ways, the career paths of sports journalists mimic those of professional baseball players. There is a defined hierarchy to pro baseball. Most players begin their careers at the lowest level of the minor leagues, either Rookie League or Single-A. As they get older and better, they progress through a team's system. The next step is High A, then Double-A, then Triple-A. Each stop is a bigger market, a little bit more like the major leagues. Finally, if a player is good enough, they earn the promotion to The Show. Stars like Mike Trout, Fernando Tatis Jr., Jacob deGrom, and Aaron Judge all spent at least some time in the minors. That time helped them develop as players and get used to the culture of pro baseball.

A similar theme traditionally runs through sports journalism. A young reporter fresh out of college gets a job at a small-town newspaper or television station. Often this means moving to a part of the country they've never lived in before. The job is mainly covering high school sports, with maybe some small-time college coverage included as circumstances allow.

Our young reporter works hard, follows the lessons they learned in journalism school, and learns some new ones in the field. They write good stories—in-depth features, maybe breaking some big news here or there—to earn a promotion to a slightly bigger market. Maybe this new job is covering college sports. Again, the reporter writes good stories, builds a file of clips (written and video; they must of course contribute to multiple media) of impressive work. Then they get promoted to a slightly bigger market. The cycle repeats itself, until they get the coveted job as a sports journalist at a major metropolitan newspaper or local television network affiliate's sports department. Then after years working there, they get promoted to columnist or anchor.

This is the path you see rhapsodized in many books on sports journalism and in books, stories, and interviews with sports reporters. And while it certainly remains a potential path, the economic realities of the industry in the digital and social media age have led to dramatic changes in the career paths available to sports journalists.

The truth is, there has never been just one career path in sports journalism. For every reporter who started out at a small paper and made it to the "big leagues," there are reporters who fell in love with small-town life and small-town journalism and didn't want to leave. Some sports journalists come from other areas of the industry. Shea Serrano, one of the most popular and successful sports writers of the 2010s who has published three *New York Times* bestsellers, started his career as a teacher who wrote freelance articles as a side job (Santos, 2017). Mina Kimes, a popular ESPN football host and writer, began her career as a financial journalist before her personal blog was noticed by ESPN.

There is no one career path for sports journalists. This chapter traces many of these paths and gives you an idea of what you can expect as you embark on your career.

The Traditional Path

Historically, journalism was not a career choice. As newspapers exploded in popularity at the turn of the 20th century (the era of yellow journalism), there were more than 500 reporters working at more than 30 papers in New York City alone. However, historian James McGrath Morris (2003) noted that most of them stayed on the job for only about five to seven years. "They saw it as a stepping-stone to a career in law, politics, or business, often through the contacts they made as reporters" (p. 108).

It was not until the middle of the 20th century that there was a growing professionalism in and around journalism as a whole and sports journalism in particular. That growing professionalism led to established career paths.

George Vecsey, a longtime *New York Times* reporter and columnist, got his job through his father, himself a journalist. Vecsey worked as a copy boy at the *New York Daily News* in the 1950s, taking stories from one physical section of the newspaper to another in the era of typewriters and engraved page proofs. "My father got jobs for me when copy-boy jobs were plentiful," he said (Vecsey, 1989, p. 289). But as the profession evolved technologically and professionally, career paths changed as well.

Typically, your first professional job as a sports journalist will not be covering one of the major pro sports. Some students do find jobs at metropolitan newspapers. Typically, these are clerk positions—low-level jobs that involve taking phone calls, collecting agate scores, and doing other clerical tasks. Even though these positions are at major newspapers in major markets, they don't typically provide young reporters with the chance to write under their own byline or do much in the way of original reporting. Vecsey (1989) writes,

> When an ambitious clerk at The Times asks how he or she can get ahead, I usually say, "Get the hell out of here. Go someplace where they'll let you write." ... Young people need clips. Six months of good clips at a local paper and you're halfway to a better job. (p. 289)

Like new broadcast journalists, who tend to begin their careers not in Top-25 Nielsen markets (the largest cities) but rather in stations in markets ranked in the high 100s or 200s of the Designated Market Area, newspaper sports journalists tend to find jobs in small towns, often far from where they would like to work. You go where the jobs are. This remains true, as Kian and his coauthors wrote in 2019:

> In reality, the majority of entry-level jobs available to most students are going to be lower-tier positions in less-than-ideal locations that pay less money than desired. There is nothing wrong with those jobs; in fact, that is where most people get their start. (pp. 44-45).

Starting at a small paper on a smaller beat is not just the way it's always been done. It is considered invaluable experience for sports journalists. Christopher Walsh wrote in 2006,

> It may also be the best training available. This is what they refer to as "paying your dues," and pretty much everyone must and should do it for at least two years. Nothing frustrates me more than hearing a young writer say, 'I don't want to cover high schools.' That person doesn't want to know how to be a good sports reporter. What you do as a high school writer is often the basis for the rest of your career. (p. 34)

On the traditional path, journalists get a chance to work on their reporting skills in a professional setting away from the bright lights of the big city. All of the skills students learned in the earlier chapters of this book—writing on a deadline, understanding news judgment, posting content online, using social media as a reporting and community-building tool, building relationships, interacting with sources and readers—are honed when you are working at a small newspaper.

Jerry Nicco, a longtime sports editor, told Steve Wilstein for the *AP Sports Writing Handbook* (2001),

> "Some of these kids just flat-out aren't ready to work (at a large paper). They need to work at a smaller paper, get their clips, make their errors, if you will. It's sort of like being a kid out of high school and going to major league baseball. That's a big jump ... they should go where they can write every day and learn how to put a newspaper out. Where they have to do some editing and be responsible for making sure phone calls are taken and prep results are getting in the paper. Somewhere where they can get the sensitivity to a community, where when they write something people read it and care ... so I tell students not to be afraid to aim a little bit small because you'll get more opportunities." (pp. 186-187).

Industry Profile

Mike Vaccaro

Mike Vaccaro

In 2002, Mike Vaccaro became a columnist for the *New York Post*. It was a job 14 years in the making. Vaccaro, who has been named the New York Sports Writer of the Year by the National Sports Media Association, took the traditional sports journalism career path. He started as an intern at the Olean (NY) *Times Herald* in 1988, eventually taking a job as a news reporter there in 1989 before moving to the sports desk for two years. He spent 18 months at the *Northwest Arkansas Times* and four years at the Middletown (NY) *Times-Herald Record* before taking a job at the *Kansas City Star*. He returned to the New York area in 1998 as a columnist for the Newark (NJ) *Star-Ledger* before being hired by the *Post*.

Vaccaro draws a direct line between those years in upstate New York and northwest Arkansas and his success in New York City.

"I don't think I'd be nearly as good at the job as I am now because my 20s were almost entirely spent getting reps, learning fundamentals, getting good at the very basics of the job—reporting, news gathering, factual writing," Vaccaro said in an email interview. "You had no choice. Also I think spending time in smaller environments allows you the opportunity to spread your wings—I started writing columns for a real newspaper at age 22. I wasn't yet a columnist by any means but by the time I truly became a full-time columnist, at 32, I had 10 full years of reps to help me develop my voice, my style and my value system as a columnist. No way you get to do that if you are "lucky" enough to get a job at the New York Post as a clerk at age 24."

Vaccaro's first professional sports journalism job was covering St. Bonaventure basketball and high school sports. He also covered high schools in Arkansas and Middletown, and the experience helps him to this day.

"One skillset I developed early out of necessity because there were always six high school results coming in at the same time was speed," Vaccaro said. "And I have retained that. I am probably the fastest writer I know on deadline (honestly not a humblebrag; ask anyone about me and that's what they'll tell you). I also think I have a better rapport with my editors because working at smaller papers I spent time on that end of the phone call and realize there is no vast conspiracy among editors to make writers' lives miserable."

Vaccaro moved up through the sports journalism ranks relatively quickly—from entry level to columnist in the nation's largest market—thanks to prodigious talents and what he deemed a maniacal work ethic and ambition.

"In retrospect I wish I would have been able to enjoy those years more than I did, but I'll own the fact that from the moment I arrived there I had my eye on my next job." said. "It was something that really stayed with me until the day I arrived at the Post."

But Vaccaro said that the traditional career path is useful, and that time at a small market newspaper is invaluable for young reporters.

"You learn basics," Vaccaro said. "You learn fundamentals. You also learn to appreciate the trappings available to you when you do reach higher planes. I still laugh when guys in press boxes bitch about the quality of the wireless. I remember begging a dozen gas station attendants to stay open so I could use their pay phones and struggle with plastic couplers in order to file a high school soccer game in the rain (and yes, it was always raining). I wouldn't swap my path with anyone else's even if you go back to 1993 and tell 26-year-old me that because I know that dumbass kid would tell you I'm lying."

As young reporters improve and create a **portfolio** of **clips** (a collection of their best stories), there will be chances for advancement to larger markets and bigger beats. Often, this first jump will be to a small city, a Division I college town, or a suburb of a major metropolitan paper. The reporter's beat will depend on the market, but as a journalist moves up the market ladder, they tend to cover higher-profile sports. Traditionally, every few years, reporters who want to move on and who are good enough move up to a bigger beat or a bigger market. The role of columnist traditionally goes to veteran reporters who have proven themselves as exceptional journalists. It's as much a reward for a job well done as it is a professional opportunity.

There is a lot of value to the traditional path. But it can also be challenging. These jobs don't traditionally pay very well, and while the pay scale in sports journalism has always been top heavy (the big stars make big money, most journalists make a living), the student loan crisis of the 2020s can make it difficult for students to take an extremely low-paying job even in their field of choice. Moving to small towns can be especially challenging for women and BIPOC journalists.

And while the traditional path certainly still exists, it is running head first into the economic realities of the newspaper industries.

The Economics of Sports Journalism

In looking at the state of sports journalism and the career paths available, it's important to understand a little about the economics of the journalism industry and of sports journalism in particular. We're not asking you to become economists. But this section will help you understand how newspapers make money and the state of the industry throughout the early 2000s.

Since the age of the **penny press** (the 1830s and 1840s), newspapers in the United States have relied primarily on advertising to cover costs and make money. This practice continued through the Industrial Age and throughout much of the 20th century. The reliance on advertising for revenues is one of the reasons sports journalism became such an important part of the newspaper—newspapers needed to capture and hold onto an audience, and that audience's attention could then be sold to advertisers.

For decades throughout the 20th century, newspapers were incredibly valuable and popular. Daily circulation was high and virtually steady. Between 1964 and 1992, the daily circulation of all newspapers in the United States was above 60 million copies, peaking in 1984 with a daily circulation of more than 63 million (Pew Research Center, 2023a).

That started to change in the 1990s. Starting in 1991 and running through 2022, total newspaper circulation in the United States dropped every single year (Pew Research Center, 2023a). Some years, the drops were relatively insignificant—in the tens or hundreds of thousands, fluctuations that were not out of line with previous years. But the drop was steady, year to year. Starting in the mid-2000s, the circulation drops became larger each year. The availability of free news online—both local and national news—led to a drop of print circulation for virtually all newspapers. By 2022, daily circulation of U.S. newspapers stood at 20.9 million—a 67 percent drop from the peak in 1984. Even taking into account digital readership, daily newspaper circulation dropped 8 percent in 2022 alone.

Newspaper online readership grew throughout the 2000s as organizations began pivoting their practices from being print based to being more digital. By 2018, newspaper online readership numbers increased 6 percent daily and 8 percent on Sundays—but that growth has been fueled by

The Original Sin of Online Journalism

Could newspapers have saved themselves? There is a persistent idea in the journalism world of newspapers' "original sin" in digital news. This is the idea that newspapers should never have published their digital editions for free. Because newspapers did this, readers were conditioned to believe that news should be free online, and they became resistant to the idea of paying for news and for journalism—which, in turn, has led to the industry's economic woes.

It's a theory that sounds and feels right. But it's one that veteran online journalist Steve Yelvington described succinctly and somewhat colorfully: "This is bullsh*t." Yelvington (2015) noted that newspapers were online before the World Wide Web, and they unsuccessfully tried to charge for the news. Once the Web came around in the mid-1990s, newspapers fought to maintain their dominance rather than embracing the new platforms.

"While newspapers were moving at the speed of newspapers, everybody else was creating the Internet," Yelvington wrote. "People with big ideas were creating big things, people with little ideas were creating little things, and people with no ideas were complaining about the Internet."

readership at major national newspapers like the *New York Times*, the *Wall Street Journal*, and the *Washington Post* (Pew Research Center, 2023b).

The falling circulation led to consistent drops in advertising revenue, and the recession of 2008 exacerbated the situation. Newspaper print ad revenue peaked in 2006 at $49 billion. By 2010, the industry's print ad revenue had fallen by nearly half ($25 billion). By 2022, newspapers were making just $9.7 billion in ad revenue, and since 2020, newspapers were making more revenue from circulation than advertising for the first time in modern history. Digital advertising at newspapers was increasing, accounting for 48 percent of the industry's revenues in 2022. The conundrum newspapers face is that the digital money coming in is significantly less than print revenue, which means that the digital gains are not making up for the print losses. The saying in the news business is that newspapers are trading print dollars for digital dimes.

Why does this matter to you?

Go back to our first lesson in this section. Newspapers have traditionally been funded by advertising. Advertising revenues are the economic engine that fuels journalism. As circulation numbers have plummeted, ad revenues have plummeted because when fewer people are reading the newspaper, it can't charge as much for advertising (this is the basic economic law of supply and demand at work).

With print advertising revenue plummeting, and digital ad revenue rising but not coming close to offsetting those losses, newspapers simply aren't making money like they used to. The result of these economic problems has been job losses. These job losses came in the form of **layoffs** (someone loses their job for financial reasons, rather than performance), **buyouts** (when a person receives a financial incentive to leave a job voluntarily), or **attrition** (when a person leaves a job and that position is not filled). Neither the Associated Press Sports Editors nor the National Sports Journalism Center at Indiana University was able to report any specific number of sports journalists who had lost their jobs. However, no area of the newsroom has been untouched.

Between 2004 and 2018, the number of newsroom jobs (reporters and editors) fell by 47 percent in the United States. Which means there are only about half as many jobs in newspaper journalism as there were barely 20 years ago.

One of the consequences of these job losses has been a reduction in coverage of some sports. Smaller sports departments have forced sports editors to cut coverage of some sports or teams that are less popular or less successful than other teams in the market (Antonen, 2009; Hardin, 2010; Klein, 2009; Petchesky, 2012a). This may be as drastic as cutting coverage altogether (where a team no longer has a beat reporter dedicated to it), or more measured steps, such as not traveling to all road games during a long professional season. One editor told *Deadspin*, "Like all news organizations, we try to get the biggest bang for our limited dollars" (Petchesky, 2012a).

What does that mean for our discussion? It means the traditional career path we described at the top of the chapter has been disrupted. Those small-town jobs that have been the starting point for so many sports journalists, that Christopher Walsh and Jerry Nico and George Vecsey wrote are so critically important for young reporters? They may not exist anymore. Or they may exist, but newsrooms are so small that those young reporters don't get the chance to write the stories that can get them noticed. Or there are no veteran

Scarcity to Abundance

What is the greatest change in media in our lifetime? If you're like a lot of people, you probably think "the Internet" or the move to more digital technology. But Vin Crosbie, a media consultant and professor at Syracuse University, sees that as a myopic point of view that misses the big picture.

"The greatest change in the history of media is that, within the span of a single human generation, *people's access to information has shifted from relative scarcity to surplus, even surfeit.*" Crosbie wrote in 2010 (italics original).

Think of this from a sports perspective. As late as the 1990s, sports news was limited to what was printed in the sports section of the daily newspaper, the news and features in magazines like *Sports Illustrated*, the highlights on ESPN, and local sportscasts. In the 2020s, you can get live updates of virtually any sporting event in the world, along with instant news updates delivered to your pocket by your phone. Sports news, like all media, has gone from an age of relative scarcity to absolute abundance.

reporters left at the paper to provide these young reporters with guidance.

Even if those small-town jobs are there, the jobs at the next level may not be there anymore. A young journalist may be able to get a job at a small-town newspaper to start their career, but the jobs at slightly larger newspapers (the ones in college towns or mid-sized markets) are disappearing as well. To extend the baseball analogy from the start of this chapter, there may jobs at the High-A level but not at the Double-A and Triple-A levels that were the key to advancement.

All of this isn't meant to scare students away from a career as a sports journalist. However, it is important that students enter the profession with a clear-eyed understanding of the state of the industry. This is a challenging era for media, with the long transition from analog to digital media upending traditional business models. But sports news remains popular with audiences. Which

Industry Profile

Christian Gooden, St. Louis Post-Dispatch

Lynn Worthy

In 2018, Lynn Worthy suddenly found himself out of a job. He had spent the previous 13 years working as a full-time sports journalist, moving from newspapers in Lowell, Massachusetts, to Binghamton, New York, to Allentown, Pennsylvania, and finally to Salt Lake City, where he covered the University of Utah's athletic department.

But in May 2018, after a little more than a year in Utah, he was one of 30 employees laid off by the *Salt Lake Tribune*.

What did Worthy do?

Got back to work.

"I remained in Salt Lake City and freelanced for the local 247Sports.com website "UteZone.com" until I was hired by The Kansas City Star to cover the Kansas City Chiefs," Worthy said in an email interview. "My first season in Kansas City coincided with the first season Patrick Mahomes served as the team's starting quarterback."

At the end of that NFL season, Worthy switched beats at the *Star* and started covering the Kansas City Royals. In 2023, he took a job at the *St. Louis Post-Dispatch*, where he covers the St. Louis Cardinals.

"I'm certainly not oblivious to the fact that many view my current position as a destination job, but I honestly try to approach each job I've had similarly," Worthy said. "Changing the name of the organization you work for or the beat you cover shouldn't drastically change the way you approach the job in terms of dedication or professionalism. There are undoubtedly more people paying attention to Cardinals' coverage than when I covered high schools. I surely get more emails and more messages directed my way on social media. That doesn't change the principles behind what we aim to do with our coverage."

Worthy's life now revolves around the St. Louis Cardinals. By the time his first season on the beat began, he had spent more time at the team's spring training site in Jupiter, Florida, than he had at his new home in St. Louis. During the season, he's part of a team of reporters and columnists covering every detail of the Cardinals season, splitting up travel duties and covering 162 games in about 187 days.

When asked for his best piece of advice for new sports journalists, Worthy echoed what he did when he suddenly lost his job in Utah. Get to work.

"The biggest thing is just to get started," Worthy said. "Get your foot in the door. The first place you work may not be the place you ultimately want to end up, but it's an important venue for you to learn, gain experience, work with editors, work with other reporters and get the repetitions you will need. Even though you're covering sports, don't forget that you're writing about people. Human beings play the games, coach, manage, officiate and operate the organizations and teams. The human element of the stories we cover shouldn't be forgotten. Often the best sports stories are unique human stories that take place in a sports setting or with sports as the backdrop."

means there still need to be sports journalists delivering that news. And while digital media is hurting traditional industries like newspapers, it is also providing new opportunities for writers.

Online Opportunities

The traditional career paths in sports journalism almost always had a print target in mind. Whether that was a magazine like *Sports Illustrated*, a major newspaper like the *Washington Post* or the *New York Times*, or as a pro sports beat writer or columnist for a major metropolitan newspaper, career trajectories in sports journalism tended to focus on print products.

That, of course, has changed.

The rise of digital and social media has upended all aspects of sports journalism, including the traditional career path. Online media have opened new opportunities for all sports writers. This section of the chapter will discuss some of the career paths available to sports journalists in the world of digital media.

Writing On Your Own

It's easy to overlook, but one of the truly revolutionary ways digital and social media have transformed the world of sports writing is by giving anybody the tools to create and publish their own work. Blogging platforms and software are available online for free and give students an opportunity to practice their craft on their own time. Some of the platforms that can be used include the following:

- Substack
- Medium
- WordPress
- Tumblr

All four of these are among the free blogging platforms that are available online. Using them is fairly intuitive for any active Internet user, and they all serve the purpose of giving writers a place to write and publish their own work for free.

Time-Out

1. Pick one of the platforms listed here or another blogging platform that allows you to start for free.
2. Create an account and begin covering a team of your choice. It can be a pro or college team that you follow, or it can be a team that is local to you and allows you greater access.
3. Aim to post three times a week for three weeks, including one post each week of original reporting.

Online Sports Journalism

While writing on your own is a valuable way to improve your writing, where digital media has truly transformed the industry is in professional opportunities.

First off, a definition. When we discuss online sports journalism, we are not talking about legacy, traditional media outlets that have begun to publish digital editions. This is not about the *Kansas City Star* or the *Los Angeles Times* publishing online, or

A Warning About Working for Free

When looking for sports writing jobs online, there's a good chance you will find plenty of websites offering you the chance to write about sports for free. The implicit promise these sites make—and sometimes it is explicit—is that young writers will gain exposure and an audience for their work. That is the trade-off they offer. You won't be paid money for your work, but the exposure will make up for that.

Be very, very, very careful about writing for these sites. Many of these sites are making money for their owners off the free labor of young, hungry writers like you. There's an inherent unfairness in this. Also, these sites tend to focus on quick posts and the kind of digital churn that do not lend themselves to the types of stories that will get young writers good sports writing jobs. The promised exposure almost never comes.

There's nothing inherently wrong with writing for free, but it is always better to do it on your terms. At the very least, be very clear about why you're doing it, what you are getting from it, and who benefits from your work.

about the digital editions of *Sports Illustrated* or the *Sporting News*. We are using the definition used by the Pew Research Center (2023b), which defined **digital news sites** as news organizations that were born online without an analog antecedent. These grew steadily through the 2000s. A study of traffic at these sites, which included sports sites like 24/7 Sports, Bleacher Report, *Deadspin*, MaxPreps and SB Nation, showed that digital news sites averaged 27 million monthly unique visitors.

In many ways, digital media have opened doors for sports writers. In part, it's simply a numbers game. There are more websites that need stories, which means more opportunities for writers. Because these digital news sites had no analog component, they were unencumbered by the traditions of print newspapers. Because they were specialized—with MaxPreps, for example, focusing on high-school sports, and Rivals.com focusing solely on college recruiting—writers had a chance to specialize in their beats, their reporting, and their writing and to build followings to niche audiences. The growth of websites meant that younger writers had far more chances to cover professional teams and high-level college sports and to be columnists far earlier in their careers than they would have in the traditional newspaper career path.

But it's important to note that even digital journalism is not immune from the economic pressures that have plagued newspapers and other traditional outlets. Online giants like ESPN and the *Huffington Post* laid off large numbers of writers and staffers in the late 2010s and early 2020s. One of the main problems is digital ad revenue. In 2018, digital advertising revenues (in all media industries, not just news) stood at $109 billion (Barthel, 2019). The problem is that nearly half of that goes to just two companies—Facebook and Google.

Digital sports journalism began in earnest in the early days of the World Wide Web. By the early 2000s, as digital sports sites began to emerge and grow, many of them made headlines by hiring big-name sports journalists who had built successful careers in newspapers and TV. Jim Kelley, who covered the NHL for decades at the *Buffalo News*, joined Fox Sports online early in the digital sports era, one of the first high-profile journalists to leave newspapers for online journalism (Farber, 2010). Yahoo! Sports was one of the first major online sports news organizations that was not affiliated with a legacy media outlet, launching in 1997 and gaining prominence with the hiring of respected sports writers Dan Wetzel in 2003 and Adrian Wojnarowski in 2007.

Time-Out

Working in small groups, list five of the online sources each of you most often use to get sports news in a given day or week. Combine your lists and examine the types of sites used, looking for patterns. How many of the sites used are digitally native sites versus legacy media sites now published online? How many sites do you pay for content on?

The Sports Guy

One of the canonical examples of a sports journalist who found success and built a career online rather than moving online after a career on the traditional newspaper path is Bill Simmons. Long before he was the CEO of a company that Spotify purchased for nearly $200 million and called "the most prominent sports writer in America" by the *New York Times* (Mahler 2011), he was the Boston Sports Guy, writing blog posts for an America Online (AOL) site in his hometown.

Bill Simmons is a unique journalist who started his career online.

Kevin Winter/Getty Images

Simmons' career path is an Internet legend. He began his journalism career as a reporter covering high school sports at the *Boston Herald* but very quickly grew frustrated with the job and the lack of advancement opportunities. The traditional career path discussed at the start of this chapter is the very thing that frustrated Simmons. "The only…way to get a column back then was to go through this whole ridiculous minor-league-newspaper system and then kind of hope that other people died," he told the *New York Times Magazine* in 2011 (Mahler, 2011).

He left the *Herald* and, while working as a bartender and waiter in Boston, wrote blogs and columns for AOL Digital City Boston for $50 each. At the time, AOL was one of the largest and most prominent Internet service providers, and it ran Digital City sites in major metropolitan areas as sort of online hubs of news and information.

Simmons' writing was raw, uncensored, and unapologetically partisan. Unlike newspaper sports journalism, which had developed a veneer of professionalism and detached objectivity, Simmons embraced his fandom, his biases, and the Wild West nature of the Internet. The column that got him noticed by editors at ESPN was a running diary of the ESPY Awards that was irreverent at best, offensive at worst (Petchesky, 2012b). His audience grew to the point where he was offered some freelance assignments by ESPN for Page 2, then a section of the site that served as a catch-all home to sports writing that did not fit the traditional mold. One of Simmons' first columns at ESPN was headlined, "Is Roger Clemens the Anti-Christ?"

Simmons' success at ESPN—within a few years, he was one of the network's most popular personalities—demonstrated the viability of online sports writing that did not conform to the traditional notions of sports journalism. In 2005, Gawker Media (publisher of the popular and influential blog *Gawker*) began publishing *Deadspin*, a sports blog created and edited by Will Leitch. *Deadspin* proudly advertised itself as creating sports news "without access, favor or discretion."

In the online sports writing world, Simmons remained the biggest star. He was one of the first big names in media to see the potential value in podcasting. In conjunction with ESPN, he launched Grantland in 2011 as a stand-alone site that featured his work as well as a staff of writers he curated. After Simmons' contract with ESPN was not renewed following a high-profile controversy, Grantland was shut down in 2015. Simmons then launched The Ringer, a site that has become the home of some of the most popular writers and podcasts in the online world (including Serrano). In 2020, just about four years after Simmons launched the site, Spotify bought The Ringer for $196 million (Spangler, 2020).

Simmons' success paved the way for a new generation of writers who come from the world outside traditional sports reporting. Shea Serrano, a staff writer for The Ringer and three-time *New York Times* bestselling author, began his career as a middle school teacher. He began writing professionally in 2008 as a way to make extra money while his wife was pregnant. "I was just literally at home Googling 'work from home jobs.' Writer was one of them," he told *GQ* (Gayomali, 2015). Serrano wrote freelance stories for various weekly newspapers until one was noticed by an editor for Grantland. That led to some freelance work with the site before he was hired full-time by the site in 2015.

Mina Kimes, who joined ESPN in 2014 as a reporter and has since become one of the network's most popular and visible NFL analysts, did not come to the self-proclaimed Worldwide Leader in Sports from another newspaper or sports outlet. Kimes worked as an award-winning business journalist for *Forbes* and *Business Insider*. In 2014, she posted an essay about her Seattle Seahawks fandom on her personal Tumblr page, and it was picked up and published on *Slate* (Nguyen, 2020), which got her noticed by ESPN.

A major part of the online sports writing world is that it opens the door for new approaches and new points of view. Serrano is Mexican American, and Kimes is half Korean, and their success stands out in an industry that is known for its lack of gender, racial, and ethnic diversity. The analytics movement described in detail in chapter 4 emerged largely from writing in the online community.

Certainly, just because Simmons and others have had success is no guarantee their respective paths would work for every student. Simmons, Serrano, and Kimes are incredibly talented as writers and thinkers about sports, and they are incredibly hard workers. In many ways, Simmons was at the right place at the right time, combining the talent and attitude at a time when it felt new to readers.

Branded Journalism and Newsletters

The mid-2010s brought about a rise in what can be called **branded journalism**—journalism websites and organizations with the public face of a high-profile journalist. Examples of this include FiveThirtyEight.com, a data journalism project led by Nate Silver, a former blogger at the *New York Times* who gained fame for his election forecasts, and Vox.com, an explanatory journalism site led by Ezra Klein, formerly of the *Washington Post*. Bill Simmons' creation of Grantland and The Ringer are two sports examples.

The so-called era of branded journalism didn't last long. While Simmons, Silver, and Klein all founded their own sites, each of them quickly established identities and reputations that transcended their founders. By 2021, The Ringer, FiveThirtyEight and Vox were all well-established digital news outlets with editorial voices and cultures that are influenced by but also independent of their founders. They stand out for the work that the journalists there produce, not for their specific founders.

But the idea of following individual reporters—something aided by the rise of social media—led to the emergence of the personal newsletter in the late 2010s and early 2020s. Rather than create a blog at a specific website that readers have to visit, a **newsletter** follows the same format but is delivered via email to readers who opt in. Newsletters have been common in the marketing world for a long time, but they've grown in popularity among journalists thanks in large part to Substack.

Substack launched in 2017, giving writers not just a digital platform on which to easily build a newsletter but also a way to monetize it. Substack

Industry Profile

Lyndsey D'Arcangelo

Lyndsey D'Arcangelo

Lyndsey D'Arcangelo's first job in journalism set the tone for the rest of her career. Granted, the *Springville Journal*, a weekly newspaper in rural western New York, is markedly different from the national websites her byline appears in now. But in that first job in the early 2000s, one of her many responsibilities was to cover the Springfield varsity women's basketball team.

"As a women's sports writer who covers primarily basketball, the early experience I gained from working at the *Journal* was invaluable," D'Arcangelo said in an email interview.

D'Arcangelo—a veteran journalist and writer based in Buffalo, New York—spent nearly six years covering the WNBA for The Athletic.

"I can only speak for myself, but it was and has been a lot of fun," she said. "I got to write a lot of feature profiles on so many great athletes, and that's where I really shine. I also dove more into the analysis side of the game, which was an area that I didn't have much experience in. So I was able to really learn and grow from that."

As a freelance journalist, D'Arcangelo has written for sites such as Fast Company, The Ringer, The Guardian, and Huffington Post. She has written for the *NBA 2K25* video game, and she has written five books, including one about the national women's football league, written with Frankie de la Cretaz. D'Arcangelo said the freedom she has as a freelancer is the best part of her current job.

"No week is the same," she said. "I could have a radio spot one day, a podcast appearance on another, interviews with athletes mixed in, and a feature to write all in the same week."

The rise in digital sites, along with the surging popularity of women's sports, has been a boon to writers like D'Arcangelo.

"Media sites are different when it comes to content," D'Arcangelo said. "I liked being able to mix it up and try different things throughout my career. Similarly, for readers, I think it's fun to be able to go to different sites for different kinds of content. Now that women's sports are exploding, there's a lot more crossover."

D'Arcangelo said her best piece of advice for young journalists is that they be open to trying new things in their careers and that they realize that the real world provides the best education.

"Everything I've learned and my growth as a writer happened because of the road my career has taken, starting with the *Springville Journal*," she said. "To see where I started to where I am now is kind of surreal. These days, a lot of journalists have to be involved with some kind of content creation. But I believe it really does come down to the writing. If you can write well, you can write anything. And it will take you places you never imagined you could go."

newsletters can be read for free, but the platform also allows journalists to charge readers a subscription fee. This allows journalists to be their own boss and their own publisher, allowing them to create their own publications and easily earn a living from their content.

One of Substack's cofounders, Hamish McKenzie, likened this model of journalism to the penny press of the 1830s and 1840s, although Michael Socolow, an associate professor at the University of Maine, likened it more to the journalism that existed before the penny press when journalism was expensive and limited to those who could afford it (Socolow, 2020).

Whether or not newsletters prove to be simply something that was trendy around 2020 or a viable platform for journalists remains to be seen. But Substack lured many of the biggest names in journalism—including Glenn Greenwald, Matt Taibbi, Andrew Sullivan, and Matthew Yglesias (Friedersdorf, 2020). On the sports side, Henry Abbott started publishing his popular and well-respected basketball blog *True Hoop*, which he started in 2005, as a Substack newsletter (Bucholtz & Koo, 2019). Tyler Dunne, who spent years covering the NFL for newspapers and websites, launched *Go Long* as a Substack newsletter in 2019.

Substack is a free tool available to anybody. Paid subscriptions are not necessary—newsletters can be free to read and subscribe to. Student journalists and young journalists can create a newsletter of their own as a home for their writing, as a chance to practice their reporting and aggregation, or simply as a means of promoting their work.

The New Online Sports Journalism

The launch and meteoric growth of *The Athletic* in the late 2010s (Perez, 2020) was one of many examples of new online sports journalism sites. In many ways, these sites can be viewed as an unbundling of the sports section from the rest of the newspaper.

One of *The Athletic*'s defining features at its launch was a complete reliance on subscriptions and a total absence of advertising. It's one of several subscription-only sports journalism sites that began in the 2010s. DK Sports in Pittsburgh formed in 2011, and the *Boston Sports Journal* began in 2017. Newspapers have started charging for sports access as well, with the *Austin American-Statesman* launching a Texas sports–focused subscription site (Willens, 2018) and the national newspaper chain McClatchy experimenting with digital sports subscriptions in several markets (Moses, 2018). ESPN launched its own subscription-based streaming service, titled ESPN+, which charged $5 a month at launch but featured access to a wide variety of domestic and international live sporting events, plus ESPN's library of documentary films, as well as original programming and access to articles by some of the company's better-known long-form feature writers like Wright Thompson and Baxter Holmes. By the end of 2020, ESPN+ had more than 10 million subscribers.

What does all this mean for you? Sites like this provide more opportunities for both new and established sports journalists to find jobs.

Future-Proof Career Advice

OK. So enough talk about career paths and business models and all that. How can I get a job in sports journalism? That's what you're thinking right now, right? As this chapter has shown, there's not only one way to do it. And offering career advice in a changing field like media and journalism is a tricky thing in a textbook, because technology changes so quickly. With that in mind, here are our top five pieces of future-proof career advice. These are tips that will serve you well no matter what the newspaper industry and digital and social media look like in the years to come.

Treat People Well

Sports journalism is a small world, and your personal reputation is just as important as that of your work, so first and foremost, don't be a jerk. Don't burn bridges. Don't be needlessly antagonistic, especially on social media. Be professional with everyone you deal with—not just sources and people who can help you in your career. This is the most important advice, not just for your career but for life in general.

Act "As If"

If you've written one sports story in your life—whether it is in a class, for a student news organization, or for your blog—you are no longer an aspiring sports journalist. You are a sports journalist. You've done the thing. Approach every aspect of your work and your career as if you are already a sports journalist, rather than its being something you want to be when you are older. This mindset will help you develop a professional attitude and focus, which will help you stand out.

Develop Your Craft

Acting "as if" does not mean acting like you already know everything and can't get better. You should always be working to get better at the craft of reporting, writing, and storytelling. Solicit feedback from mentors, and listen to that feedback. Focus not on getting the next job but on getting better as a journalist. That doesn't guarantee advancement, but it helps. Follow Steve Martin's career advice: Be so good they can't ignore you.

Create a Portfolio and Keep It Updated

The only piece of technological advice we'll give, since this area changes so much, is create a simple online portfolio of your best work that is easy to update and easy to share. Make sure you update it often with new stories. It doesn't have to have any kind of fancy design to it. But it is an easy way to share your work with editors, and it is an incentive for you to continue to do good work so that you can have new stories there.

Say Yes to Opportunities

When presented with a new opportunity—a summer internship, a first job in a new city, an assignment covering an unfamiliar sport—make your default answer yes. Saying yes gives you the chance to meet new people, develop new skills, and get chances to do new things. This doesn't mean do every single thing to the detriment of your physical and mental health. Balance is important. But changing your default answer to yes rather than no or maybe will open doors for you to develop your craft and advance in your career.

Summary

This chapter has shown you the career paths available to sports journalists. It has traced the traditional path that young journalists take in their careers, from small town reporter to big-city columnist. It examined how the newspaper industry in general and the sports journalism industry specifically has been affected by the rise of digital and social media, and it has detailed the new opportunities that online media have provided to students and young reporters.

What this chapter has also demonstrated is that there is no single career path in sports journalism. It's not like baseball, where every player is seeking the same goal by the same path. There are countless roads available for young journalists to take in their careers.

Discussion Questions

1. What is the traditional career path for sports journalists? What are some of the advantages and disadvantages of this path?
2. This chapter details the economic challenges the newspaper industry has faced in the 2000s due to the emergence of digital and social media. Was there anything that the newspaper industry could have done to avoid this fate? Going forward, what can news organizations do to reverse the trends and improve their financial health?
3. What opportunities do digital and social media provide young journalists? Along the same lines, what pitfalls should young reporters avoid or be aware of?

Applied Activity

Imagine yourself 25 years from now. Your sports journalism career has gone according to script. You've got your dream job, the one you always wanted to have. And now, you've been invited back to your alma mater to speak to journalism students.

Write a speech that looks back at your imagined career. Describe the path you took to your dream job. Tell the students the skills you have developed to get this job, and what you have learned about journalism from your imagined career.

Your speech should be between 750 and 1,000 words, should draw from the lessons you have learned in this chapter, and should trace a career path that is at least somewhat realistic based on what you have read.

The Future of Sports Journalism

Chapter Objectives

After completing this chapter, you will be able to do the following:

- Discuss challenges facing sports journalism practitioners in the 21st century.
- Discuss the benefits and pitfalls of technological developments in media and how they affect sports journalism instruction and practice.
- Make informed predictions about the future of sports journalism.
- Describe sports journalism as a business that can at times be unpredictable.

During the 2022 FIFA Men's World Cup tournament in Qatar, longtime *Sports Illustrated* soccer and NCAA men's basketball reporter Grant Wahl passed away in the press box while covering the world's most popular sporting event. Wahl's fame among sports fans led to open and rampant speculation on social media about the manner of his passing. With discussion mostly occurring on Twitter (now known as X), fans pointed out that Wahl had been an outspoken critic of Qatar's various human rights violations (Scribner, 2022). Spurred by an emotional video posted online by Wahl's brother, Twitter users questioned whether Wahl had been the victim of foul play because of his criticism of Qatar's government. Eric Wahl soon recanted his original claim of possible criminality in his brother's passing (Shlendorio, 2022).

Wahl had also been an open supporter of COVID-19 vaccines, and his wife, Dr. Celine Gounder, is an infectious disease specialist who also supported the vaccines in television appearances (Hastings, 2023). Twitter users circulated a popular online conspiracy theory about COVID-19 vaccines, blaming Wahl's passing on his being vaccinated against COVID-19. When Gounder announced that postmortem examination revealed that Wahl had died of an aortic aneurysm, that did little to stem the deluge of posts that blamed nefarious causes without evidence or reason (Hastings, 2023).

Less than a month after Wahl's passing, Buffalo Bills defensive back Damar Hamlin collapsed on the field after making what looked like a routine tackle during a nationally televised *Monday Night Football* game (Stacy, 2023). Hamlin had medical care administered to him on the field, and the game was canceled as he was taken to the hospital. Video of his collapse circulated widely, with social media channels again animated by baseless speculation about a possible vaccine-related issue. Hamlin did not play again that season, and even after his brief public appearances to support his teammates in the postseason, some social media users still chose to speculate whether Hamlin had actually died and the NFL had simply replaced him with an actor.

While online platforms have helped sport to move forward in positive ways, there is also a need for sports journalism to combat misinformation. Social media have given legions of sports fans a voice, and some of the voices that are perceived as strong or have gained a large following don't have formal media training.

Often, the form misinformation takes in the sports world is relatively harmless. A fake Adrian Wojnarowski feed tweets a bogus NBA trade deadline transaction. An account purporting to be a famous athlete tweets that they have always hated the team's fan base.

These instances are no big deal; just some false postings likely meant as jokes. However, the Wahl and Hamlin situations demonstrate that there is potential for harmful disinformation to become part of the fabric of the sports narrative. Sports-related rumors can percolate and spread widely on social media platforms. As more media and more voices appear, sports journalists face growing challenges determining whether they have the time and resources to check out each rumor, each bit of innuendo, each potential hoax. In addition to developing and applying their skills in reporting, finding nonhuman sources, and writing and broadcasting information on multiple media, sports journalists must learn to deal with a veritable deluge of false information.

The lead author of this book often notes that on the very first day of his first journalism course, the professor stated that every college curriculum should include a journalism course, "to help everyone become better and more informed consumers of media." The need to deal with misinformation is just one part of the future of sports journalism. In this chapter, you will examine the past, current, and future state of the industry and the craft, and you will have the opportunity to come up with your own ideas and solutions. This all comes with the strong caveat that predictions about the future are often affected by unexpected events.

Time-Out

When pursuing any career, it's important to see others doing the work you would like to do. Make a list of the first 10 sports journalists who come to mind. Answer the following questions about each one.

- Where did they study journalism (if anywhere)? If they did not study journalism, what did they study?
- Where do they work? What is their background? (Look them up on Google and LinkedIn.)
- What do they cover?
- What draws you to their work?
- What comprises their social media presence?
- Would you say these people are more traditional or nontraditional sports journalists?
- Describe how these journalists may have influenced your own career goals.

A Quick Look at the State of the Profession

There are no magic spells that will restore the sports journalism industry, business, or craft to what it was in the past. However, a look into the future must include a thorough discussion of the challenges sports journalism has faced as an industry.

We must tell you that since at least the mid-1990s, layoffs have become a fact of life in sports media. As recently as three decades ago, newspapers were still in a somewhat strong competitive position. Around that time, it became clear to media observers that media companies were beginning to actively cut costs, but it was not because they were losing money. Rather, these shortcuts in the newsgathering operation—which included cutting jobs in increasingly large numbers—were undertaken to preserve higher profit margins (Ureneck, 1999). At the same time, newspaper circulation, which had been steady from 1940 to 2000 (peaking around 1990), dropped precipitously after the turn of the century (Pew Research, 2021).

The continuing decline of newspapers led to several developments. After the *New York Times* purchased *The Athletic* (Arbel & Reedy, 2022), the legendary newspaper announced that it would reassign its sports journalists and use coverage from *The Athletic* in its sports sections (Folkenkirk, 2023). This followed an announcement of layoffs at *The Athletic* a month earlier (Associated Press, 2023). In early 2024, the *Los Angeles Times* announced mass layoffs, including beat writers for the Angels and Clippers as well as a longtime NHL columnist (Jenkins, 2024). In addition, the *Times'* Dodgers beat writer announced on X that he had been laid off before tweeting weeks later that his job had been restored (Bucholtz, 2024).

As newspapers have declined in popularity, the opportunities for trained and experienced journalists to be compensated for their work have moved online, and many have been with official team sites as well as traditional media platforms. But online ventures have not always proven to be stable. Fox Sports, for instance, had rounds of notably high layoffs two decades apart (Nakamura, 2020). When *The Athletic* announced a new round of layoffs in June 2023, it let go 4 percent of the outlet's total workforce (Perez, 2023).

The layoffs at *The Athletic* occurred in the wake of similar downsizing events at online sports media enterprises SB Nation and Jomboy Media. As media commentary site *Awful Announcing* pointed out, ventures including Grantland, *The Players' Tribune*, and Bleacher Report all sought to establish a new

Industry Profile

Courtney Cronin, ESPN

Courtney Cronin

While in Indianapolis to cover the 2018 NFL Draft Combine, ESPN reporter Courtney Cronin received some off-field inspiration. Working there in her capacity as a Minnesota Vikings reporter, Cronin saw that at least one group of sports journalists planned regular meetings during the combine for networking and support purposes. The following year, she organized the first Women of the NFL Combine event, which began with approximately 30 attendees and grew to more than 150 in 2024.

Women of the NFL Combine includes women—as well as supportive men—who work as reporters and in official capacities in and around the NFL. Cronin noted that she has heard from people who have made career moves based on connections made at the event.

"The hope is that the event continues to make waves that way, gives people opportunities to network so they can find jobs," Cronin said (personal correspondence, March 2024). "I think that representation certainly matters, and when you see people who are women doing our jobs, you don't feel as alienated or alone. You feel like, 'OK, if they can do it, I can do it too.'"

Cronin has spent her career being someone who sets multiple examples of a sports journalist at work. After five seasons in Minneapolis, Cronin returned home to the Chicago area to work for ESPN covering the Bears and a whole lot more. Multiple times a week, Cronin can be found on ESPN's afternoon debate show *Around the Horn*, and she has also appeared on *Get Up* as well as *First Take* and *SportsCenter*. In addition, Cronin regularly fills in as a co-host on national ESPN Radio shows.

"I've never tried to be a one-trick pony, I never wanted to be," Cronin said. "So for me to be able to do the writing on top of the on-camera stuff, to early in my career, behind the camera, and also being able to talk on radio, that was huge for me. And I felt like that was going to be my path to being the best version of myself as a journalist, that I wouldn't be just a writer, just a TV person, just a podcaster. I truly feel like you have to be proficient in all areas to do all of these things well, and to make your platform as big as it is."

After focusing mostly on broadcasting in college, Cronin started to hone her journalistic writing skills in her first professional position at the Jackson *Clarion-Ledger* in Jackson, Mississippi, where she covered high school and college sports. From there, she moved to a primarily video position at the San Jose *Mercury News*, where she was thrust into covering first the NBA and then the NFL. As part of that NFL coverage, she took a photo of then-49ers quarterback Colin Kaepernick's socks, which depicted pigs in police hats, thinking at first the socks depicted dogs. Within days, that photo was everywhere in the wake of Kaepernick's pregame protest of kneeling during the national anthem.

"Being at the heart of this really opened my eyes to how you have to cover this sort of topic, which is so foreign to sports reporters, when politics, more or less, come into play," Cronin said. "That was truly an eye-opening experience. I don't know if I ever would have had the opportunity to do something like that again. It really taught me a lot. It's overwhelming, thinking back to how that became as much of a story as the NFL product itself."

As a reporter who has covered multiple high-profile beats, Cronin is familiar with the challenges and experiences inherent in being not only a journalist on multiple platforms, but also in being a female in the still male-dominated world of sports. She noted that even basic interactions with sports newsmakers are potentially fraught; a female reporter must make sure a text is worded a certain way, or that any in-person interactions occur in public places. Cronin also said that when facing criticism, it's important to have a good support system, like the one she and her colleagues have cultivated through the annual Women of the NFL Combine gathering.

> *continued*

Courtney Cronin > *continued*

"Being able to have a solid foundation of knowing who you are, and knowing what you stand for, will help you combat those days where the imposter syndrome comes in," Cronin said. "That's probably the biggest challenge of being a woman, when you haven't played the sport. You could be the most well-read person, well-researched, well-sourced, etc. Somebody makes that one comment that makes you feel awful about yourself, you're gonna question everything."

To students, Cronin advises that it's important to be willing to go where the jobs are, with the important caveat that one must focus on the tasks at hand and not be constantly searching for the next big career jump. And never stop learning.

"Read and consume everything; it doesn't just have to be sports," Cronin said. "Read books, read your favorite authors, read about subjects that you don't know about that you want to learn about, because you'll become a better writer. By doing that, you'll become better at articulating what you've covered."

way of covering sport and presenting sports journalism. And all ended up scaling back their operations after initial excitement and frenzies of hiring (Pantuosco, 2023). In addition, once-pioneering sports blog site *Deadspin*, after undergoing a decade of ownership-related turmoil, laid off its entire staff in spring 2024 (Spangler, 2024).

Perhaps the most noteworthy legacy sports media entity to have experienced job and space cuts in recent years has been *Sports Illustrated*. The once-indisputable juggernaut of weekly sports magazines now publishes only a handful of times per year, with attendant drops in personnel and prestige. In early 2024, the magazine's ownership announced a nearly complete purging of staff members.

Where Do We Go From Here?

In describing the dangers of layoffs and the challenges that can come from media ownership changing hands, we want to provide as clear and complete an assessment of the sports journalism business as we can. This includes the historical notes scattered throughout this book as well as descriptions of more recent challenges. Ideally, students and their mentors will have honest and thorough discussions about the state of the sports journalism business so they can prepare for the possibilities. We should also note that after a lengthy period of transition—which pushed at least one of the authors to decide to leave newspaper sports journalism for academia—sports journalism has largely stabilized. While previous generations could specialize in specific skills (e.g., writing, video production), the current and predicted world of sports journalism features more well-rounded workers with knowledge and a certain level of expertise in multiple techniques for news and data gathering. This book has spotlighted those techniques. At the same time, students who have completed their studies are invited to predict the future of sports journalism themselves.

Online Media

Sports journalism's uneasy relationship with online media outlets has been an issue since around the beginning of the 21st century, when Web 2.0 and Internet functionality allowed users to easily create content. The challenge of separating reliable, professionally generated news reports from user-generated reports emerged as consumers began to regard non-mainstream media as equal to mainstream media (Kwak et al., 2010). Concurrently, sports blogs gained a place alongside mainstream media in the perceptions of readers.

The uneasy truce between mainstream sports media and the blogosphere may have reached a flash point in early 2013. Notre Dame's football team had a resurgent season, going undefeated all year on its way to a loss in the BCS National Championship against Alabama. During the season, the media focus was on star linebacker Manti Te'o. As the linchpin of the Fighting Irish's defense, his was the story that everyone sought to tell. That story included a long-distance relationship with a young woman named Lennay Kekua, who became very ill and died within a week of Te'o's grandmother also passing away (Polzer, 2012). Due to Notre Dame's status as a program with a national following of both fans and college football enthusiasts, the story was covered by pretty much every sports news outlet. The heart-wrenching story of perseverance in the face of profound loss had clearly struck a chord.

However, just prior to the national championship game, popular sports blog *Deadspin* exposed the Kekua story as a lie; she had never existed in the first place. Through meticulous reporting, writers Timothy Burke and Jack Dickey debunked the widely covered story with a single lengthy blog (Burke & Dickey, 2013). While sports blogs had been securing press passes for professional and college sporting events for years by early 2013, that *Deadspin* blog marked the moment that no mainstream outlet could continue to scoff at sports blogs offhand without taking a moment to examine the story that was being reported.

A footnote on the future of sports media occurred here as well. Nearly a decade after the original story had been reported, streaming service Netflix aired a documentary update that featured Te'o speaking about the impact the experience had on him. In addition, the family friend who had impersonated Kekua—and placed the Internet term "catfished" into the sports vernacular—also sat for an interview. The documentary was not about any kind of damage control; rather, it was about clarification through another medium, that of documentary filmmaking. At that moment, an outlet that had often been derided for posting photos of athletes partying (Frank, 2022; Leitch, 2008), and which had caused the sports journalism industry in the United States no small amount of embarrassment on a massive story, had earned a final validation. *Deadspin* originally made its name with irreverence through headlines such as "Matt Leinart Is Taking His Offseason Film Work Quite Seriously" over a photo of the then-Arizona Cardinals quarterback drinking with others in a hot tub. Now it was treated as a mainstream outlet that had broken a massive story, in a documentary that featured the writers of the Te'o story being interviewed just as older documentaries might put *New York Times* or *Los Angeles Times* reporters on camera to talk about old Super Bowls. The sports blog had arrived twice now as a mainstream outlet, first with the Te'o story, and then again with Netflix providing an update.

Advancements in Technology and New Competitors

The evolution and development of journalism have been studied by scholars for decades. In the modern era, not only advances in technology but also changes in society itself have been examined for their effects on the industry and the profession (Deuze, 2004). It is important, then, to consider the potential effects of these forces on the future of sports journalism both as a profession and as an industry.

Journalism leaders and analysts have long known that the ongoing march of technology would be something they needed to prepare for. They needed to consider not only how they might use that technology but also how it might lead to new and unexpected competition. If non-sports-based streaming services such as Netflix and cable television juggernauts like Max are producing documentaries and journalistic investigations into sports-related issues, then the level of potential competition has risen exponentially from the days of worrying about being in a two-newspaper town or in a larger market with four major television networks.

For decades, CBS, NBC, and ABC dominated the television airwaves. The Fox network began in the late 1980s, and in 1993, spurred by profitability brought on by popular original programming and expansion, Fox bid for the National Football League's National Football Conference TV package. The fledgling network wrested the sport from longtime home NBC just in time for the NFL to cement its hegemony as the 1994 MLB season was canceled by a players' strike (Goehler, 2022). Before the 1990s were over, Fox also secured broadcasting rights to the National Hockey League, solidifying its status as a major player in sports broadcasting.

The expansion of sports broadcast opportunities rose to meet the increase in the number of platforms (see table 2.1). The entire NCAA men's basketball tournament appears on television. CBS partners with TNT, TBS, and TruTV—in perhaps the only weekend where sports fans need to know which channel on their cable provider is TruTV—to present every game.

Concurrently, streaming television platforms have emerged as another option for sports properties that are seeking broadcast partners. With these new deals, the world of sports broadcasting has become even more fragmented as fans often need multiple streaming services to be able to view games (Chemneera, n.d.). Paramount+ has become a home for international soccer as well as European club soccer. Apple TV+ carries weekly MLB broadcasts and has also created an extra subscription service as part of a deal to become Major League Soccer's main live carrier. NBA games have become part of the enticement for subscribing to YouTube TV, which also carries NFL Sunday Ticket. Amazon Prime is the home of Thursday Night Football. Major League Baseball offers all 162 games of a subscriber's favorite team or every team for tiered pricing (blackout rules apply).

While keeping track of so many streaming services just to watch sports can be costly, consumers must also consider where sports streaming fits with their subscriptions to Netflix, Hulu, Disney+, and other entertainment-focused platforms. In perhaps a nod to consumers' desire to consolidate, ESPN, Fox, and Warner Brothers Discovery announced in 2024 a joint streaming service for launch in fall 2024. While no name—or price—was stated in the initial disclosure, the service was expected to feature content from at least 15 networks, including those dedicated to airing content from the Big Ten, SEC, and ACC (Associated Press, 2024). Disney CEO Bob Iger proclaimed that the service would cost less than it would to subscribe to the various partnering platforms separately, with analysts estimating it would be between $30 and $60 at launch (Maglio, 2024).

How does this movement to and creation of new outlets apply to students of sports journalism? Ultimately, students who study broadcast journalism will find that there are many aspects to television and radio that do not involve being on-camera talent. The proliferation of new sports entities as well as their broadcast partners will continue to create opportunities for students who bring a varied set of skills and experiences to the field. To put this in perspective, when the authors of this book were engaged in their undergraduate studies during the late 1990s and early 2000s, streaming services did not exist, YouTube and easy streaming online video were just an idea, and online video required both a fast Internet connection and often a lot of patience. Major League Soccer and the WNBA were still in their infancy with uncertain futures. Some leagues that have broadcast deals as of this writing, including the National Women's Soccer League, XFL, and Major League Lacrosse, did not exist. MMA events, including the hugely popular UFC, had almost no media presence. It would be easy to think that there can be no more sports that someone would want to broadcast. You might consider this while viewing coverage of the American Cornhole League on ESPN.

Online Media

The migration of sports journalism from traditional printed media to the online platform has been occurring since the Internet became ubiquitous in the late 1990s (Kian & Zimmerman, 2012). Considering the ongoing drop in newspaper circulation (Pew Research, 2021), it is likely that the future of sports journalism will be online in every way. The platforms on which this journalism is created and consumed may change, though not as quickly as they did in the early part of the 21st century. However, the increasing ubiquity of pocket supercomputers (i.e., smartphones) also creates an opportunity for sports journalists to continue to explore different ways of presenting stories.

The online speculative video *EPIC 2014* (Farivar, 2014), originally created in 2004, contained a somewhat humorous shot at legacy media outlets among its predictions of how media would evolve. After envisioning a merger of two notable online companies to create a behemoth called "Googlezon" in a battle against legacy media, the creators said that in response to online dominance by the newer companies, the *New York Times* would become a print-only outlet "for the Elite, and the Elderly." While this has not yet occurred, the demographics of newspaper readership are not skewing toward a younger audience, as every student reading this textbook can attest.

Time-Out

This book discusses the past, present, and future of sports journalism. Based on your own studies, viewpoints expressed in this book and outside of class, and what you would like to see, do the following exercises:

1. List three to five new ideas (e.g., technology, workloads, newsroom-related items) that you expect will emerge in sports journalism in the next five years.
2. Identify three to five aspects of sports journalism that seem strong now but that may fall away.
3. In both cases, elaborate on why you expect these things to develop or disappear. Is there anything you think must be preserved? What should happen to improve sports journalism, in your view?

Though it has proven manifestly difficult to accurately predict the future of sports media, *EPIC 2014* did get some predictions correct. For instance, the creators said that individual consumers would be offered the chance to curate their own news feeds online. This has shown itself in (for instance) the functionality of ESPN's website as well as *The Athletic*. Users can choose to follow news from specific teams and organizations, with those appearing on their feed or as buttons to click for more information and a list of the most recent stories.

There is also reason to believe that previously or currently dismissed forms of communication will find a place within the sports media ecosystem. Most notably, online blogs were initially frowned upon, only to be accepted as part of the overall sport-related conversation (McCarthy, 2014). Eventually, in the wake of *Deadspin*'s coming of age mentioned earlier, some independent blogs reached a level of respect that led to their being credentialed for events, including press conferences and games. It is therefore easy to expect that just as Twitter and Instagram became venues for supplemental storytelling or behind-the-scenes information, a platform such as TikTok, often maligned as a place for adversarial elements both on the videos and in terms of its ownership, might end up being a location for media outlets to place their content. Many athletes already use TikTok as a place to disseminate their thoughts, as seen perhaps most prominently during the 2021 Tokyo Olympic Games.

Before the rise of the Internet, the limited number of media outlets lacked the personnel or the reach to cover all sports to the extent that fans and followers would have liked to see. McCarthy (2014) surveyed bloggers who focused on tennis and gymnastics and found that the gymnastics bloggers especially were motivated to produce content on their favorite sport due to a notable lack of regular coverage in the mainstream media. In addition, while the Internet in the form of Web 2.0 has allowed for and encouraged open conversation between large groups of people, individual bloggers can create a platform in which they are the experts speaking with knowledge to the audience, essentially re-creating the old one-to-many media production model (McCarthy, 2014). Soccer's rise in popularity occurred at the same time the Internet was finding its way into every home; perhaps no sport has benefited more from the American sports blogosphere. Online coverage, presentations, and discussions of mixed martial arts, Olympic sport, and various niche sports have also proliferated.

Participation in online communities devoted to sport has been a key motivator for bloggers and other online content creators (McCarthy, 2014). The camaraderie and social benefits of connecting with others who share similar interests has spurred the creation of fan groups on social media platforms, as well as the use of hashtags in X and Instagram discussions and posts. This is likely to continue; social identity theory (Tajfel & Turner, 1979) points out that the need for connection is important. This especially applies to sporting realms because sport itself often includes community and belonging as a major selling point. As social media have developed from message boards to comment sections to MySpace, Facebook, Twitter, Instagram, and beyond, sport organizations and media outlets that were used to disseminating messages in a one-to-many mode had to change their approach. Now companies that had been slow to adapt to the idea of many-to-many conversations occurring in increasingly global spaces have sought to increase engagement through social platforms. For media outlets, reporters' X handles and contact information are often included next to their bylines, inviting news consumers to engage in conversation as well as sending story ideas or tips.

Artificial Intelligence

In 2023, *Sports Illustrated* publisher Arena Group Holdings began publishing stories generated by artificial intelligence (AI) in the lifestyle and fitness magazine *Men's Journal*. While the use of AI to produce media had been anticipated for some time (Galily, 2018), this was the most mainstream application to date. AI's stated benefits include the ability to create more content in less time. However, there are concerns about the need to identify and correct factual errors and about the overall quality of content. However, multiple media outlets have decided to test the utility of AI as a content producer (Vincent, 2023).

The unique voices and personalities that come through in sports journalists' work have been a part of its appeal. Will the brave new world of AI cause sports journalism to sacrifice readability and personality in favor of cold facts? At the time of this writing it remains uncertain whether this technological tool will produce a radical change in how content created or whether it will just be a passing idea that will eventually yield to the next fresh thing (Galily, 2018). (See chapter 5 for more discussion on the role of AI in sports journalism.)

What role will AI have in the future of sports journalism?
Lionel Bonaventure/AFP via Getty Images

Needed Skills

How will all of this affect students' learning of journalism skills? In a 2014 survey of newspaper sports editors and television directors, researchers found that those newsroom leaders preferred to hire journalists with a wide array of skills, and they found that student journalists should ideally strive to have a diverse skill set (Ketterer et al., 2014). As traditional media outlets such as newspapers and television stations have sought to cut costs by reducing personnel, journalists working for such outlets have increasingly needed to fill multiple roles. While a television reporter might once have expected to always have a producer on-site, reporters now increasingly set out to do live shots alone. A newspaper reporter is expected to carry a camera. Sport public relations practitioners must often produce journalism-type content for the team website and social media accounts, in addition to the standard PR tasks of creating press releases, compiling statistics, and pitching stories to mainstream media.

While the tools of journalism and media production are including more and more technology, the core ability to write well remains paramount for aspiring media practitioners because it is still important to those who do the hiring at media outlets (Ketterer et al., 2014). Indeed, while it may seem easy to podcast or broadcast—simply turn on the microphone and the recorder, and go!—having a written plan is the wisest course of action. Scripts and schedules (as well as good research and reporting) are necessary for a television newscast or audio show to maintain coherence and stay on point. It is therefore obvious that the ability to write and disseminate ideas and reportage—to tell stories in a compelling manner—through words on a screen, on paper, or in a script, will remain critical for students seeking future success in sports journalism.

Not only is the ability to write well important, hiring managers also want reporters to be able to do it multiple times a day (Ketterer et al., 2014). The constant need to produce and keep up with news and events is known as the 24-hour news cycle. It can also be viewed as a 25-hour, eight-day-a-week news cycle, as competition and available technology mean that there is no waiting for stories to be produced for the next newscast or print product. This drive to create frequent content will remain a prominent part of sports reporting, with the competitiveness for scoops leading to a need for journalists to constantly remain plugged in.

If the ability to write and create a compelling story will continue to be a preferred skill among hiring managers, objective reporting that feeds and provides structure for those stories will also be key going forward (Ketterer et al., 2014). This includes cultivating sources through professionalism and building strong reporter-source relationships.

Sports Media Startups

While the impact of online sports coverage site *The Athletic* was covered in previous chapters, it is a topic that forces its way into any discussion of the future of sports journalism because the site has achieved a level of longevity that has thus far been uncommon in sports media startups. Launched in 2016, *The Athletic* has, as of this writing, continued to thrive. While the site has had rounds of layoffs (Draper, 2020) and shuffled editors in reassignments within the organization (Perez, 2021), *The Athletic*'s presence as a sports media outlet remains strong. In early 2022, the former startup found long-term stability when the New York Times Company purchased *The Athletic* for $550 million. Despite having at that time never turned a profit, *The Athletic* added to the *Times'* subscriber base with 1.1 million sports fans to bring the *Times* closer to its eventual goal of 15 million total subscribers (Perez, 2022).

The Athletic had been criticized for poaching editors and writers from traditional media outlets (Draper, 2020), but it found staying power amid the ongoing decline of print media. However, it is questionable whether many other sports media startups can duplicate its success. For example, after a decade of providing commentary and investigations on sport with what can be described as a robust comment section, *Deadspin* closed under legal and financial difficulties. Much of its personnel reassembled under a subscription model at a new site called Defector, while *Deadspin* itself hired new staff and lost much of its foothold in the sports media space. Notably, the comment section was eliminated, while some postings by the revamped *Deadspin* continue to produce negative social media responses and personal attacks on the new writers.

An appropriate contemporary comparison for *The Athletic*'s success may be the Bill Simmons–led Ringer. Rising from the ashes of Grantland.com, The Ringer leans more heavily on podcasts, but it also features a significant amount of written content on its main page. The emphasis on podcasts has proved prescient and lucrative. Among the site's initial investors was cable TV giant HBO, but The Ringer leapt forward in 2020 when online streaming service Spotify purchased the site for $200 million (Jarvey, 2020; Leskin, 2020). Another notable—though non-sports—example is Newsy.com, a video news aggregation startup that began at the University of Missouri in 2008 and evolved into a news outlet that was purchased by the E.W. Scripps Company in 2014 for $35 million (Lunden, 2013).

Each of these acquisitions had at least one specific purpose. The *New York Times* purchased *The Athletic* partially to expand its overall subscriber base. Spotify added The Ringer's podcast lineup to its already-massive slate of audio offerings. Scripps picked up Newsy as part of the expansion of its news-based organization. In each case, an established media company made a move that could help solidify its standing in the media marketplace. However, for every time a media startup manages to find strong financial footing, there are many examples of attempts that survive—think of your favorite fan blog or social media feeds—but never find the financial footing to be more than a side project for engaged fans who support themselves financially in other ways.

This is therefore somewhat of a cautionary tale in terms of startup media companies. Can a general site succeed? Will every sports site succeed? The answers remain inconclusive and notably individualized to each site.

Women and Minoritized Groups in Sports Journalism

Sports journalism has long been a male-dominated field. Franks and O'Neill (2016) noted that in the United Kingdom, opportunities for women to cover sports lagged behind other countries. While the demographics have changed in terms of featuring more diversity in backgrounds and gender, students who consume a typical amount of sports media may have noticed that the bylines and on-camera positions could feature a wider variety of voices. In their examination of the number of female sports journalists in the United Kingdom, Franks and O'Neill (2016) found that there was no significant increase in the decade prior to the 2012 Summer Olympic Games in London.

Academic research is ongoing regarding the future of diversity in journalism, including sports journalism. Diversity in newsrooms has proven to be important in its influence on how coverage is determined (Lapchick, 2021). In 2022, Pew Research surveyed 12,000 journalists across all coverage areas. Responses indicated that some felt that in

> **Time-Out**
>
> In the earlier Time-Out exercise, how many of the journalists you named were female or people of color? If not many, why not? Name the first 10 female sports journalists who come to mind. If you cannot immediately name that many, do some research to create your list.
>
> After completing the following questions for your first list, name the first 10 sports journalists of color who come to mind. Again, if you cannot immediately name that many, do some research to create your list.
>
> - Where did they study journalism (if anywhere)? (What did they study, if not journalism, or in addition to journalism?)
> - What is their background? (Look them up on Google and LinkedIn.)
> - Where do they work?
> - What do they cover?
> - What draws you to their work?
> - What comprises their social media presence?
> - Would you say these people are more traditional or nontraditional sports journalists?
> - Discuss the impact of these journalists, if any, on your own career goals.

their newsrooms, gender and age-related diversity was somewhat solid, while racial and ethnic diversity needed a lot of improvement (Gottfried et al., 2022).

Since 2006, the Institute for Diversity and Ethics in Sport at the University of Central Florida has produced a report every few years examining diversity in sports media. The latest edition, published in 2021, examined more than 100 newspapers and websites, including all circulation and readership levels. The researchers reported that in every category (i.e., editors, assistant editors, reporters, copy editors, columnists, web specialists), more than 70 percent were White or male or both (Lapchick, 2021). The study on newsrooms is one of multiple similar efforts the group does, with examinations of racial and gender-related hiring practices in professional sports leagues also among their work. The lead author of the report said that the progress made by the Associated Press Sports Editors (APSE) in terms of diversified hiring had been notably slow compared to the professional sports leagues (Beard, 2021). While the percentages of women in sports newsroom positions had risen since the previous report in 2018, a former APSE president noted as part of the report that sports journalism needed to increase the number of women (Lapchick, 2021).

Companies and some college journalism programs have sought to create more opportunities for women and minoritized groups in journalism. In a nonsports vein, entities including Dow Jones, Columbia University's Journalism School, the *Wall Street Journal*, Politico, NBC News, and the *New York Times* have established programs meant specifically to train student journalists of color in covering politics and finance (Marcus, 2023). To achieve a more diversified representation, the APSE in 1993 established the Sports Journalism Institute. The program, which involves a short boot camp at a central location before student journalists scatter to their respective summer outlets, has since graduated more than 300 students, including individuals who have worked in print as well as television and online (Sports Journalism Institute, n.d.).

Notably, the numbers regarding newsroom diversity would have skewed even more toward White males if ESPN hadn't been included. For instance, five of 20 female sports editors worked for ESPN in 2021. When considering both gender and racial minority representation in newsrooms, ESPN had a positive effect in the percentages of reporters, columnists, and editors employed in sports journalism as of the report's 2021 publication (Lapchick, 2021).

Local Engagement

The sports department of a media company drives engagement, usually in a positive way. One possible path forward that was suggested by a writer at Poynter.org involved sports journalism as an important aspect of presenting more news coverage of local issues. In a piece headlined, "How high school sports coverage can save democracy," the

High school sports provide an opportunity for sports journalists to engage the local community.
Brittany Murray/MediaNews Group/Long Beach Press-Telegram via Getty Images

writer pointed out that high school sports coverage can help drive stories about events and issues that are more localized to communities. At a time when media coverage of local governments, local sports, and local events have all declined in mainstream media due to shrinking news holes and personnel cuts, the writer noted that a sense of community might increase as a result of an increase in local journalism, with high school sports at the center (Waldman, 2023).

The idea that local coverage is the key to the future of journalism has been brought up over the years as the number of news sources has lessened. However, placing high school sports coverage at the core of such an approach is usually not part of the discussion. Waldman (2023) noted Pew Research studies had indicated that people who follow local news have an increased sense of their community. Can telling the stories of individuals and teams involved in high school sports help create a stronger sense of belonging to a community? Anyone who has driven across parts of the United States has probably seen a sign upon entering a small town that promotes it as the "Home of the 2003 Girls Basketball State Champs" or similar sports-related source of local pride.

Many who pursue sports journalism as a career, whether as writers, broadcasters, or editors, likely do not include coverage of high school athletics as a significant part of their ambitions for the future. However, most writers and broadcasters will engage in high school sports coverage during their careers in sports journalism, creating opportunities to tell individual stories that will resonate with their communities for years to come.

Time-Out

In chapter 1, you were asked to list your top five desired careers and locations in sports journalism. Now, please do so again. What, if anything, has changed? What remains the same? At the very least, you should have gained a better understanding of what pursuing your desired careers might entail.

Summary

While the ongoing development of technology will remain a major part of sports journalism in the future, other challenges will also continue to emerge. Trained and conscientious sports journalists might also invest in combating disinformation, promoting more diverse ideas in the newsroom, and hammering local coverage. Sports journalism, like journalism itself, is constantly at a crossroads, and through experience and training, sports journalists can continue to adjust and adapt to events and developments both predictable and unpredictable.

Discussion Questions

1. What do you think sports journalism will look like in a decade?
2. What kinds of technologies do you believe will dominate the creation and consumption of sports journalism content? Can this kind of future be predicted with any level of confidence or accuracy?
3. Are you more or less confident in your own predictions after having read this book?

Applied Activity

In chapter 1, you were asked to choose three pieces of sports journalism that you have consumed (i.e., read or watched or listened to) in the past week. Then you answered the following questions: What made these the topics or media you chose? Have you decided to focus on producing content in a specific medium? Why or why not? These answers should be shared in a class discussion.

This time, after answering the preceding questions, also answer the following:

- What has changed, if anything, in terms of your sports media consumption compared to the start of the semester?
- Why do you think your tendencies have or haven't changed?
- What do you notice now about sports media that you didn't perceive at the start of the semester?
- How does practicing the creation of sports media content affect your viewpoints?

GLOSSARY

active public—Group that has a relationship with an organization and opens communication with it.

agenda-setting—The power of media to steer discussion and attention toward certain topics; a manipulation of topics without expressing a viewpoint or opinion.

alternative leads—Ways to structure and start stories that move beyond the basic who-what-when-where-why-how structure of the inverted pyramid. They expand our storytelling options.

analytics—The use of advanced statistics to evaluate teams and players.

anecdotal lead—A type of lead that starts with a tale connected to the article.

attrition—This occurs when a person leaves a job and that position is not filled.

aware public—Group that is aware that it has a relationship to an organization through a problem or issue but chooses not to act.

backpack journalism—A type of journalism that involves a single person carrying multiple news-gathering devices. A laptop, camera, FireWire, and tape recorder would all be contained in a backpack.

beat writer—A journalist who provides the day-to-day coverage of a team, conference, or league.

bias—The presence of prejudice or favoritism in the presentation of information.

bias by omission—When important information is left out, leading to a skewed or incomplete representation of a story.

bias by placement—When the placement of a story within a publication or news broadcast influences its perceived importance.

bias by story selection—Certain stories or angles that favor a particular perspective or agenda, contributing to a biased narrative.

bizarreness—A news value that entails anything that's weird, wacky, or way out of the ordinary.

blog—A form of user-generated content that includes news and stories that allow the blogger's individual voice or opinions to be published online in a frequently updated forum.

Box Plus/Minus (BPM)—A box-score estimate of the points per 100 possessions a basketball player contributed above a league-average player, translated to an average team.

branded journalism—Journalism websites and organizations with the public face of a high-profile journalist.

buyout—This occurs when someone receives a financial incentive to leave their job voluntarily.

change in direction—A type of lead that is an abrupt shift in the story.

citizen journalism—Journalism practiced not by official or "mainstream" outlets, but by local unaffiliated individuals who are interested in providing coverage and sometimes viewpoints.

clips—A sports journalists' best stories, which are sent to editors when looking for a new job.

columnists—The opinion writers of the sports pages. They write regularly, though not every day, and write personality-driven pieces.

conflict—A news value that looks for disagreement between people or groups and thus makes for news.

contrasting posts—Posts that are more constructed and promotional in nature.

convergence—The uncomfortable merging of various media styles.

copyright—The protection for the creator or the owner of intellectual property of the exclusive legal right to copy, disseminate, and distribute their work.

Corsi—A statistic of offensive success in ice hockey. Counts the numbers of all shots toward the goal, including shots saved by the goalie and shots blocked by opposing players.

crisis communication—Response to an event that could have negative implications for the organization.

crisis communications plan—An internal organization plan that provides clear, step-by-step actions for an organization to follow in a crisis situation.

crowdsourcing—Seeking information via social media posts that solicit information.

currency—A news value that looks at a subject, topic, or person that is being discussed and is generally culturally relevant. Examples include the AIDS crisis in the 1980s and the climate crisis in the 2000s.

defamation—The communication of false statements that harm the reputation of an individual or entity.

Defense Independent Pitching Stats (DIPS)—Baseball stats that separate how well a pitcher performs from how well (or poorly) the team plays.

deontology—An ethical framework that focuses on the inherent nature of actions rather than their consequences.

digital news sites—News organizations that were born online without an analog antecedent.

discrimination—The unjust or prejudicial treatment of individuals or groups based on factors such as race, gender identity, age, sexual identity, or other characteristics.

disinformation—Deliberate misinformation; falsehoods disseminated with the intent to mislead people who see the material.

DVOA, or Defense-adjusted Value Over Average—A method of evaluating football teams and players that compares each play to the league average based on the given situation.

DYAR, or Defensive Yards Above Replacement—A method of evaluating football player value.

Effective Field Goal Percentage—A calculation of a basketball player's shooting percentage that accounts for the fact that a three-point basket is worth more than a two-pointer.

episodic framing—Coverage that treats each occurrence of an incident as being independent of others.

ethics—Branch of philosophy that is interested in understanding what is the good.

Even-Strength Save Percentage—A hockey stat that measures a goalie's save percentage when both teams are at even strength.

Expected Goals—A soccer metric that tries to quantify the quality of a shot.

fabrication—The creation of false or misleading information, quotes, or events and presenting them as genuine or truthful in journalism.

feature writers—Writers who focus their work on longer-form pieces. These can be profiles (stories about people), stories about trends and issues, or other pieces that don't necessarily fall into the day-to-day grind of a beat.

Fenwick—A statistic of offensive success in ice hockey. Counts the numbers of all shots toward the goal, including shots saved by the goalie.

Fielding Independent Pitching (FIP)—A measure of a pitcher's effectiveness at striking batters out and preventing home runs, walks, and hit by pitches.

framing—Presenting readers and viewers with a clear and stated point of view about a topic.

freedom of the press—The constitutional right guaranteed by the First Amendment that allows journalists and media organizations to publish information without government interference.

Fremeau Efficiency Index (FEI)—An advanced metric used to rank college football teams.

Goals Saved Above Expected—A statistic used to evaluate a soccer goalkeeper.

impact—A news value that addresses who this story affects, how many people it affects, and what that effect is.

intellectual property—Creations of the mind, such as inventions, literary and artistic works, designs, symbols, names, and images used in commerce, for which exclusive rights are recognized.

intriguing statement—A coy, interesting, ironic sentence that begins the story and intrigues the reader.

inverted pyramid—Standard way of writing a news story, beginning with the most important information and ending with the least important.

key publics—Targeted audiences relevant to the organization.

latent public—Group with a relationship to an organization through some issue, but the public is not aware of the issue.

layoff—This occurs when someone loses their job for financial reasons, rather than performance.

lead—Opening paragraph of a written news story, intended to pique the reader's interest and containing the most important information.

lean question—A question type that is short and conceptually simple.

libel—A form of defamation that occurs through written or published statements, images, or content that falsely harms the reputation of an individual or organization.

listicle—Article based on a listing of items around a certain topic.

media guide—Printed or online book of information about a sports entity, with bios of players, coaches, and owners as well as statistics, historical records, and schedules.

misinformation—Misleading information, not necessarily deliberate, that can be conveyed through carelessness.

mobile journalism—Journalism practiced outside the office using modern technology. Also refers to journalism practiced primarily with a smartphone.

NET rankings—A ranking system created by the NCAA to evaluate men's and women's basketball teams for postseason seeding purposes.

neutral question—A question type that doesn't include leading language.

newsletter—A means for writers to deliver their work directly to readers via email.

news peg—Information that connects the subject to the reader. It's the answer to the question, "Why are you writing about this person today?"

news release—An internal organization document produced to communicate key information to multiple publics, including the news media. Also referred to as a press release.

news value—What journalists use to determine whether an event is worthy of coverage. Examples of news values include impact, timeliness, prominence, proximity, conflict, currency, and bizarreness.

nonpublic—Group that has no relationship with an organization and thus has little to no impact on it.

nut graph—The second or third graph of a story, meant to present the core issues and topics.

On-Base Percentage (OBP)—How often a baseball player reaches base. The statistic takes the sum of hits, walks, and times the batter was hit by pitches and divides that total by the number of plate appearances by the batter.

open question—A question type that allows for answers beyond yes or no.

OPS—On-Base Percentage plus Slugging Percentage. Measures batters in MLB.

OPS+—OPS with a stadium adjustment added in and standardized by 100.

organizational media—Media produced by the organization to generate positive awareness with key publics, including news media.

organizational spokesperson—Individual or individuals responsible for acting as the voice of the organization and answering questions from the media.

packet switching—Transferring smaller pieces of data across networks to help speed up the transfer.

Passes Per Defensive Action—A soccer statistic used to measure a team's defensive pressure.

penny press—The era of American newspaper journalism when newspapers were sold for a penny, and when the newspapers began making a majority of their revenue from advertising.

PITCHf/x—A system that uses multiple cameras to track the speed, location, and movement of every pitch thrown in every Major League Baseball game.

plagiarism—The act of presenting someone else's ideas, words, or work as one's own without proper attribution or permission.

Player Efficiency Rating (PER)—A basketball statistic designed by John Hollinger that measures a player's all-around efficiency and contributions.

podcasts—Audio discussions that are recorded and can be downloaded. The name derives from their popularity that grew with that of the iPod.

portfolio—A physical or digital collection of a journalist's clips.

Possession Value—In soccer, the chance that a goal will be scored at any point while a team possesses the ball.

probabilistic thinking—A way to make and evaluate decisions in sports based on analytics and the likelihood of success, rather than basing judgment solely on the outcome.

profile—A feature story that is about a specific person, telling their life or career story.

prominence—A news value that looks at the societal importance of the people involved in a potential story.

proximity—A news value that takes into account how geographically close to your readers an event happens. The closer the event, the more newsworthy it tends to be.

public relations—The management and relationship functions between an organization and its publics.

publics—Groups that interact with a brand or company.

Range Factor—A defensive stat in baseball that divides a player's putouts and assists by number of defensive games played.

relationship building—Creating an ongoing conversation with your target publics.

right to privacy—An individual's legal and ethical entitlement to keep their personal information, actions, and relationships confidential and protected from intrusion or public disclosure without consent.

RPI (Ratings Percentage Index)—In college basketball, a metric used to rank teams that relies heavily on strength of schedule.

sabermetrics—The name given by Bill James to the statistical analysis and study of baseball.

shield law—A legal provision that protects journalists from being compelled to reveal confidential sources or disclose unpublished information in court.

Shotlink—A system in golf that measures the entire course of a PGA tournament.

situational lead—A type of lead that describes the scene of the story.

slander—A form of defamation that involves making false spoken statements that harm the reputation of an individual or organization.

Slugging Percentage—A stat that measures a baseball player's power beyond the raw numbers of home runs, taking the total number of bases reached and dividing it by the number of at-bats.

social media—Forms of electronic communication through which users create online communities to share information, ideas, personal messages, and other content.

so what?—A question that must be answered in terms of the importance of a story. Usually answered by the nut graph.

SP+—A measure of a college football team's overall efficiency, designed to predict future performance.

spin—Slang term for public relations activities.

sport public relations—A brand-centric communication function designed to manage and advance relationships between a sport organization and its key publics.

sports journalism—The practice of media around topics related to the sports world.

statistics—Numerical measures of performances in sports.

story ideation—The skill of coming up with ideas for articles, for knowing what can be categorized as "news."

Strokes Gained—In golf, a comparison of a player's score to the average score of every other player in the field.

The Athletic—Subscriber-based online sports media outlet featuring national and international sports coverage.

"The Decision"—Sponsored event televised by ESPN at which NBA superstar LeBron James announced his free-agent destination.

The Players' Tribune—Derek Jeter–founded online outlet on which amateur and professional athletes can tell their own stories in their own words.

thematic framing—Presenting an ongoing issue, with events being viewed in relation to that issue.

timeliness—A news value that looks at how recently something happened.

Total QBR (Total Quarterback Rating)—A stat developed by ESPN to measure an NFL quarterback's efficiency.

toy department—Pejorative nickname given to the sports section at newspapers.

True Shooting Percentage—Mathematically combines a player's shooting percentages on two-pointers, three-pointers, and free throws to determine shooting efficiency.

two-way symmetrical model of communication—Communication on social media platforms that is reciprocal and designed to provide direct communication between organizations and their key audiences.

Ultimate Zone Rating (UZR)—An advanced baseball metric designed to determine a player's total defensive value by evaluating how many opposing runs that player saves.

Usage Rate—A basketball stat that indicates how often a player is involved in a team's plays.

utilitarianism—An ethical theory that posits that the best action is the one that maximizes the good for the greatest number of people.

valence—The power or importance of a message.

Value Over Replacement Player (VORP)—An advanced stat used in basketball and baseball that estimates a given player's worth when compared to a league-average player.

virtue ethics—An ethical approach that emphasizes the development of good character traits or virtues, such as honesty, integrity, and compassion, as the foundation for ethical behavior.

Walks and Hits per Inning Pitched (WHIP)—The sum of a pitcher's walks and hits divided by total innings pitched. It measures how good a pitcher is at keeping runners off base.

WAR—Wins Above Replacement, an MLB statistic for assessing player value.

Web 1.0—Traditional websites that facilitated content consumption.

Web 2.0—Web-based applications that facilitated two-way forms of communication and user-generated content, such as message boards and blogs.

Win Shares—A basketball statistic that helps quantify each player's impact on their team by estimating how many of a team's victories an individual is responsible for.

REFERENCES

PREFACE

Hutchins, B., & Boyle, R. (2017). A community of practice: Sport journalism, mobile media and institutional change. *Digital Journalism*, 5(5), 496-512.

Serazio, M. (2010). When the sportswriters go marching in: Sports journalism, collective trauma, and memory metaphors. *Critical Studies in Media Communication*, 27(2), 155-173.

CHAPTER 1

Anderson, W.B. (2001). Does the cheerleading ever stop? Major League Baseball and sports journalism. *Journalism & Mass Communication Quarterly*, 78(2), 355-382.

Beck, D., & Bosshart, L. (2003). Sports and media. *Communication Research Trends*, 22(4).

Berr, J. (2018, May 28). NFL's tangled ties with national anthem don't run deep. *CBS News*. www.cbsnews.com/news/the-nfls-tangled-ties-with-the-national-anthem-dont-run-deep/

Boyle, R. (2013). Reflections on communication and sport: On journalism and digital culture. *Communication & Sport*, 1(1-2), 88-99.

Brugar, K.A. (2016). *30 for 30*: An inquiry into sports documentaries to engage in social history. *The History Teacher*, 49(2), 285-299.

Chapman, M. (2023, July 10). The *New York Times* disbands sports department and will rely on coverage from *The Athletic*. Associated Press. https://apnews.com/article/new-york-times-sports-athletic-83d7b725499fb3572d-c5dde766d5a0be

DiCaro, J. (2021, March 16). Under the bridge: A female journalist's life among the sports troll army. *The Guardian*. www.theguardian.com/sport/2021/mar/16/dont-feed-the-trolls-its-terrible-advice-for-female-sports-journalists

English, P. (2016). Twitter's diffusion in sports journalism: Role models, laggards and followers of the social media innovation. *New Media & Society*, 18(3), 484-501.

ESPN+ hits 26 million subscribers. (2023, November 8). *Sports Business Journal*. www.sportsbusinessjournal.com/Articles/2023/11/08/unpacks-espn-plus-subs

Feringa, M. (2024, January 21). Emma Hayes claims England "more sexist" than USA after attacks on women in football. *Daily Mirror*. www.mirror.co.uk/sport/football/news/emma-hayes-england-sexist-usa-31931741

Gregory, M. (2020, August 16). Military no longer pays NFL for acts of patriotism, but it's not because of kneeling. *WUSA9*. www.wusa9.com/article/news/verify/verify-military-nfl-acts-of-patriotism-kneeling-national-anthem/65-730024a0-3286-4d28-afe8-996606547da7

Hardin, M., & Shain, S. (2005). Strength in numbers? The experiences and attitudes of women in sports media careers. *Journalism & Mass Communication Quarterly*, 82(4), 804-819.

Hogg, D. (2015, November 4). The military paid pro sports teams $10.4 million for patriotic displays, troop tributes. *SB Nation*. www.sbnation.com/2015/11/4/9670302/nfl-paid-patriotism-troops-mcain-flake-report-million

Hong, S. (2012). Online news on Twitter: Newspapers' social media adoption and their online readership. *Information Economics and Policy*, 24(1), 69-74.

Jenkins, T. (2013). The militarization of American professional sports: How the sports–war intertext influences athletic ritual and sports media. *Journal of Sport and Social Issues*, 37(3), 245-260.

Lenthang, M. (2023, November 17). Charissa Thompson sparks backlash after saying she'd "make up" coaches' comments during NFL sideline reports. *NBC News*. www.nbcnews.com/news/us-news/charissa-thompson-fox-sports-fabricated-reports-pardon-my-take-rcna125703

MacLean, M. (2017). Review of the book *ESPN: The making of a sports media empire* by T. Vogan. *Sport in History*, 37(3), 388-390.

McCarthy, B. (2013). Consuming sports media, producing sports media: An analysis of two fan sports blogospheres. *International Review for the Sociology of Sport*, 48(4), 421-434.

Messner, M.A., Dunbar, M., & Hunt, D. (2000). The televised sports manhood formula. *Journal of Sport and Social Issues*, 24(4), 380-394.

Messner, M.A., & Montez de Oca, J. (2005). The male consumer as loser: Beer and liquor ads in mega sports media events. *Signs: Journal of Women in Culture and Society*, 30(3), 1879-1909.

Oates, T.P. (2016). Race, economics, and the shifting politics of sport media: The case of Jimmy the Greek. *Radical History Review*, 2016(125), 159-167.

Orellana-Rodriguez, C., & Keane, M.T. (2018). Attention to news and its dissemination on Twitter: A survey. *Computer Science Review*, 29, 74-94.

Perez, A.J. (2024, January 19). *Sports Illustrated*'s publisher guts staff. Future unclear. *Front Office Sports*. https://frontofficesports.com/sports-illustrateds-publisher-lays-off-entire-staff-future-unclear/

Reedy, J. (2023, November 7). NFL host Charissa Thompson says on social media she didn't fabricate quotes by players or coaches. Associated Press. https://apnews.com/article/charissa-thompson-nfl-sideline-reports-47757f5ce4e80fc208f63acec7bfd9bf

Reedy, J. & Bauder, D. (2024, January 19). *Sports Illustrated* staff could be laid off as the iconic magazine's publisher faces money troubles. Associated Press. https://apnews.com/article/sports-illustrated-layoffs-fd731d842f378305b4ddbb115538ed58

Reilly, L. (2023, July 10). The *New York Times* will shut down its sports desk and shift coverage to *The Athletic*. CNN. www.cnn.com/2023/07/10/media/new-york-times-sports-desk-closure-the-atlantic/index.html

Rowe, D. (2007). Sports journalism: Still the 'toy department' of the news media? *Journalism*, 8(4), 385-405.

Rowe, D. (2017). Sports journalism and the FIFA scandal: Personalization, co-optation, and investigation. *Communication & Sport*, 5(5), 515-533.

Rucker, J. (2023, March 6). A conversation with ESPN: How the company is elevating their diversity standards. One37pm.com. www.one37pm.com/sports/conversation-with-espn

Serazio, M. (2010). When the sportswriters go marching in: Sports journalism, collective trauma, and memory metaphors. *Critical Studies in Media Communication*, 27(2), 155-173.

Smith, R. (2006). *Sports Illustrated*'s African American athlete series as socially responsible journalism. *American Journalism*, 23(2), 45-68.

Suggs, D.W., Jr. (2016). Tensions in the press box: Understanding relationships among sports media and source organizations. *Communication & Sport*, 4(3), 261-281.

Weedon, G., Wilson, B., Yoon, L., & Lawson, S. (2018). Where's all the "good" sports journalism? Sports media research, the sociology of sport, and the question of quality sports reporting. *International Review for the Sociology of Sport*, 53(6), 639-667.

Wile, R. (2024, January 19). Mass layoffs hit *Sports Illustrated* staff. NBC News. www.nbcnews.com/business/business-news/sports-illustrated-layoffs-staff-why-media-job-losses-rcna134760

CHAPTER 2

Adgate, B. (2023, October 23). Next NBA TV deal could set new standard for sports streaming rights. *Forbes*. www.forbes.com/sites/bradadgate/2023/10/23/how-the-next-nba-media-rights-negotiations-will-be-different/?sh=4dda0f424ead

Associated Press. (2024, February 6). ESPN, Fox, Warner Bros. to launch sports streaming platform. ESPN.com. https://www.espn.com/espn/story/_/id/39472710/espn-fox-warner-bros-launch-sports-streaming-platform

Baker, T.A. III, & Brison, N.T. (2015). From board of regents to O'Bannon: How antitrust and media rights have influenced college football. *Marquette Sports Law Review*, 26, 331.

Banagan, R. (2011). The decision, a case study: LeBron James, ESPN and questions about US sports journalism losing its way. *Media International Australia*, 140(1), 157-167.

Beck, D., & Bosshart, L. (2003). Sports and media. *Communication Research Trends*, 22(4).

Billings, A.C., & Hundley, H.L. (2010). *Examining identity in sports media* (pp. 1-15). Sage.

Bird, S. (2019, July 2). So the president f*cking hates my girlfriend. *The Players' Tribune*. www.theplayerstribune.com/articles/sue-bird-megan-rapinoe-uswnt

Blackistone, K. (2012, May 31). Sports journalism. *Oxford African American Studies Center*. https://oxfordaasc.com/display/10.1093/acref/9780195301731.001.0001/acref-9780195301731-e-50283

Blystone, D. (2020, June 6). The story of Instagram: The rise of the No. 1 photo-sharing application. *Investopedia*. www.investopedia.com/articles/investing/102615/story-instagram-rise-1-photo0sharing-app.asp

Boyle, R. (2006). *Sports journalism: Context and issues*. Sage.

Bryant, J., & Holt, A. (2006). A historical overview of sports and media in the United States. In A.A. Raney & J. Bryant (Eds.), *Handbook of sports and media* (pp. 22-45). Routledge.

Caron, E. & Crupi, A. (2020, December 10). ESPN signs $3 billion deal for SEC football as CBS era nears end. *Sportico*. https://sports.yahoo.com/espn-signs-3-billion-deal-230050450.html

Clavio, G., & Moritz, B. (2021). Here's why I joined: Introductory letters from new hires to *The Athletic* and the framing of paywall journalism. *Communication & Sport*, 9(2), 198-219.

Clavio, G.E., & Zimmerman, M.H. (2024). Governance and the sport media industry. In B. Tiell & K. Cebula, *Governance in sport: Analysis and Application*. Human Kinetics.

Clemens, B. (2023, January 30). Diamond Sports Group's bankruptcy could rock the baseball revenue boat. *FanGraphs*. https://blogs.fangraphs.com/diamond-sports-groups-bankruptcy-could-rock-the-baseball-revenue-boat

Columbia University Athletics. (2009, May 17). Columbia vs. Princeton: First televised sporting event marks 70th anniversary. *GoColumbiaLions.com*. https://gocolumbialions.com/news/2009/5/17/3738874.aspx

Cormode, G., & Krishnamurthy, B. (2008). Key differences between Web 1.0 and Web 2.0. *First Monday*, 13(6). http://firstmonday.org/article/view/2125/1972

Crupi, A. (2023, December 10). Ohtani's payday fueled by Dodgers' lucrative local TV business. *Sportico*. www.sportico.com/business/media/2023/ohtani-dodgers-lucrative-los-angeles-tv-rsn-sportsnet-1234755676

Curtis, B. (2017, July 3). What "pivoting to video" really means. The Ringer. www.theringer.com/2017/7/3/16045198/fox-sports-mtv-news-vocativ-layoffs-pivot-to-video-77e441a49cb7

Curtis, B. (2020a, March 10). Locked out: How the coronavirus could change American sportswriting forever. The Ringer. www.theringer.com/2020/3/10/21173499/coronavirus-locker-room-mlb-nba-nfl-sportswriting

Curtis, B. (2020b, March 16). What do we do now? Sports media ponders the coronavirus. The Ringer. www.theringer.com/2020/3/16/21181180/coronavirus-media-espn-nba-utah-jazz-scott-van-pelt-jim-rome

Curtis, C. (2018, December 7). Fox Sports is bringing John Tesh's iconic 'Roundball Rock' back to basketball broadcasts. *For the Win*. https://ftw.usatoday.com/2018/12/fox-sports-roundball-rock-nba-on-nbc-theme-john-tesh-video

Draper, K. (2017, October 23). Why *The Athletic* wants to pillage newspapers. *The New York Times*. www.nytimes.com/2017/10/23/sports/the-athletic-newspapers.html

Draper, K. (2020, June 5). *The Athletic* lays off 8 percent of staff. *The New York Times*. www.nytimes.com/2020/06/05/sports/the-athletic-layoffs.html

Eighmey, J., & McCord, L. (1998). Adding value in the information age: Uses and gratifications of sites on the World Wide Web. *Journal of Business Research, 41*(3), 187-194.

Farivar, C. (2014, November 2). *EPIC 2014*: Recalling a decade-old imagining of the media's future. *ARS Technica*. https://arstechnica.com/information-technology/2014/11/epic-2014-recalling-a-decade-old-imagining-of-the-tech-driven-media-future

Finn, C. (2021, April 25). ABC's 'Wide World of Sports' debut 60 years ago. It would go on to change sports television as we know it. *Boston Globe*. www.boston.com/sports/tv/2021/04/25/abc-wide-world-of-sports-debut-60-years-ago

Fisher, E. (2023, December 12). Questions about MLB's streaming future loom as Peacock deal ends. *Front Office Sports*. https://frontofficesports.com/questions-about-mlbs-streaming-future-loom-as-peacock-deal-quietly-ends

Folk, Z. (2024, January 17). Bally Sports coming to Amazon Prime Video in proposed deal: What to know. *Forbes*. www.forbes.com/sites/zacharyfolk/2024/01/17/bally-sports-coming-to-amazon-prime-video-in-proposed-deal-what-to-know/?sh=4aa382e67d30

French, A., & Kahn, H. (2011, June 13). The greatest paper that ever died. Grantland.com. https://grantland.com/features/the-greatest-paper-ever-died

Friend, T. (2024, February 26). NBA teams look beyond national media rights deal to state of local rights. *Sports Business Journal*. www.sportsbusinessjournal.com/Articles/2024/02/26/nba-rights

Gisondi, J. (2011). *Field guide to covering sports*. CQ Press.

Holton, B. (2023, August 10). Explaining ACC's grant of rights deal and what it means as conference realignment continues. *Louisville Courier-Journal*. www.courier-journal.com/story/sports/college/louisville/2023/08/10/acc-grant-of-rights-conference-realignment-college-sports-ncaa/70554279007

Hong, S. (2012). Online news on Twitter: Newspapers' social media adoption and their online readership. *Information Economics and Policy, 24*(1), 69-74.

Hutchins, B., & Boyle, R. (2017). A community of practice: Sport journalism, mobile media and institutional change. *Digital Journalism, 5*(5), 496-512.

James, L., & Jenkins, L. (2014, July 11). LeBron: I'm coming back to Cleveland. *Sports Illustrated*. www.si.com/nba/2014/07/11/lebron-james-cleveland-cavaliers

Kelleher, K. (2017, August 27). Let's call "pivot to video" what it really is: Desperation. *Venture Beat*. https://venturebeat.com/2017/08/27/lets-call-pivot-to-video-what-it-really-is-desperation/

Krawczynski, J. (2017, June 1). Lakers-Celtics in 1980s paved the way for the Cavs-Warriors. Associated Press. www.registercitizen.com/nba/article/Lakers-Celtics-in-1980s-paved-the-way-for-the-11960451.php

Kurkjian, T. (2010, August 14). Sad end to a man's quest for knowledge. ESPN.com. www.espn.com/mlb/columns/story?columnist=kurkjian_tim&id=5420098

MacLean, M. (2017) Review of *ESPN: The making of a sports media empire* by Travis Vogan, *Sport in History, 37*(3), 388-390.

Marchand, A. (2020, September 25). Fox Sports is pivoting back. *New York Post*. https://nypost.com/2020/09/25/fox-sports-is-pivoting-back

Mawson, L.M., & Bowler, W.T. (1989). Effects of the 1984 Supreme Court ruling on the television revenues of NCAA Division I football programs. *Journal of Sport Management, 3*(2), 79-89.

McChesney, R.W. (1989). Media made sport: A history of sports coverage in the United States. In L.A. Wenner (Ed.), *Media, sports, and society* (pp. 49-69). Sage.

Messner, M.A., Dunbar, M., & Hunt, D. (2000). The televised sports manhood formula. *Journal of Sport and Social Issues, 24*(4), 380-394.

Oriard, M. (1998). *Reading football: How the popular press created an American spectacle*. University of North Carolina Press.

Ozanian, M. (2023, August 30). Why the NFL could reap more than $126 billion in TV money by 2033. *Forbes*. www.forbes.com/sites/mikeozanian/2023/08/30/

why-the-nfl-could-reap-more-than-126-billion-in-tv-money-by-2033/?sh=5eca56f815b5

Pesca, M. (2009, July 30). The man who made baseball's box score a hit. National Public Radio. www.npr.org/templates/story/story.php?storyId=106891539

Pew Research. (2023, November 10). Newspapers fact sheet. Pew Research Center. www.pewresearch.org/journalism/fact-sheet/newspapers

Quillen, I.N. (2022, December 14). Breaking down the new MLS 4-year TV deal with Fox Sports. *Forbes*. www.forbes.com/sites/ianquillen/2022/12/14/breaking-down-the-new-mls-4-year-tv-deal-with-fox-sport/?sh=c05bc822787a

Reedy, J. (2023, August 30). Big Ten is ready for maximum exposure with games on NBC, CBS and Fox. Associated Press. https://apnews.com/article/big-ten-nbc-cbs-fox-d783dda33a1ec02b0376151b682d65d0

Rodriguez, S. (2019, September 24). As calls grow to split up Facebook, employees who were there for the Instagram acquisition explain why the deal happened. CNBC.com. www.cnbc.com/2019/09/24/facebook-bought-instagram-because-it-was-scared-of-twitter-and-google.html

Russo, R.D. (2024, March 19). Clemson joins Florida State, becomes second school to sue ACC as it seeks to exit conference. Associated Press. https://apnews.com/article/clemson-sues-acc-ec231745cfe4690ec282050c33c144ed

Sandomir, R. (2011, January 14). *Sporting News* will take over AOL FanHouse content. *The New York Times*. www.nytimes.com/2011/01/14/sports/14fanhouse.html

Schram, C. (2021, April 27). NHL finalizes U.S. TV deals as Turner Sports joins ESPN/Disney. *Forbes*. www.forbes.com/sites/carolschram/2021/04/27/nhl-finalizes-us-tv-rights-deals-as-turner-sports-joins-espndisney/?sh=4a2c9d8841f1

Serazio, M. (2010). When the sportswriters go marching in: Sports journalism, collective trauma, and memory metaphors. *Critical Studies in Media Communication*, 27(2), 155-173.

Shales, T., & Miller, J.A. (2011). *Those guys have all the fun: Inside the world of ESPN*. Little, Brown.

Sheridan, P. (2023, May 16). How a 1921 baseball radio broadcast marked the dawn of sportscasting. *History Channel*. www.history.com/news/first-mlb-game-radio-kdka-harold-arlin-pirates-padres

Slater, K., & Zimmerman, M.H. (2021). Sport communication. In S.P. Brown (Ed.), *Fundamentals of Kinesiology*. Kendall Hunt.

Squawk Box. (2024, April 8). WNBA commissioner on the "Caitlin Clark effect" impact on women's sports and equal pay push. CNBC. www.cnbc.com/video/2024/04/08/wnba-commissioner-on-the-caitlin-clark-effect-impact-on-womens-sports-and-equal-pay-push.html

Steinberg, R. (2023, May 16). The ACC's looming grant of rights' question: What is it and what's at stake? *Boardroom*. https://boardroom.tv/atlantic-coast-conference-acc-grant-of-rights

Thomas, J. (2020, June 17). Just being "not racist" isn't good enough. *The Players' Tribune*. www.theplayerstribune.com/articles/joe-thomas-systemic-racism-nfl

Vecsey, G. (1989). *A year in the sun: The games, the players, the pleasure of sports*. Crown.

Velloso, C. (2022). Making soufflé with metal: Effects of the coronavirus pandemic on sports journalism practices. *Journalism*, 23(12), 2591-2607.

Wolcott, M. (2008, May 1). What is Web 2.0? CBS News. www.cbsnews.com/news/what-is-web-20

Zimmerman, M.H., Clavio, G.E., & Lim, C.H. (2011). Set the agenda like Beckham: A professional sports league's use of YouTube to disseminate messages to its users. *International Journal of Sport Management and Marketing*, 10(3-4), 180-195.

CHAPTER 3

Anderson, A. (2018, January 19). Notre Dame women's basketball uses epic rally to beat Tennessee. *South Bend Tribune*. www.southbendtribune.com/sports/college/notredame/womensbasketball/notre-dame-womens-basketball-uses-epic-rally-to-beat-tennessee/article_d8f30e1e-fd20-11e7-b387-a3787e322bdb.html

Buttry, S. (2009). Elevate your journalism career. *The Buttry Diary*. https://stevebuttry.wordpress.com/2009/09/20/elevate-your-journalism-career/

Culpepper, C. (2016, April 4). Kris Jenkins hits buzzer-beating three-pointer to lift Villanova past North Carolina for NCAA title. *Washington Post*. www.washingtonpost.com/sports/colleges/kris-jenkins-hits-buzzer-beating-three-pointer-to-lift-villanova-past-north-carolina-for-ncaa-championship/2016/04/04/d9a0a136-fa99-11e5-886f-a037dba38301_story.html

Eskenaz, G. (2016, January 5). A look at some of sports journalism's best leads. *Columbia Journalism Review*. www.cjr.org/first_person/lead_or_lede_idk.php

ESPN News Services. (2012, May 2). Jonathan Vilma banned for year. ESPN.com. www.espn.com/nfl/story/_/id/7881761/nfl-bans-four-players-new-orleans-saints-bounty-roles

Fainaru-Wada, M., & Fainaru, S. (2013, January 9). Doctors: Junior Seau's brain had CTE. ESPN.com. www.espn.com/espn/otl/story/_/id/8830344/study-junior-seau-brain-shows-chronic-brain-damage-found-other-nfl-football-players

Fedler, F. (1993). *Reporting for the print media* (5th ed.). Harcourt Brace.

Filak, V. (2019). *Dynamics of news reporting & writing*. CQ Press.

Fleming, D. (2012, August 12). Neither saint nor sinner. ESPN.com. www.espn.com/nfl/story/_/id/8287033/former-saints-lb-scott-fujita-post-bounty-scandal-role-safety-advocate-espn-magazine

Gay, J. (2012, May 2). John Sawatsky is highly questionable. ESPN.com. www.espn.com/blog/poynterreview/post/_/id/320/john-sawatsky-is-highly-questionable

Gisondi, J. (2011). *Field guide to covering sports*. CQ Press.

Goffman, E. (1974). *Frame analysis: An essay on the organization of experience*. Harvard University Press.

Gordon, A. (2013, September 15). When ESPN cheered violence. Salon.com. www.salon.com/2013/09/15/keep_your_helmet_on_espns_jacked_up_in_retrospect_partner

Gross, K. (2008). Framing persuasive appeals: Episodic and thematic framing, emotional response, and policy opinion. *Political Psychology*, 29(2), 169-192.

Lloyd, R., & Guzzo, G. (2008). *Writing and reporting the news as a story*. Pearson.

Mayo Clinic Staff. (2021, May 25). Chronic traumatic encephalopathy. Mayo Clinic. www.mayoclinic.org/diseases-conditions/chronic-traumatic-encephalopathy/symptoms-causes/syc-20370921

McCombs, M.E., & Shaw, D.L. (1972). The agenda-setting function of mass media. *Public Opinion Quarterly*, 36(2), 176-187.

Merrill, E. (2012, May 8). The tragedies of the 1994 Chargers. ESPN.com. www.espn.com/nfl/story/_/id/7904536/junior-seau-adds-tragedies-befallen-1994-san-diego-chargers-super-bowl-team

Moritz, B. (2007, July 30). B-Mets fail to stop sweep. *Press & Sun-Bulletin*, 1c.

Moritz, B. (2014). *Rooting for the story: Institutional sports journalism in the digital age*. [Unpublished doctoral dissertation]. Syracuse University.

Moritz, B. (2019a). The amazing and the impossible with Joe Posnanski (No. 100). *The other 51* [Audio podcast]. www.sportsmediaguy.com/the-other-51/2019/8/21/episode-100-the-amazing-and-the-impossible-with-joe-posnanski

Moritz, B. (2019b). Paying close attention with Steve Politi (No. 92). *The other 51* [Audio podcast]. www.sportsmediaguy.com/the-other-51/2019/4/11/episode-92-paying-close-attention-with-steve-politi

Nalder, E. (2010). Loosening lips. The art of the interview. *Exposé: America's investigative reports*. WNET. www.thirteen.org/wnet/expose/2008/12/loosening-lips-the-art-of-the.html

Paterno, S. (2002, October). The question man. *American Journalism Review*. https://ajrarchive.org/Article.asp?id=676

Ruiz, S. (2019, September 30). Deshaun Watson's thorough breakdown of the Panthers defense might break your mind. *USA Today*. https://ftw.usatoday.com/2019/09/nfl-texans-deshaun-watson-press-conference-panthers-defense

Shoemaker, P.J., & Reese, S.D. (2013). *Mediating the message in the 21st century: A media sociology perspective*. Routledge.

Smith, R. (n.d.). ESPN Classic—Thomson authored an unlikely ending. Retrieved January 17, 2020, from www.espn.com/classic/s/smith_on_thomson.html

UNCP (n.d.). The seven news values held by news media gatekeepers. Retrieved January 17, 2020, from www2.uncp.edu/home/acurtis/Course

Vecsey, G. (1989). *A year in the sun: The games, the players, the pleasure of sports*. Crown.

Wilstein, S. (2002). *Associated Press sports writing handbook*. McGraw-Hill.

Wolken, D. (2021, February 18). Opinion: Time is running out for Serena Williams to win Grand Slam No. 24—and she knows it. *USA Today*. www.usatoday.com/story/sports/columnist/dan-wolken/2021/02/17/serena-williams-future-australian-open-naomi-osaka/6796450002

Zimmerman, M.H., Clavio, G.E., & Lim, C.H. (2011). Set the agenda like Beckham: A professional sports league's use of YouTube to disseminate messages to its users. *International Journal of Sport Management and Marketing*, 10(3-4), 180-195.

CHAPTER 4

1920_mediaguide_v3.pdf. (n.d.). Retrieved December 7, 2020, from www.nba.com/resources/static/team/v2/sixers/pdfs/1920_mediaguide_v3.pdf

Albom, M. (2012, November 16). Cabrera's MVP a win for fans, defeat for stats geeks. *USA Today*. www.usatoday.com/story/sports/mlb/tigers/2012/11/16/miguel-cabrera-detroit-tigers-mvp-triple-crown/1709271

BBHOF. (n.d.). Henry Chadwick. Baseball Hall of Fame. Retrieved March 1, 2021, from https://baseballhall.org/hall-of-famers/chadwick-henry

Buffalo Sabres won-loss records. (n.d.). Hockey-Reference.com. Retrieved December 7, 2020, from www.hockey-reference.com/teams/BUF/head2head.html

Connolly, B. (2020, December 6). SP+ rankings after week 15. ESPN.com. www.espn.com/college-football/insider/story/_/id/30513461/college-football-sp+-rankings-week-15-north-carolina-enters-top-10

Football Outsiders. (n.d.-a). 2020 college football FEI ratings. Retrieved December 15, 2020, from www.footballoutsiders.com/stats/ncaa/fei/overall/2020

Football Outsiders. (n.d.-b). Methods to our madness. Retrieved December 15, 2020, from www.footballoutsiders.com/info/methods#dvoa

Fromal, A. (2012, January 26). Understanding the NBA: Explaining advanced offensive stats and metrics. Bleacher Report. https://bleacherreport.com/articles/1039116-understanding-the-nba-explaining-advanced-offensive-stats-and-metrics

Gaudios, F. (2019, December 9). KenPom rankings explained & how to better evaluate Rutgers basketball. On the Banks. www.onthebanks.com/2019/12/9/21002735/

kenpom-rankings-explained-how-to-better-evaluate-rutgers-basketball-big-ten-ncaa-steve-pikiell

Harrington, M. (2014, December 25). Formulas for success: Everyone jumping on board with analytics. *Buffalo News*.

Hollinger, J. (2007, April 26). Hollinger: What is PER? ESPN.com. www.espn.com/nba/columns/story?columnist=hollinger_john&id=2850240

Ioakimidis, M. (2010). Online marketing of professional sports clubs: Engaging fans on a new playing field. *International Journal of Sports Marketing & Sponsorship*, 11(4), 271-282.

Jaffe, J. (2017). *The Cooperstown casebook*. Thomas Dunne Books.

Kane, C., Thompson, P., Collier, J., Gonzales, M., Pope, L., Sullivan, P., Greenstein, T., Ryan, S., & Mikula, J. (2020, August 25). The strangest thing has been ___. Zoom calls with coaches and athletes are ___. 9 writers answer 4 topics about covering Chicago sports during COVID-19. Chicagotribune.com. www.chicagotribune.com/sports/ct-cb-chicago-sports-covid-19-20200825-3zakhjx3zbadpcqjkgywimswwu-story.html

Katz, S., & Burke, B. (2016, September 8). Total QBR: An explainer. ESPN.com. www.espn.com/blog/statsinfo/post/_/id/123701/how-is-total-qbr-calculated-we-explain-our-quarterback-rating

Law, K. (2017). *Smart baseball: The story behind the old stats that are ruining the game, the new ones that are running it, and the right way to think about baseball*. William Morrow.

Lindbergh, B., & Miller, S. (2016). *The only rule is it has to work: Our wild experiment building a new kind of baseball team*. Macmillan.

Lucia, J. (2012). The ignorant Jason Whitlock attempts to slay sabermetricians. The Outside Corner. http://thecomeback.com/theoutsidecorner/2011-articles/the-ignorant-jason-whitlock-attempts-to-slay-sabermetricians.html

Mallon, T. (2010, November 28). Off the rim. *The New Yorker*. www.newyorker.com/magazine/2010/12/06/off-the-rim

MLB.com. (n.d.-a). Statcast. Major League Baseball. Retrieved December 15, 2020, from http://m.mlb.com/glossary/statcast

MLB.com. (n.d.-b). What is an error? Major League Baseball. Retrieved December 15, 2020, from http://m.mlb.com/glossary/standard-stats/error

MLB.com. (n.d.-c). What is a range factor? Major League Baseball. Retrieved December 15, 2020, from http://m.mlb.com/glossary/advanced-stats/range-factor

MLB.com. (n.d.-d). What is a save? Major League Baseball. Retrieved December 15, 2020, from http://m.mlb.com/glossary/standard-stats/save

Minkus, K. (2020, April 16). Soccer analytics 101. MLSsoccer.com. www.mlssoccer.com/soccer-analytics-guide/2020/soccer-analytics-101?utm_source=social_share&utm_medium=share_button&utm_campaign=social_share_button

Moritz, B. (2020). *Bubble adjacent with Tim Bontemps. The Other 51* (Audio podcast). Retrieved December 15, 2020, from https://podcasts.apple.com/us/podcast/bubble-adjacent-with-tim-bontemps/id1123850813?i=1000495646132

NBA win shares. (n.d.). Basketball-Reference.com. Retrieved December 15, 2020, from www.basketball-reference.com/about/ws.html

Official Indiana Fever website. (n.d.). Retrieved January 2, 2024, from https://fever.wnba.com

PGATour.com (n.d.). Strokes gained: How it works. PGATour. Retrieved March 1, 2021, from www.pgatour.com/news/2016/05/31/strokes-gained-defined.html

Serrano, S. (2017). *Basketball (and other things)*. Abrams Image.

Shotlink.com. (n.d.). Retrieved March 1, 2021, from www.shotlink.com

Silver, N. (2012). *The signal and the noise: Why so many predictions fail—but some don't*. Penguin.

Slowinski, S. (2010a). FIP. Sabermetrics Library. https://library.fangraphs.com/pitching/fip

Slowinski, S. (2010b). UZR. Sabermetrics Library. https://library.fangraphs.com/defense/uzr

Slowinski, S. (2010c). What is PITCHF/x? Sabermetrics Library. https://library.fangraphs.com/misc/pitch-fx

Slowinski, S. (2011). DIPS. Sabermetrics Library. https://library.fangraphs.com/principles/dips

Tremlett, S. (2019, September 6). What is strokes gained? *Golf Monthly*. www.golfmonthly.com/features/the-game/what-is-strokes-gained-185460

What is a win (W)? (n.d.). Major League Baseball. Retrieved December 15, 2020, from http://m.mlb.com/glossary/standard-stats/win

Who was the first football club to have an official website? (2016, October 26). *The Guardian*. www.theguardian.com/football/2016/oct/26/who-were-the-first-football-club-to-have-an-official-website

Wilbon, M. (2016, May 24). Mission impossible: African-Americans & analytics. The Undefeated. https://theundefeated.com/features/mission-impossible-african-americans-analytics

CHAPTER 5

Amazon Web Services. (n.d.). What is the Internet of Things (IoT)? https://aws.amazon.com/what-is/iot/#:~:text=with%20AWS%20IoT-,What%20is%20the%20Internet%20of%20Things%20(IoT)%3F,as%20between%20the%20devices%20themselves

Associated Press. (2023, April 28). ATP dropping line judges, to use all electronic calls by 2025. www.espn.com/tennis/story/_/id/36312616/atp-dropping-line-judges-use-all-electronic-calls-2025

Basaeed, S. (2023). Journalism in the age of artificial intelligence. *Journal of Organisational Creativity*, 2(1), 23.

Bauder, D. (2023, November 29). *Sports Illustrated* found publishing AI generated stories, photos and authors. Associated Press. www.pbs.org/newshour/economy/sports-illustrated-found-publishing-ai-generated-stories-photos-and-authors

Bennett, R. [@rogbennett] (2020, June 21). PULISIC ON SINCE THE FIRST TIME IN JANUARY. AND HE SCORES. WITHIN MINUTES. BEST THING THAT HAS HAPPENED TO AMERICA IN FAR TOO LONG [Retweet; thumbnail link to original tweet]. Twitter https://twitter.com/rogbennett/status/1282354828962926599

Beveridge, C. (2022, March 24). 19 Facebook demographics to inform your strategy in 2022. *Hootsuite*. https://blog.hootsuite.com/facebook-demographics/

Bostwick, D. (n.d.). Ethics in journalism and strategic media: A guidebook of lessons and resources. https://uark.pressbooks.pub/journalismethics/chapter/chapter-15/

Buzzelli, N.R., Gentile, P., Sadri, S.R., & Billings, A.C. (2022). "Cutting editors faster than we're cutting reporters": Influences of *The Athletic* on sports journalism quality and standards. *Communication & Sport*, 10(3), 417-437.

Cameron, D. (2009). Mobile journalism: A snapshot of current research and practice. *The End of Journalism: News in the Twenty-First Century*, 63-72.

Castillo, C., El-Haddad, M., Pfeffer, J., & Stempeck, M. (2014, February). Characterizing the life cycle of online news stories using social media reactions. In *Proceedings of the 17th ACM conference on computer supported cooperative work & social computing* (pp. 211-223).

Cernohous, S. (2006). Considering a new avenue of communication: The weblog. *Athletic Therapy Today*, 11(4), 32-33.

Clavio, G. (2021). *Social media and sports*. Champaign, IL: Human Kinetics.

Clavio, G., & and Mortiz, B.P. (2022). Podcasting and sports journalism. In *The Routledge Handbook of Digital Sport Management* (pp. 180-191). Routledge.

Cossich, V.R., Carlgren, D., Holash, R.J., & Katz, L. (2023). Technological breakthroughs in sport: Current practice and future potential of artificial intelligence, virtual reality, augmented reality, and modern data visualization in performance analysis. *Applied Sciences*, 13(23), 12965.

Dart, J.J. (2009). Blogging the 2006 FIFA World Cup Finals. *Sociology of Sport Journal*, 26(1), 107-126.

Dixon, S. (2023, November 13). Number of X (formerly Twitter) users worldwide from 2019 to 2024. *Statista*. www.statista.com/statistics/303681/twitter-users-worldwide/

Dixon, S.J. (2024, March 20). Countries with the most Facebook users 2024. *Statista*. www.statista.com/statistics/268136/top-15-countries-based-on-number-of-facebook-users/

Dowsett, B. (2024, May 2). AI is helping referee games in major sports leagues, but limitations remain. *Scientific American*. www.scientificamerican.com/article/ai-is-helping-referee-games-in-major-sports-leagues-but-limitations-remain

Ellis, K.K. (2019). Is a shorter video length more engaging on Facebook? Retrieved June 13, 2020, from www.newswhip.com/2019/03/video-length-engaging-facebook/

Frangonikolopoulos, C.A., & Chapsos, I. (2012). Explaining the role and the impact of the social media in the Arab Spring. *Global Media Journal: Mediterranean Edition*, 7(2).

Gee, C. (2019). Audience preferences in determining quality news production of backpack journalism. *Electronic News*, 13(1), 34-55.

Geissler, D., Beiderbeck, D., Schmidt, S.L., & Schreyer, D. (2024). Emerging technologies and shifting consumer motives: Projecting the future of the top-tier sports media product. *Technological Forecasting and Social Change*, 203, 123366.

Gutierrez Lopez, M., Porlezza, C., Cooper, G., Makri, S., MacFarlane, A., & Missaoui, S. (2023). A question of design: Strategies for embedding AI-driven tools into journalistic work routines. *Digital Journalism*, 11(3), 484-503.

IBM. (n.d.). What is the Internet of Things (IoT)? www.ibm.com/topics/internet-of-things

Jackson, D. (2020). Know your limit: The ideal length of every social media post. Retrieved June 13, 2020, from https://sproutsocial.com/insights/social-media-character-counter/#facebook

Jarvis, J. (2024, January 11). Which rights do AI and journalists have in common? Nieman Lab. www.niemanlab.org/2024/01/which-rights-do-ai-and-journalists-have-in-common/

Kang, S. (2020). Going beyond just watching: The fan adoption process of virtual reality spectatorship. *Journal of Broadcasting & Electronic Media*, 64(3), 499-518.

Kassing, J.W., & Sanderson, J. (2010). Fan-athlete interaction and Twitter tweeting through the Giro: A case study. *International Journal of Sport Communication*, 3(1), 113-128.

Kwak, H., Lee, C., Park, H., & Moon, S. (2010, April). What is Twitter, a social network or a news media? In *Proceedings of the 19th international conference on World Wide Web* (pp. 591-600).

Latar, N.L. (2018). *Robot journalism: Can human journalism survive?* World Scientific.

Linehan, M. [@itsmeglinehan] (2020, July 21). EVEN MORE. @juhrman and @alexisohanian join me for a bonus episode of Full Time with Meg Linehan to discuss @weareangelcity. #NWSL. [Tweet; thumbnail video to embedded podcast, links to podcast content]. Twitter https://twitter.com/itsmeglinehan/status/1285557876535197700

López González, H., Guerrero Solé, F., & Larrea Estefanía, O. (2014). Community building in the digital age: Dynamics of online sports discussion. *Communication & Society, 27*(3): 83-105.

McEnnis, S. (2013). Raising our game: Effects of citizen journalism on Twitter for professional identity and working practices of British sport journalists. *International Journal of Sport Communication, 6*(4).

McLean, S., Read, G.J., Thompson, J., Hancock, P.A., & Salmon, P.M. (2022). Who is in control? Managerial artificial general intelligence (MAGI) for football. *Soccer & Society, 23*(1), 104-109.

Mendoza, J. (2023, February 21). Vanderbilt University apologizes for using ChatGPT for "disgusting" email on Michigan State shooting. *USA Today.* www.usatoday.com/story/news/education/2023/02/21/vanderbilt-apologizes-chatgpt-email-msu-shooting/11314144002/

Merriam-Webster. (n.d.). Social media. *Merriam-Webster.com dictionary.* Retrieved June 13, 2020, from www.merriam-webster.com/dictionary/social%20media

Moreland, J. (2024, January 8). Artificial intelligence in sports photojournalism leads to ethical questions. WKAR. www.wkar.org/wkar-news/2024-01-08/artificial-intelligence-in-sports-photojournalism-leads-to-ethical-questions

Nielsen Sports. (2022). *Year in review: Sports consumption evolution.* https://nielsensports.com/year-in-review-sports-consumption-evolution/

Nwanakwaugwu, A.C., Matthew, U.O., Okey, O.D., Kazaure, J.S., & Nwamouh, U.C. (2023). News reporting in drone Internet of Things digital journalism: Drones technology for intelligence gathering in journalism. *International Journal of Interactive Communication Systems and Technologies, 12*(1), 1-22.

Oliver, L. (2008). Reuters using mobile journalism for US Political coverage. *Journalism.co.uk.* Retrieved from www.journalism.co.uk/2/articles/532258.php

Passan, J. (2024, May 2). Early MLB takeaways: Best and worst teams, umpires, trends. *ESPN.* www.espn.com/mlb/insider/story/_/id/40064274/2024-mlb-season-passan-early-takeaways-offense-strikeouts-umpires

Perreault, G., & Bell, T.R. (2022). Towards a "digital" sports journalism: Field theory, changing boundaries and evolving technologies. *Communication & Sport, 10*(3), 398-416.

PRSA. (2023, November). Promise and pitfalls: The ethical use of AI for public relations practitioners. https://www.prsa.org/docs/default-source/about/ethics/ethicaluseofai.pdf?sfvrsn=5d02139f_2

Regret Iyer, S., Pavlik, J., & Jin, S.V. (2022). Leveraging virtual reality (VR) for sports public relations and sports journalism: Qualitative analyses of VR content productions for "Russia 2018"and "Qatar 2022" FIFA World Cups. *Journal of Sport & Tourism, 26*(4), 335-362.

Rupprecht, P.M. (2020). A phenomenological study exploring the meaning of global engagement among former participants of a backpack journalism program. *The Journal of Public Interest Communications, 4*(1), 61-61.

Sandomier, R. (2008). A confrontation on "Costas Now" worthy of a blog. *The New York Times.* Retrieved July 2, 2020, from www.nytimes.com/2008/05/01/sports/football/01sandomir.html

Schultz, B., & Sheffer, M.L. (2007). Sports journalists who blog cling to traditional values. *Newspaper Research Journal, 28*(4), 62-76.

Segarra-Saavedra, J., Cristòfol, F.J., & Martínez-Sala, A.M. (2019). Artificial intelligence (AI) applied to informative documentation and journalistic sports writing: The case of BeSoccer. *Doxa Comunicación, 29,* 275-286

Singer, J.B. (2011). Journalism and digital technologies. In W. Lowrey and P. J. Gade (Eds.), *Changing the news: The forces shaping journalism in uncertain times* (pp. 213-229). Routledge.

Society of Professional Journalists. (2023, February 1). The ethics of using AI. *SPJ Ethics Central.* https://ethicscentral.org/the-ethics-of-using-ai/

Staley, L., Dvorak, M., Ewing, M.E., Hall, H.K., Hoeft, J.R., & Myers, C. (2023, November 20). *PROMISE & PITFALLS: The ethical use of AI for public relations practitioners.* Public Relations Society of America.

Thomas, S. & Sooknanan, P. (2019). Citizen uournalism and civil society: Attitudes of mainstream journalists to user-generated content (UGC) on social media. *Journal of Eastern Caribbean Studies, 44*(3), 115-155.

Torrijos, J.R. (2019). Automated sports coverages. Case study of bot released by the *Washington Post* during Río 2016 and Pyeongchang 2018 Olympics. *Revista Latina de Comunicación Social, 74,* 1729-1747.

ViaSport (2020). Facebook 101 for sport communicators. Retrieved June 13, 2020, from www.viasport.ca/social-media-toolkit/Facebook-101-for-sport-communicators

Watson, H. (2013). Citizen journalism as data for disaster research. *International Journal of Mass Emergencies & Disasters, 31*(2).

Webb, A. (2019). 4 ways to customize your Facebook link posts for more clicks. Retrieved June 13, 2020, from www.socialmediaexaminer.com/4-ways-to-customize-facebook-link-posts-for-more-clicks/

Wojnarowski, A. [@wojESPN] (2020, July 9). Tom Thibodeau—the leading candidate for the New York Knicks coaching job—had his formal interview with the organization today. [Tweet]. https://twitter.com/wojespn/status/1281346909286924289

Zhang, Y., & Zhao, J. (2023). Integrating the Internet of Things and computer-aided technology with the construction of a sports training evaluation system. *Computer-Aided Design and Applications, 20*, 89-98.

CHAPTER 6

Beverland, M. (2005). Crafting brand authenticity: The case of luxury wines. *Journal of Management Studies, 42*(5), 1003-1029.

Business Research Company. (2023, January). The Business Research Company. Retrieved from www.thebusinessresearchcompany.com/report/sports-global-market-report#:~:text=The%20global%20sports%20market%20grew,least%20in%20the%20short%20term

Cawley, C. (2021, February 13). What is social media management? https://tech.co/digital-marketing/social-media-management-guide

Charlton, A., & Cornwell, T.B. (2019). Authenticity in horizontal marketing partnerships: A better measure of brand compatibility. *Journal of Business Research, 100*, 279-298.

Dozier, D.M., Grunig, L.A., &, Grunig, J.E. (1995). *Manager's guide to excellence in public relations and communications management.* Lawrence Erlbaum Associates.

Facebook for Business. (2021, February 28). Facebook for Business. Retrieved on February 28, 2021, from www.facebook.com/business/news/audience-insights

Favorito, J. (2007). *Sports publicity: A practical approach.* Elsevier.

Grunig, J.E. (1993). Image and substance: From symbolic to behavioural relationships. *Public Relations Review 19*(2), 121-139.

Grunig, J.E., & Hunt, T. (1984). *Managing public relations.* Holt, Rinehart & Winston.

Grunig, J.E., & Repper, F.C. (1992). Strategic management, publics, and issues. In J.E. Grunig (Ed.), *Excellence in public relations and communication management* (pp. 117 157). Lawrence Erlbaum Associates.

Harlow, R.F. (1976). Building a public relations definition. *Public Relations Review, 2*(4), 34-42. https://doi.org/10.1016/S0363-8111(76)80022-7

Helitzer, M. (2000). *The dream job: $port$ publicity, promotion, and marketing* (3rd ed.). University Sports Press.

Hopwood, M. (2010). Public relations and communication in sport. In M. Hopwood, P. Kitchen, & J. Skinner (Eds.), *Sport public relations and communication* (pp. 13-32). Butterworth-Heinemann.

Jefkins, F., 1994. *Public relations techniques* (2nd ed.). Butterworth Heinemann.

Kelly, K.S. (2001). Stewardship: The fifth step in the public relations process. In Heath, R. (Ed.), *Handbook of public relations* (pp. 279–290). Sage Publications.

Ledingham, J.A., & Bruning, S.D. (2000). *Public relations as relationship management: A relational approach to the study and practice of public relations.* Lawrence Erlbaum Associates.

Maloney, J., & Kaskey-Blomain, M. (2020, December 11). Nets' Kyrie Irving responds to $25,000 fine from NBA for not speaking to media: "I do not talk to pawns." CBS Sports.com. www.cbssports.com/nba/news/nets-kyrie-irving-responds-to-25000-fine-from-nba-for-not-speaking-to-media-i-do-not-talk-to-pawns/

Martin, J. (2016, November 3) Believe it! Chicago Cubs end the curse, win 2016 World Series. CNN.com. https://edition.cnn.com/2016/11/02/sport/world-series-game-7-chicago-cubs-cleveland-indians/index.html

NFL Communications. (2021, February 28). NFL Communications.com. Retrieved on February 28, 2021, from https://nflcommunications.com/Pages/Home.aspx

Public Relations Society of America. (2021, February 28). About public relations. PRSA.com. Retrieved February 28, 2021, from www.prsa.org/about/all-about-pr

Seiter, C. (2015, March 12). 61 key social media metrics defined. *Buffer.* Retrieved April 19, 2024 from https://buffer.com/resources/social-media-metrics/

Sharp, K. (2015, August 26). Marshawn Lynch fined $75K for not talking to media after NFC Championship. SB Nation.com. www.sbnation.com/nfl/2015/8/26/9211425/marshawn-lynch-fined-talking-media-packers-appeal

The Shed. (2021, February 28). Chelsea FC.com. Retrieved February 28, 2021, from https://theshed.chelseafc.com

Shilbury D., & Rowe, K. (2010). Sport relationship management. In M. Hopwood, P. Kitchen, & J. Skinner (Eds.), *Sport public relations and communication* (pp. 13-32). Butterworth-Heinemann.

Simko-Bednarski, E., & Vera, A. (2021, February 26). Ex-USA Gymnastics coach John Geddert found dead after being charged with human trafficking and sex crimes, officials say. CNN.com. https://edition.cnn.com/2021/02/25/us/john-geddert-usa-gymnastics-coach-charged/index.html

Smith, R.D. (2017). *Strategic planning for public relations* (4th ed.) Erlbaum.

Stoldt, G.C., Dittmore, S.W., Ross, M., & Branvold, S.E. (2020). *Sport public relations.* Human Kinetics.

Thompson, W. (1996). *Targeting the message: A receiver-centered process for public-relations writing.* Longman.

Treadwell, D., & Treadwell, J.B. (2000). *Public relations writings: Principles and practice.* Allyn and Bacon.

Twitter Analytics. (2021, February 28). Twitter analytics. Retrieved February 28, 2021, from https://analytics.twitter.com/about

Venus Williams hit with $5,000 fine for skipping post-match press conference. (2021, February 28). *The Guardian*. Retrieved on February 28, 2021 from https://www.theguardian.com/sport/2016/jan/20/venus-williams-hit-with-5000-fine-for-skipping-post-match-press-conference

CHAPTER 7

ABC13 Houston [@abc13houston]. (2020, January 6). Houston Dash trade J.J. Watt's fiancée to Chicago [Tweet; thumbnail link to article; photograph]. Twitter. https://twitter.com/abc13houston/status/1214386381180588032?s=12

Anderson, W.B. (2001). Does the cheerleading ever stop? Major League Baseball and sports journalism. *Journalism & Mass Communication Quarterly*, 78(2), 355-382. https://doi.org/10.1177/107769900107800210

Aristotle (1999). *Nicomachean ethics*. (W. D. Ross, Trans.) Batoche Books. https://socialsciences.mcmaster.ca/econ/ugcm/3ll3/aristotle/Ethics.pdf (Original work published ca. 350 BCE)

Arnold, K. (2020, February 4). "I was scrolling on Twitter": How NBA players found out they were traded. NBA. www.nba.com/news/when-players-find-out-theyve-been-traded-social-media

Associated Press Sports Editors (n.d.). Ethics guidelines. www.apsportseditors.com/apse-ethics-guidelines/

Bartlett, L. (n.d.). SPJ Ethics Committee position papers: Plagiarism. Society of Professional Journalists. www.spj.org/ethics-papers-plagiarism.asp

Bentham, J. (1781). *An introduction to the principles of morals and legislation*. www.earlymoderntexts.com/assets/pdfs/bentham1780.pdf

Bieber, C. (2022, October 17). Libel vs. slander: what's the difference? *Forbes*. https://www.forbes.com/advisor/legal/personal-injury/libel-vs-slander/

Bissada, M. (2022, January 25). Baseball writers reject Barry Bonds and other "steroid era" MLB stars from Hall of Fame for final time. *Forbes*. www.forbes.com/sites/masonbissada/2022/01/25/baseball-writers-reject-barry-bonds-other-steroid-era-mlb-stars-from-hall-of-fame-for-final-time/?sh=3424526098c6

Boczek, K., Dogruel, L., & Schallhorn, C. (2023). Gender byline bias in sports reporting: Examining the visibility and audience perception of male and female journalists in sports coverage. *Journalism*, 24(7), 1462-1481. https://doi.org/10.1177/14648849211063312

Brennan, M.L. (1979). Civil rights in the locker room: Ludtke v. Kuhn. *Hastings Communication and Entertainment Law Journal*, 2(4), 645.

Brown, N.A., & Billings, A.C. (2013). Sports fans as crisis communicators on social media websites. *Public Relations Review*, 39(1), 74-81.

Brito, C. (2023, November 17). NFL broadcaster Charissa Thompson says she made up sideline reports during games. CBS News. https://www.cbsnews.com/news/charissa-thompson-nfl-thursday-night-football-fox-sports-sideline-reports/

Church, B. (2023, November 17). Host Charissa Thompson apologizes after saying she fabricated NFL sideline reports; faces mounting criticism. CNN. https://www.cnn.com/2023/11/17/sport/charissa-thompson-sideline-reports-spt-intl/index.html

Curtis, B. (2017, October 2) Sports has a fake news problem. The Ringer. www.theringer.com/sports/2017/10/2/16400992/donald-trump-fake-news-sports-nfl

Devine, J.W. (2019). Gender, steroids, and fairness in sport. *Sport, Ethics and Philosophy*, 13(2), 161-169.

Eastman, S.T., & Billings, A.C. (2000). Sportscasting and sports reporting: The power of gender bias. *Journal of Sport and Social Issues*, 24(2), 192-213.

Eastman, S.T., & Billings, A.C. (2001). Biased voices of sports: Racial and gender stereotyping in college basketball announcing. *Howard Journal of Communications*, 12, 183-201.

Eliason, R.D. (2007). Striking out: The BALCO reporters shielded a lying lawyer. They are no heroes. *Legal Times*, 30(19), 1-3. https://openargs.com/wp-content/uploads/Eliason-2007-BALCO-bad.pdf

Fink, J.S. (2013) Female athletes, women's sport, and the sport media commercial complex: Have we really "come a long way, baby"? *Sport Management Review*, 18(3), 331-42.

Funt, D. (2021, Summer). All in: How gambling swallowed sports media. *Columbia Journalism Review*. www.cjr.org/special_report/sports-betting.php

Gentzkow, M., & Shapiro, J.M. (2006). Media bias and reputation. *Journal of Political Economy*, 114(2), 280-316.

Green, L.C. (2016, January 22). Is sports gambling moral? You bet, Americans say. Lifeway Research. https://research.lifeway.com/2016/01/22/is-sports-gambling-moral-you-bet-americans-say/

Hardin, M., & Shain, S. (2005). Female sports journalists: Are we there yet? "No." *Newspaper Research Journal*, 26(4), 22-35. https://doi.org/10.1177/073953290502600403

Hardin, M., & Zhong, B. (2010). Sports reporters' attitudes about ethics vary based on beat. *Newspaper Research Journal*, 31(2), 6–19. https://doi.org/10.1177/073953291003100202

Harris, J. and Clayton, B. (2002). Femininity, masculinity and physicality in the British tabloid press: The case of Anna Kournikova. *International Review for the Sociology of Sport*, 37(3-4), 397-415.

Hull, K., Walker, D., Romney, M., & Pellizzaro, K. (2022). "Through our prism": Black television sports journalists' work experiences and interactions with black athletes. *Journalism Practice*. DOI: 10.1080/17512786.2022.2050468

Hylton, J.G. (2011). The over-protection of intellectual property rights in sport in the United States and elsewhere. *Journal of Legal Aspects of Sport*, 21(1), 43-74.

Jones, A.S. (1992, April 10). Report of Ashe's illness raises an old issue for editors. *The New York Times*. www.nytimes.com/1992/04/10/us/report-of-ashe-s-illness-raises-an-old-issue-for-editors.html

Jurkowitz, M. (2006, April 5). Muckrakers in the outfield. The Phoenix. https://thephoenix.com/Article.aspx%-3Fid=8312&page=4

Kant, I. (1785). Groundwork for the metaphysic of morals. www.earlymoderntexts.com/assets/pdfs/kant1785.pdf

Kian, E., Schultz, B., Clavio, G. & Sheffer, M.L. (2018). *Multimedia sports journalism: A practitioner's guide for the digital age*. Oxford University Press.

Kim, Y., & Billings, A.C. (2017). A hostile sports media? Perceived nationalism bias in online sports coverage. *Electronic News*, 11(4), 195-210.

Langin, K. (2018, March 8). Fake news spreads faster than true news on Twitter—thanks to people, not bots. *Science*. www.science.org/content/article/fake-news-spreads-faster-true-news-twitter-thanks-people-not-bots

Lapchick, R. (2020). *2020 racial and gender report card*. The Institute for Diversity and Ethics in Sport. www.tidesport.org/_files/ugd/138a69_bee975e-956ad45949456eae2afdc74a2.pdf

Lapchick, R. (2021). *The 2021 sports media racial and gender report card: Associated Press Sports Editors (APSE)*. The Institute for Diversity and Ethics in Sport. www.tidesport.org/_files/ugd/138a69_e1e67c118b784f-4caba00a4536699300.pdf

Laucella, P.C. (2009). Arthur Ashe, privacy, and the media: An analysis of newspaper journalists' coverage of Ashe's AIDS announcement. *International Journal of Sport Communication*, 2(1), 56-80.

Lavin, M. (1987). Sports and drugs: Are the current bans justified? *Journal of the Philosophy of Sport*, 14(1), 34-43.

Liptak, A., & Draper, K. (2018, May 14). Supreme Court ruling favors sports betting. *The New York Times*. www.nytimes.com/2018/05/14/us/politics/supreme-court-sports-betting-new-jersey.html

Low, C. (2009, November 12). Key freshman among Vols arrested. ESPN. www.espn.com/college-football/news/story?id=4647094

McGlone, M.S. (2005). Contextomy: The art of quoting out of context. *Media, Culture & Society*, 27(4), 511-522. https://doi.org/10.1177/0163443705053974

Merullo, J., Yeh, L., Handler, A., Grissom II, A., O'Connor, B., & Iyyer, M. (2019). Investigating sports commentator bias within a large corpus of American football broadcasts. https://doi.org/10.48550/arXiv.1909.03343

Mirer, M., Duncan, M.A., & Wagner, M.W. (2018). Taking it from the team: Assessments of bias and credibility in team-operated sports media. *Newspaper Research Journal*, 39(4), 481-495. https://doi.org/10.1177/0739532918806890

Moritz, B. (2022, 11). What happens to sports media when everyone's a gambler? *Global Sport Matters*. https://globalsportmatters.com/business/2022/01/11/what-happens-sports-media-sports-betting/

O'Brien, T., & He, E. (2021, December 16). The sports gambling gold rush is absolutely off the charts. *Bloomberg Opinion*. www.bloomberg.com/graphics/2021-opinion-online-sports-betting-future-of-american-gambling/

Olesker, M. (1992, April 8). Ashe's revelation is journalism's newest shame. *Baltimore Sun*. www.baltimoresun.com/news/bs-xpm-1992-04-09-1992100009-story.html

Petrotta, B.A. (2023). From prohibition to promotion: Framing and sourcing the legalization of sports betting in the U.S. *Communication & Sport*. https://doi.org/10.1177/21674795231193132

Pettus, E.W. (2023, October 30). Judge dismisses Brett Favre defamation suit, saying Shannon Sharpe used hyperbole over welfare money. *Associated Press*. https://apnews.com/article/mississippi-welfare-lawsuit-favre-sharpe-nfl-34e777728532c0d6f779b308c16b0a7b

Ponterotto, D. (2014). Trivializing the female body: A cross-cultural analysis of the representation of women in sports journalism. *Journal of International Women's Studies*, 15(2), 94-111.

Rada, J.A., & Wulfemeyer, K.T. (2005). Color coded: Racial descriptors in television coverage of intercollegiate sports. *Journal of Broadcasting and Electronic Media*, 49(1), 65-85.

Reed, W. (2021, June 9). The Pete Rose betting scandal and why he should be in the Hall of Fame. Baseball Spotlight. www.baseballspotlight.com/why-pete-rose-should-be-in-the-hall-of-fame/

Rosenthal, G. (2011, September 20). Fox Sports admits fabrication of newspaper headlines. NBC Sports. https://profootballtalk.nbcsports.com/2011/09/20/fox-sports-admits-they-fabricated-newspaper-headlines/

Rowe, D. (2005) Fourth estate or fan club? Sports journalism engages the popular. In S. Allan (Ed.), *Journalism: Critical issues* (pp. 125-136). Open University Press.

Society of Professional Journalists. (2014). SPJ code of ethics. www.spj.org/ethicscode.asp

Soong, K. (2014, July 23). Prominent British tennis reporter admits to plagiarism. *Washington Post.* www.washingtonpost.com/news/early-lead/wp/2014/07/23/prominent-british-tennis-reporter-admits-to-plagiarism/

Strupp, J. (2006, October 1). Sportswriters say they dropped the ball on steroids in Major League Sports. *Editor & Publisher.* www.editorandpublisher.com/stories/sportswriters-say-they-dropped-the-ball-on-steroids-in-major-league-sports,38061

Suggs, D.W., Jr. (2016). Tensions in the press box: Understanding relationships among sports media and source organizations. *Communication & Sport, 4*(3), 261-281.

Tracy, M. (2020, January 27). In haste to confirm Kobe Bryant news, news media stumbles. *The New York Times.* www.nytimes.com/2020/01/27/business/tmz-kobe.html

Traina, J. (2021, March 23). Steve Kerr "angry" over out-of-context report regarding Kevin Durant: Traina thoughts. *Sports Illustrated.* www.si.com/extra-mustard/2021/03/23/steve-kerr-calls-out-reporter-over-out-of-context-kevin-durant-quote

Trotter, J. (2021, February 24). Is race still a part of the equation? NFL. www.nfl.com/news/sidelines/does-race-remain-a-factor-in-the-evaluation-of-nfl-quarterbacks

Twietmeyer (2019). *Fundamentals of sports ethics* (2nd ed.). Kendall Hunt Publishing.

Watt, J.J. (2020, January 7). This headline is trash. Kealia Ohai (which is her name by the way, since you didn't even bother to mention. [Quote Tweet]. Twitter. https://twitter.com/jjwatt/status/1214547782121512961?s=12

Weedon, G., Wilson, B., Yoon, L. & Lawson, S. (2018). Where's all the 'good' sports journalism? Sports media research, the sociology of sport, and the question of quality sports reporting. *International Review for the Sociology of Sport, 53*(6), 639-667.

CHAPTER 8

Antonen, M. (2009). Shrinking newsrooms put squeeze on MLB coverage. *USA Today.* Retrieved from http://usatoday.com

Barthel, M. (2019, July 23). 5 key takeaways about the state of the news media in 2018. Pew Research Center. www.pewresearch.org/short-reads/2019/07/23/key-takeaways-state-of-the-news-media-2018

Bucholtz, A., & Koo, B. (2019). Henry Abbott talks how ESPN released the TrueHoop name to him and why the site has returned as a subscription newsletter. *Awful Announcing.* https://awfulannouncing.com/nba/henry-abbott-truehoop-return-newsletter.html

Crosbie, V. (2010, June 8). The greatest change in the history of media. *Digital Deliverance.* www.digitaldeliverance.com/2010/06/08/the-greatest-change-in-the-history-of-media

Farber, M. (2010, December 1). Jim Kelley, the writer and the man. *Sports Illustrated.* Retrieved from www.si.com/more-sports/2010/12/01/jim-kelleytribute

Friedersdorf, C. (2020). Why Matthew Yglesias left Vox. *The Atlantic.* www.theatlantic.com/ideas/archive/2020/11/substack-and-medias-groupthink-problem/617102/?scrolla=5eb6d68b7fedc-32c19ef33b4

Gayomali, C. (2015, October 26). How Grantland's Shea Serrano became a *New York Times* best-selling author. *GQ.* Retrieved February 28, 2021, from www.gq.com/story/how-grantlands-shea-serrano-became-a-new-york-times-best-selling-author

Hardin, M. (2010). A shrinking sports beat: Women's teams, athletes. *Nieman Reports.* https://niemanreports.org/articles/a-shrinking-sports-beat-womens-teams-athletes/

Kian, E., Schultz, B., Clavio, G., & Sheffer, M.L. (2019). *Multimedia sports journalism: A practitioner's guide for the digital age.* Oxford University Press.

Klein, J. (2009, Sept. 5). In ever-shrinking N.H.L. coverage, even Islanders are cutting back. *The New York Times.* https://www.nytimes.com/2009/09/06/sports/hockey/06islanders.html

Mahler, J. (2011, May 31). Can Bill Simmons win the big one? *The New York Times Magazine.* www.nytimes.com/2011/06/05/magazine/can-bill-simmons-win-the-big-one.html?_r=1&emc=eta1&pagewanted=all

Morris, J.M. (2003). *The Rose Man of Sing Sing: A true tale of life, murder, and redemption in the age of yellow journalism.* Fordham University Press.

Moses, L. (2018, September 10). With an eye on *The Athletic*'s growth, newspapers roll out sports-only subscriptions. *Digiday.* https://digiday.com/media/athletic-expands-newspapers-roll-sports-subscriptions/

Nguyen, T.N. (2020, September 8). How Mina Kimes turned her football passion into a profession. *Los Angeles Times.* www.latimes.com/sports/story/2020-09-08/how-mina-kimes-turned-her-passion-for-football-into-a-profession

Perez, A.J. (2020, December 8). Has sports news site *The Athletic* hit middle age? *Front Office Sports.* https://frontofficesports.com/the-athletic-financial-outlook-2021/

Petchesky, B. (2012a, January 30). Here's the AOL column that got Bill Simmons hired by ESPN, in which he calls the ESPYs a "TV holocaust." *Deadspin.* https://deadspin.com/heres-the-aol-column-that-got-bill-simmons-hired-by-esp-5880534

Petchesky, B. (2012b, August 23). Does a last-place team really need beat reporters? *Deadspin.* Retrieved from www.deadspin.com.

Pew Research Center. (2023a). Newspapers fact sheet. Retrieved March 28, 2024, from https://www.pewresearch.org/journalism/fact-sheet/newspapers/

Pew Research Center. (2023b). Digital news fact sheet. Retrieved June 17, 2024, from https://www.pewresearch.org/journalism/fact-sheet/digital-news/

Santos, B.D.L. (2017). How Shea Serrano went from schoolteacher to leader of a Twitter army. Mashable. Retrieved February 28, 2021, from https://mashable.com/2017/10/26/shea-serrano-foh-army-twitter

Socolow, M. (2020). Substack isn't a new model for journalism—it's a very old one. *Salon*. Retrieved from www.salon.com/2020/12/23/substack-isnt-a-new-model-for-journalism--its-a-very-old-one_partner

Spangler, T. (2020, February 12). Spotify is paying up to $196 million in cash to acquire Bill Simmons' The Ringer. *Variety*. https://variety.com/2020/digital/news/spotify-acquires-the-ringer-196-million-cash-bill-simmons-1203502471

Vecsey, G. (1989). *A year in the sun: The games, the players, the pleasure of sports*. Crown.

Walsh, C.J. (2006). *No time outs: What it's really like to be a sportswriter today*. Taylor Trade Pub.

Willens, M. (2018, March 12). Why subscription sports sites have scored early wins. *Digiday*. https://digiday.com/media/subscription-sports-sites-scored-early-wins

Wilstein, S. (2001). *Associated Press sports writing handbook*. McGraw-Hill.

Yelvington, S. (2015, June 7). Revisionist online journalism history and the "original sin" myth. Yelvington.com. www.yelvington.com/content/06-07-2015/revisionist-online-journalism-history-and-original-sin-myth

CHAPTER 9

Arbel, T., & Reedy, J. (2022, January 6). *New York Times* buys sports site *The Athletic* for $550M. Associated Press. https://apnews.com/article/technology-sports-business-newspapers-new-york-times-co-455a48d77ce840f-f695796a7178e5586

Associated Press. (2023, June 12). *The Athletic* cuts nearly 20 jobs, 4% of newsroom for *New York Times*-owned sports site. https://apnews.com/article/athletic-journalists-layoffs-new-york-times-dc19421672246328a58f-cd2c856a8e7f

Associated Press. (2024, February 6). ESPN, Fox, Warner Bros. to launch sports streaming platform. www.espn.com/espn/story/_/id/39472710/espn-fox-warner-bros-launch-sports-streaming-platform

Beard, A. (2021, September 22). Diversity study: APSE's gender-hiring scores continue to lag. The Associated Press. https://apnews.com/article/sports-business-media-f2c10fcaaf0f828456d948ec56e70905

Bucholtz, A. (2024, February 4). *Los Angeles Times*' Dodgers writer Jack Harris says he'll return to that beat, weeks after tweeting he was laid off. *Awful Announcing*. https://awfulannouncing.com/mlb/jack-harris-dodgers-los-angeles-times-return.html

Burke, T., & Dickey, J. (2013, January 13). Manti Te'o's dead girlfriend, the most heartbreaking and inspirational story of the college football season, is a hoax. *Deadspin*. https://deadspin.com/manti-teos-dead-girlfriend-the-most-heartbreaking-an-5976517

Chemneera. (n.d.). Risk of a fragmented future in sports broadcasting. www.chemneera.com/news-and-resources/risk-of-a-fragmented-future-in-sports-broadcasting

Deuze, M. (2004). What is multimedia journalism? *Journalism Studies*, 5(2), 139-152.

Draper, K. (2020, June 5). *The Athletic* lays off 8 percent of staff. *New York Times*. www.nytimes.com/2020/06/05/sports/the-athletic-layoffs.html

Farivar, C. (2014, November 2). EPIC 2014: Recalling a decade-old imagining of the media's future. *Ars Technica*. https://arstechnica.com/information-technology/2014/11/epic-2014-recalling-a-decade-old-imagining-of-the-tech-driven-media-future/

Folkenkirk, D. (2023, July 11). *New York Times* disbands its sports desk. Will rely on a sports website it acquired. National Public Radio. www.npr.org/2023/07/11/1186916676/new-york-times-disbands-its-sports-desk-will-rely-on-a-sports-website-it-acquire

Frank, N. (2022, July 21). The rise and fall of *Deadspin*: How "jerks in Brooklyn" changed sports journalism. *The Guardian*. www.theguardian.com/sport/2022/jul/21/the-rise-and-fall-of-deadspin-how-jerks-in-brooklyn-changed-sports-journalism

Franks, S., & O'Neill, D. (2016). Women reporting sport: Still a man's game? *Journalism*, 17(4), 474-492.

Galily, Y. (2018). Artificial intelligence and sports journalism: Is it a sweeping change? *Technology in Society*, 54, 47-51.

Goehler, A. (2022, February 21). Reliving the 1994 MLB strike 28 years later. *Sports Illustrated*. www.si.com/mlb/guardians/opinion/reliving-the-1994-mlb-strike-as-2022-labor-negotiations-continue

Gottfried, J., Mitchell, A., Jukowitz, M., & Liedke, J. (2022, June 14). Journalists give industry mixed reviews on newsroom diversity, lowest marks in racial and ethnic diversity. Pew Research. www.pewresearch.org/journalism/2022/06/14/journalists-give-industry-mixed-reviews-on-newsroom-diversity-lowest-marks-in-racial-and-ethnic-diversity/

Hastings, D. (2023, January 12). Grant Wahl's wife fights vaccine misinformation in the wake of her husband's death. PBS. www.pbs.org/newshour/show/grant-wahls-wife-fights-vaccine-misinformation-in-the-wake-of-her-husbands-death

Jarvey, N. (2020, February 12). Spotify to pay as much as $195M for Bill Simmons' The Ringer. *The Hollywood Reporter*. www.hollywoodreporter.com/business/digital/spotify-pay-as-as-195-million-bill-simmons-ringer-1279077/

Jenkins, B. (2024. January 26). *Sports Illustrated, L.A. Times* layoffs reflect wounded state of sports journalism. *San Francisco Chronicle*. www.sfchronicle.com/sports/jenkins/article/sports-illustrated-l-a-times-layoffs-mark-18628730.php

Ketterer, S., McGuire, J., & Murray, R. (2014). Contrasting desired sports journalism skills in a convergent media environment. *Communication & Sport*, 2(3), 282-298.

Kian, E.M., & Zimmerman, M.H. (2012). The medium of the future: Top sports writers discuss transitioning from newspapers to online journalism. *International Journal of Sport Communication*, 5(3), 285-304.

Kwak, D.H., Kim, Y.K., & Zimmerman, M.H. (2010). User-versus mainstream-media-generated content: Media source, message valence, and team identification and sport consumers' response. *International Journal of Sport Communication*, 3(4), 402-421.

Lapchick, R. (2021, September 22). Sports media remains overwhelmingly white and male, study finds. ESPN.com. www.espn.com/espn/story/_/id/32254145/sports-media-remains-overwhelmingly-white-male-study-finds

Leitch, W. (2008, March 31). Matt Leinart is taking his offseason film work quite seriously. *Deadspin*. https://deadspin.com/matt-leinart-is-taking-his-offseason-film-work-quite-se-373940

Leskin, P. (2020, February 12). Bill Simmons scores massive sale as Spotify buys his publication, The Ringer, for nearly $200 million. *Business Insider*. www.businessinsider.com/spotify-ringer-deal-price-250-million-podcasting-bill-simmons-report-2020-2/

Lunden, I. (2013, December 9). Scripps buys Newsy for $35M to expand from TV and newspapers to digital video. *Tech Crunch*. https://techcrunch.com/2013/12/09/scripps-buys-newsy-for-35m-to-expand-from-tv-and-newspapers-to-digital-video/

Maglio, T. (2024, February 9). Everything on ABC, Fox, and TNT will have a new home—if the new sports mega-streamer lets you find them. *Indie Wire*. www.indiewire.com/news/analysis/how-much-sports-streaming-service-cost-1234951774/

Marcus, J. (2023, November 17). Newsrooms want to diversify. These programs can help. *Nieman Reports*. https://niemanreports.org/articles/newsroom-diversity-pipeline/

McCarthy, B. (2014). A sports journalism of their own: An investigation into the motivations, behaviours, and media attitudes of fan sports bloggers. *Communication & Sport*, 2(1), 65-79.

Nakamura, R. (2020, July 24). Fox Sports hit with layoffs amid restructuring. *The Wrap*. www.thewrap.com/fox-sports-hit-with-layoffs-amid-restructuring/

Pantuosco, J. (2023, June 15). The Athletic's layoffs are latest in a vicious cycle killing sports journalism. *Awful Announcing*. https://awfulannouncing.com/athletic/layoffs-vicious-cycle-killing-sport-journalism.html

Perez, A.J. (2021, January 14). Sources: *The Athletic* reassigns local editors in major shift. *Front Office Sports*. https://frontofficesports.com/sources-the-athletic-nixes-local-editors-in-major-shift/

Perez, A.J. (2022, January 6). *New York Times* acquires *The Athletic* for $550M. *Front Office Sports*. https://frontofficesports.com/new-york-times-acquires-the-athletic-for-550m/

Perez, A.J. (2023, June 12). *The Athletic* lays off 20 journalists in reorganization. *Front Office Sports*. https://frontofficesports.com/the-athletic-lays-off-20-journalists-in-reorganization/

Pew Research. (2021, June 29). Newspapers fact sheet. www.pewresearch.org/journalism/fact-sheet/newspapers/

Polzer, T. (2012, September 14). Notre Dame LB Manti Te'o to play while mourning two deaths. *Sports Illustrated*. www.si.com/si-wire/2012/09/14/notre-dame-manti-teo-mourning-grandmother-girlfriend-death

Sblendorio, P. (2022, December 13). Grant Wahl's brother no longer suspects foul play in soccer journalist's death. *New York Daily News*. www.nydailynews.com/news/national/ny-grant-wahl-brother-no-longer-suspects-foul-play-20221213-2d6i6lprmja55jtrr35tvnru64-story.html

Scribner, H. (2022, December 10). "An inspiration to many": Journalist Grant Wahl dies while covering World Cup in Qatar. *Axios*. www.axios.com/2022/12/10/grant-wahl-dies-fifa-world-cup-qatar

Spangler, T. (2024, March 11). *Deadspin*'s entire staff laid off as G/O Media sells sports news site to European startup. *Variety*. https://variety.com/2024/digital/news/deadspin-staff-laid-off-site-sold-1235938325/

Sports Journalism Institute. (n.d.) About SJI. www.sportsjournalisminstitute.org/about-2/about-sji

Stacy, M. (2023, January 3). Bills' Hamlin in critical condition after collapse on field. The Associated Press. https://apnews.com/article/damar-hamlin-collapse-buffalo-bills-cincinnati-bengals-c9f684bdac-cd1e3f77bda6c77baca75e

Tajfel, H., & Turner, J.C. (1979). An integrative theory of intergroup conflict. In W.G. Austin & S. Worchel (Eds.), *The social psychology of intergroup relations* (pp. 33-37). Brooks/Cole.

Ureneck, L. (1999, June 15). Newspapers arrive at economic crossroads. *Nieman Reports*. https://niemanreports.org/articles/newspapers-arrive-at-economic-crossroads/

Vincent, J. (2023, February 3). *Sports Illustrated*'s publisher is using AI to generate fitness advice. *The Verge*. www.theverge.com/2023/2/3/23584305/ai-language-tools-media-use-arena-group-sports-illustrated-mens-journal

Waldman, S. (2023, June 5). How high school sports coverage can save democracy. Poynter. www.poynter.org/commentary/2023/high-school-sports-coverage-can-save-democracy/

INDEX

Note: The italicized *f* and *t* following page numbers refer to figures and tables, respectively.

A
Abbott, Henry 133
Abdo, Mike 32-33
Abdul-Jabbar, Kareem 54
ACC (Atlantic Coast Conference) 18
acquisition efforts (social media analytic) 102
active public 88
activity (social media analytic) 102
AdobeSpark 102
advanced stats
   American football 59-60
   baseball 57-58
   basketball 52-55
   defined 51
   golf 61-62
   hockey 61
   soccer 60-61
adversity, in feature stories 41
advertising
   cross-promotional 8
   digital revenue 130
   newspaper revenues 126-127
agate page 48-49
agenda-setting 42-43
AI (artificial intelligence) 81-84, 141
Albom, Mitch 45
alternative leads 29-32
American football
   college team rankings 60
   NFL 16, 16*t*, 115
   statistics 59-60
analytics (social media) 101, 102
analytics (sport)
   benchmarks for 52
   criticism of 45, 49-50
   defined 49
   sport specific 51-62
Anderson, Anthony 32
anecdotal leads 30
anti-analytics 45, 49-50
Apple TV+ 139
APSE (Associated Press Sports Editors) 110, 120, 144
AP Sports Writing Handbook (Wilstein) 124
Arab Spring (2011) 70
Aristotle 109

artificial intelligence (AI) 81-84, 141
Art Ross Trophy (Hockey) 61
Ashe, Arthur 107, 108, 109, 110
assists statistic
   baseball 57
   soccer 60
Associated Press Sports Editors (APSE) 110, 120, 144
athletes
   access to 4, 24, 35-37, 89-90, 117
   narrative control 11, 19-20
Athletic, The
   acquisition of 8, 143
   history of 23-25, 133
   layoffs 24, 136
Atlantic Coast Conference (ACC) 18
attrition 127
augmented reality 82
Austin American-Statesman 133
authenticity, in social media 101
aware public 88

B
backpack journalism 65
Bally Sports 18
Baseball Hall of Fame 108, 119
Baseball Prospectus 62
baseball statistics 56-58
Baseball Writers' Association of America 107-108
basketball
   broadcast contracts 16, 16*t*
   college team rankings 55-56
   statistics 52-55
bating average 49
beat writers 28
benchmarks, for statistics 52
Bentham, Jeremy 108
bias
   readers' perceptions of 114-115
   types of 115-118
bias by omission 116
bias by placement 116
bias by story selection 116
Big Ten Conference 16*t*, 18
Bird, Sue 20
Bissinger, Buzz 78
bizarreness (news value) 33-34, 90

Bleacher Report 136-137
blogs and bloggers
   as career opportunity 129
   defined 78
   journalists' use of 79
   for key public communication 99
   mainstreaming of 138-139, 141
   versus traditional media 2-3, 78-80
body, in story structure 29*f*
bolstering strategy 104
Bonds, Barry 57, 58, 108, 113
Boston Sports Journal 133
Bountygate 43-44
Box Plus/Minus (BPM) 54
box score 19, 48
Brady, Tom 59-60
branded journalism 131-132
brand identity
   cross-promotion 8
   organizational 101
   personal 75, 76*t*
broadcast contracts 16, 16*t*
brochures 97
B-roll 92
Bryant, Kobe 118-119
Buttry, Steve 41
buyouts 127

C
card stats
   American football 59
   baseball 56-57
   basketball 52
   defined 51
   golf 61
   hockey 61
   soccer 60
careers
   economics and 126-129
   future-proof advice on 133-134
   job descriptions 4
   online opportunities 129-133
   in public relations 85
   skills needed in 142-143
   traditional path 124-126
   trajectories of 123-124
   working for free 129

Carlos, John 7
Chadwick, Henry 19, 48
Chamberlain, Wilt 54
change in direction 32
charitable associations 98
chronic traumatic encephalopathy (CTE) 43
citizen journalism 65-66
Clemens, Roger 113
clichés 39
clips 125, 134
coaches, access to 89-90
college sports
   basketball team rankings 55
   broadcast contracts 18
   football team rankings 60
   locker room or athlete access 36-37
columnists 28, 42
communication channels. *See also* digital media; social media
   news media tools 90-95
   organizational media 96-97
conflict (news value) 33, 34, 90
conflict, in feature stories 41
Connolly, Bill 60
consequentialist ethic 108
content creators 2-3, 67-68, 77. *See also* blogs and bloggers; social media
context (news value) 34
contrasting posts 73
control of narrative 11, 18-20
convergence of media 67
conversational podcasts 80
conversion rate (social media analytic) 102
copyright laws 112
Corsi 61
COVID-19 pandemic 24, 46
crisis communication 85, 102-105
crisis communications plans 103-104
Cronin, Courtney 137-138
cross promotion 8
crowdsourcing 23
CTE (chronic traumatic encephalopathy) 43
Culpepper, Chuck 31
currency (news value) 33, 34
Cutler, Jay 112

D

databases 48, 62
D'Arcangelo, Lyndsey 132
Deadspin
   layoffs 138
   mainstreaming of 138-139
   in media evolution 3, 80, 131
   revamping of 143
"Decision, The" 11, 20
defamation 112-113

Defense-adjusted Value Over Average (DVOA) 59
Defense Independent Pitching Stats (DIPS) 58
Defensive Yards Against Replacement (DYAR) 60
Deford, Frank 20
Delle Donne, Elena 54
demographics, in social media 70t, 101
denial posture 104
deontology 108-109
digital media. *See also* social media
   blogs 2-3, 78-80, 99, 129
   career opportunities 129-133
   digital news sites 130
   evolution of 4-6, 21-24, 138-143
   podcasts 80, 81t, 99, 131
   websites 47, 48f, 97-98, 118
diminishment strategy 104
DIPS (Defense Independent Pitching Stats) 58
discrimination 6-7, 116-117
disinformation or misinformation 68, 112, 119, 135-136
diversity, in sports journalism 6-7, 143-144
DK Sports 133
donors 98
driving distance 61
Dunne, Tyler 133
Durant, Kevin 113
DVOA (Defense-adjusted Value Over Average) 59
DYAR (Defensive Yards Against Replacement) 60

E

earned run average (ERA) 57
Effective Field Goal Percentage 55
Ellerman, Troy 114
Embiid, Joel 54
emergency plans, versus crisis plans 103
engagement (social media analytic) 102
English Premier League 16t
EPIC 2014 13, 140-141
episodic framing 43
ERA (earned run average) 57
errors (baseball statistic) 57
ESPN
   agenda-setting 43-44
   evolution of 15-16
   influence of 1
   joint streaming service 140
   newsroom diversity 144
   prominent journalists 131
   statistics resources 62
   Total QBR statistic 60

ESPN+ 133
ethics
   AI use and 83
   bias management 114-118
   defined 108
   dilemma scenarios 120-121
   media controversies in 107-108
   versus objectivity 107
   philosophies of 108-110
   social media and 118-119
   sports gambling and 119-120
   in sports writing 110-114
Even-Strength Save Percentage 61
excuse-based strategy 104
Expected Goals 60
external crisis communication plans 103

F

fabrication 112, 119
Facebook
   advertising revenue 130
   in Big Four 22
   curated feeds 75
   description and use of 70t, 71-74
Facebook Insights 101
Facebook Messenger 70t
fact checking 83, 119
Fainaru-Wada, Mark 114
fairways hit 61
fake news 75, 119. *See also* disinformation or misinformation
FanGraphs 62
FanHouse 20
Favre, Brett 112
feature stories 40-41
feature writers 28
FEI (Fremeau Efficiency Index) 60
Fenwick 61
Fielding Independent Pitching (FIP) 58
fielding percentage 57
film, as learning aid 6
First Amendment (U.S. Constitution) 107
FiveThirtyEight.com 131-132
football. *See* American football; soccer statistics
Football Outsiders 59, 62
Fox network 139, 140
Fox Sports 23, 112, 136
framing theory 43
freedom of the press 107
free speech 107, 113
Fremeau Efficiency Index (FEI) 60
Fromal, Adam 55

G

game notes 35, 97
game programs 97

game stories
    defined 14
    writing 27-32
gender bias 6-7, 115-117. *See also* diversity
goals (soccer statistic) 60
Goals Saved Above Expected 60-61
Gobert, Rudy 54
golf statistics 61-62
Go Long 133
Google 130
Grantland 131, 132, 136-137
greens-in-regulation 61
Griner, Brittney 54
Gutman, Matt 118-119

H
Hamlin, Damar 135
hardware, for social media production 81*t*
Harman, Neil 112
Harrington, Mike 36
Hasek, Dominik 61
hearing, in reporting 40
high school sports 36, 144-145
hiring practices, discriminatory 117
history, in feature stories 41
hockey statistics 61
Hollinger, John 54
Holtzman, Jerome 56
home runs 56
humorous lead 32

I
impact (news value) 33, 34, 90
information access 127
insider trading 120
Instagram
    analytics 101
    in Big Four 22
    description and use of 70*t*, 76-78
Institute for Diversity and Ethics in Sport 144
intellectual property laws 112
internal crisis communication plans 103
Internet. *See also* digital media
    for crisis communication 104
    development of 21-23
Internet of Things (IOT) 82
internships 4
interview podcasts 80
interviews 35-40, 94, 113-114
intriguing statement 31-32
inverted pyramid 28-29, 29*f*
IOT (Internet of Things) 82
Irving, Kyrie 90

J
Jackson, Lamar 115
Jackson, Lauren 54

James, Bill 49, 58
James, LeBron 11, 20
Jenkins, Lee 20
Jeter, Derek 19-20
jobs, in sports journalism 4, 85
Jokić, Nikola 54
Jomboy Media 136
Jordan, Michael 54
justification strategy 104

K
Kant, Immanuel 109
Kekua, Lennay 138-139
KenPom ratings 56
Kerr, Steve 113
key players (news value) 34
key plays (news value) 34
key publics
    communication with 89-102
    identification of 88
    relationships with 87-88
Kian, E. 124
Kimes, Mina 123, 131
Klein, Ezra 131-132
Koluder, John 93

L
Las Vegas Review-Journal 120
latent public 88
Law, Keith 56-57
laws, and sports writing 112-113
layoffs, of journalists 8, 23, 127, 136-138
lead (or lede) 28-32, 29*f*
lean questions 38
Lewis, Michael 46
libel 112
life stories 40-41
Lindbergh, Ben 51
local sports coverage 144-145
locker room access 4, 24, 36, 117
Los Angeles Times 136
Love, Kevin 54
Ludkte, Melissa 117
Lynch, Marshawn 90

M
magazines 13-14
Major League Baseball (MLB) 16, 16*t*. *See also* baseball entries
Major League Soccer (MLS) 18. *See also* soccer statistics
Martinez, Pedro 58
mass media
    in crisis communication 104
    news access in 127
Matthewson, Christy 58
McAfee, Pat 112, 113
McCoughtry, Angel 54
McCracken, Voros 58
McGwire, Mark 113

McKenzie, Hamish 133
media convergence 67
media days 94
media ethics. *See* ethics
media evolution 3-6, 13-18, 21-24, 139-143
media guides 47, 96
media ownership 2
media policy 89-90
media theory 42-44
Miller, Sam 51
minorities, in sports journalism 143-144. *See also* women
misinformation or disinformation 68, 112, 119, 135-136
MLB (Major League Baseball) 16, 16*t*. *See also* baseball entries
MLS (Major League Soccer) 18. *See also* soccer statistics
mobile journalism 66-67
moments, in feature stories 41
Moneyball (Lewis) 46
MTV 23
Musk, Elon 75
MVP Machine, The (Lindbergh, Sawchik) 51

N
Nalder, Eric 37
National Basketball Association (NBA) 16, 16*t*. *See also* basketball
National Football League (NFL). *See also* American football
    broadcast contracts 16, 16*t*
    racial bias in 115
National Hockey League (NHL) 16, 16*t*. *See also* hockey statistics
National Sports Daily, The 20-21
NET rankings 56
neutral questions 38
news advisory 95
news availability 127
news conferences 95
news consumers 67
news cycle 68, 118, 142
news gathering
    news values in 32-34
    research and reporting 35-40, 65-67
newsletters 97, 132-133
news media tools 90-95
newspapers
    circulation and revenue declines 126-127, 136
    job losses 127-128
    as sport medium 13, 14
news peg 41
news releases 90-91, 91*f*, 92*f*
news values 32-34

newsworthiness 33, 90
Newsy.com 143
New York Times 8, 136, 143
NFL. *See* National Football League (NFL)
NHL (National Hockey League) 16, 16*t*. *See also* hockey statistics
Nicco, Jerry 124
nonhuman sources 46-48
nonpublic 88
nut graph 29, 29*f*

O

objectivity, versus ethics 107
OBP (On-Base Percentage) 57
Ogwumike, Nneka 54
Ohai, Kealia 116
Ohtani, Shohei 58
On-Base Percentage (OBP) 57
online media. *See* digital media
online resources 47-48, 48*f*, 62
Only Rule Is It Has to Work, The (Lindbergh, Miller) 51
open questions 38
OPS (On-Base Percentage plus Slugging Percentage) 58
OPS+ 58
organizational branding 101
organizational media 96-97
organizational spokesperson 89, 104
organizational websites 97-98

P

packet switching 21
Paramount+ 139
passer rating 59
Passes Per Defensive Action 61
PED use 107-108, 113, 114
penny press 126, 133
PER (Player Efficiency Rating) 54
Perez, A.J. 17
personal branding, on X 75, 76*t*
photography 81*t*
photos 94
Pinterest 70*t*
pitcher wins 49-50, 56
PITCHf/x 56
plagiarism 110-112
Player Efficiency Rating (PER) 54
Players' Tribune, The 19-20, 136-137
plus-minus (hockey statistic) 61
podcasts 80, 81*t*, 99, 131
Politi, Steve 41
Pomeroy, Ken 56
portfolio of clips 125, 134
Posnanski, Joe 38
Possession Value 61
posters 97
Powers, Scott 69
Press Agency Model 88, 88*f*

press kits 95
press releases 90-91, 91*f*, 92*f*
print journalists 4
print sport media 13-14
probabilistic thinking. 53
Professional and Amateur Sports Protection Act 119
professional sports 36-37. *See also specific sports or leagues*
profiles 40-41
prominence (news value) 33, 34, 90
promotion
 cross promotion 8
 using social media 100
 on websites 98
proximity (news value) 33, 34, 90
PSRA (Public Relations Society of America) 83-84, 86
psychographics, in social media 101
Public Information Model 88, 88*f*
public relations 25, 86. *See also* sport public relations
public relations practitioners 4, 118
Public Relations Society of America (PSRA) 83-84, 86
public relations transfer process 86, 86*f*
publics, defined 87. *See also* key publics
putouts 57

Q

quotations, using 38-40, 113

R

racial bias 115, 117. *See also* diversity
radio broadcasts 14
radio journalists 4
Range Factor 58
Rasmussen, Bill 1
Ratings Percentage Index (RPI) 55-56
RBI (runs batted in) 56
reach (social media analytic) 102
rebuilding strategy 104
reciprocity 88
relationship building 85
relationship nurturing 88
relevance, in feature stories 41
reporting 35-40, 65-67, 88
repurposed content podcasts 80
reputation management 86
research 35-40
responsibility, in stewardship 88
results (news value) 34
retention metrics (social media analytic) 102
right to privacy 107
Ringer, The (blog site) 131, 132, 143
Rivals.com 118
Rose, Pete 119

RPI (Ratings Percentage Index) 55-56
runs batted in (RBI) 56
Ruth, Babe 58

S

sabermetrics 49
SABR (Society of American Baseball Research) 49
saves statistic
 baseball 56-57
 soccer 60
Sawatsky, John 37-38
Sawchik, Travis 51
SB Nation 136
Schatz, Aaron 59
schedule cards 97
score (golf) 61
Scripps Company 143
scripted podcasts 80
Seau, Junior 43
SEC (Southeastern Conference) 18
senses, in reporting 40
Serrano, Shea 46, 123
sexual discrimination 6-7
Sharpe, Shannon 112, 113
Sharrett, Cody 72
shield laws 114
Shiller, Drew 113
Shotlink system 62
shots, shots on goal (soccer statistics) 60
show, don't tell 41
sight, in reporting 40
Silver, Nate 50, 131-132
Simmons, Bill 130-131, 132
situational leads 30-31
slander 112
slash line 58
Slugging Percentage 57-58
Smart Baseball (Law) 56-57
smell, in reporting 40
Smith, Red 42
Smith, Tommie 7
Snapchat 70*t*
soccer statistics 60-61
social justice 7
social media. *See also specific platforms*
 analytics 101, 102
 defined 68-69
 effect on news cycle 68, 118
 ethics and 118-119
 hardware and software for 81*t*, 102
 journalists use of 70-71
 main platforms 22, 70*t*
 negative aspects of 7
 role in traditional sports journalism 3, 4, 23
 in sport public relations 100-102
social media practitioners 4

Society of American Baseball Research (SABR) 49
Society of Professional Journalists (SPJ) 83, 110, 112, 120
software, for social media production 81t, 102
Sosa, Sammy 113
sources. *See also* analytics (sport)
    access to 4, 24, 35-37, 46
    misquoting 113
    nonhuman 46-49, 62
    relationships with 1, 113-114
Southeastern Conference (SEC) 18
So what? 29
SP+ 60
spin 85, 87
SPJ (Society of Professional Journalists) 83, 110, 112, 120
spokesperson 89, 104
sport communication 86-87
sport communication channels. *See also* digital media; social media
    news media tools 90-95
    organizational media 96-97
sport marketing 86
sport media. *See* digital media; social media; traditional media
sport media startups 143
sport public relations
    careers in 4, 85
    defined 86
    digital media use 97-99
    key publics 88
    media policy 89-90
    news media tools 90-95
    organizational media use 96-97
    social media use 100-102
    spokesperson 89, 104
    stewardship practices 88
sports gambling 119-120
Sports Illustrated
    AI use 83, 141
    James' narrative and 20
    layoffs and decline of 8, 23, 138
    locker room access suit 117
    social justice reporting 7
    in sports media history 13
sports journalism. *See also* careers; digital media; ethics; public relations; sports writing; traditional media
    control of narrative in 11, 18-20
    economics of 126-129
    future of 135-146
    lack of diversity in 6-7, 143-144
    market for 24
    media evolution 3-6, 13-18, 21-24, 139-143
    promotion in 8
    public relations and 25, 85
    role and value of 1-2
    storytelling in 7, 8
Sports Journalism Institute 144
sports journalists
    attitude of 6
    competition with non-journalists 67-68
    female 6-7, 143-144
    layoffs of 8, 23, 127, 136-138
    relationship to sources 1, 113-114
    technology advancements and 65-67
    types of 4, 28
Sports Reference 62
sports writing
    alternate leads for 29-32
    defamation in 112-113
    for digital media 81t
    fabrication in 112
    ignoring information in 113
    news values in 33-34
    originality in 41
    plagiarism in 110-112
    quotations in 38-40, 113
    research and reporting 35-40, 65-67
    story forms 40-42
    story ideation 33
    story structure 27-29, 29f
    working for free 129
Spotify 143
statistics 48-49. *See also* analytics (sport)
steroid use in sport 107-108, 113, 114
stewardship practices 88
story ideation 33
storytelling 7, 8, 33
storytelling podcasts 80
streaming platforms 18, 139-140
Strokes Gained 62
Substack 132-133
Swoopes, Sheryl 54
symmetry model 86

T
team-operated media 117-118
Team Value Index 56
team websites 47, 48f, 118
technological evolution. *See* media evolution
television broadcasts 12, 14-15
television journalists 4
Tennessee Volunteers 118
Te'o, Manti 138-139
"The Decision" 11-20
thematic framing 43
The Ringer (blog site) 131, 132, 143
30 for 30 (ESPN) 6
Thomas, Joe 20

Thompson, Charissa 7, 112
TikTok 70t, 141
timeliness (news value) 33, 34, 90
TIPCUP acronym 90
Total QBR (Total Quarterback Rating) 60
touch, in reporting 40
toy department reputation 1-2
traditional media
    changes and challenges in 11-13, 20-23, 136-138
    narrative control 18-19
Trimble, Joe 31-32
True Hoop 133
True Shooting Percentage 54
24-hour news cycle 142
Twietmeyer, Gregg 111
Twitter. *See* X (formerly Twitter)
Two-Way Asymmetrical Model 88, 88f
Two-Way Symmetrical Model 86, 88, 88f, 100

U
UGC (user-generated content) 2-3, 67-68, 77
Ultimate Zone Rating (UZR) 58
unusualness (news value) 33-34, 90
Usage Rate 54
USA Today 107, 108, 109, 110
U.S. Constitution 107
user-generated content (UGC) 2-3, 67-68, 77
utilitarianism 108
UZR (Ultimate Zone Rating) 58

V
Vaccaro, Mike 125
valance 71
Value Over Replacement Player (VORP) 54
Vecsey, George 124
video news release 92
video production and use 81t, 98-99
virtual reality 82
virtue ethics 109-110
visuals 92-94
VORP (Value Over Replacement Player) 54
Vox.com 131-132

W
Wahl, Grant 135
Walks and Hits per Inning Pitched (WHIP) 58
Walsh, Christopher 124
Walt Disney Company 2
WAR (Wins Above Replacement) 58
Warner Brothers Discovery 140
Watson, Deshaun 39
Watt, J.J. 116

Web 1.0 22
Web 2.0 22-23
websites 47, 48*f*, 97-98, 118
Westbrook, Russell 54
Wetzel, Dan 130
WhatsApp 70*t*
WHIP (Walks and Hits per Inning Pitched) 58
Whitaker, Tricia 5
White, Shad 112
Whitlock, Jason 45
Wide World of Sports 15
Wilbon, Michael 45
Williams, Lance 114
Williams, Venus 90
Wilson, A'ja 54
Wilstein, Steve 124
win-loss record (baseball) 56
Wins Above Replacement (WAR) 58
Win Shares 54
WNBA (Women's National Basketball Association) 16, 16*t*
Wojnarowski, Adrian 130
Wolken, Dan 30
women, in sports journalism 6-7, 115-117, 143-144
Women's National Basketball Association (WNBA) 16, 16*t*
women's sports 115-116
Worthy, Lynn 128

X
X (formerly Twitter)
    analytics 101
    in Big Four 22
    characteristics of 70*t*
    description and use of 74-76, 76*t*
X-Pro 102

Y
Yahoo! Sports 130
yards (American football statistic) 59
Yelvington, Steve 126
YouTube 22, 70*t*, 76-78
YouTube TV 139

ABOUT THE AUTHORS

Matthew Zimmerman, PhD, is an assistant professor of sports media analytics at Virginia Tech. Previously, he taught sport administration and sport communication for eight years at Mississippi State University. Following a six-year stint in sports journalism, he has spent more than a decade in academia studying the effects of new media on the overall sports conversation between fans and organizations. He teaches courses on sport analytics and sports media production. As a researcher, he has published in multiple journals. He is a member of the International Association for Communication and Sport.

Lauren Burch, PhD, is a senior lecturer and the program director for the sports analytics and technologies program in the Institute for Sport Business at Loughborough University London in England. She teaches courses such as Digital Storytelling for Sports and Sport PR & Communication. Her research interests focus on examining the gendered construction of brand identity, athlete activism, and the examination of discourse and sentiment on social media. Burch's current research has examined online abuse from a racial or gendered perspective in sport on social media. Her work has been published in *International Journal of Sport Communication* and *Communication and Sport*. She is a member of the International Association of Communication in Sport.

Brian Moritz, PhD, is an associate professor and director of the online journalism master's programs in sports journalism and digital journalism at St. Bonaventure University. Previously, he taught for seven years as an associate professor of digital media production and online journalism at State University of New York (SUNY) at Oswego and spent 10 years as an award-winning sports journalist and columnist in western and central New York. His research, which focuses on both the work routines of sports journalists and the economic models of digital sports journalism, has been published in the *International Journal of Sport Communication* and *Communication and Sport*. He is also the author of the *Sports Media Guy* blog. He is a member and past president of the Sports Communication Interest Group within the Association for Education in Journalism & Mass Communication (AEJMC) and a member of the International Association for Communication and Sport.